high note 3

Workbook

Pearson
KAO TWO
KAO Park
Hockham Way
Harlow, Essex
CM17 9SR
England
and Associated Companies throughout the world

www.english.com/highnote

First published 2020
Tenth impression 2024
ISBN: 978-1-292-20964-7
Set in Akko Pro

Printed and bound by CPI Group (UK) Ltd, Croydon, CR0 4YY

Image Credit(s)

The publisher would like to thank the following for their kind permisson to reproduce their photographs:

123RF.com: Cathy Yeulet 54, Chupina Yuliia 5, Evgenii Zadiraka 81, Fabio Lotti 45, Hyunsu Kim 65, Iakov Filimonov 10, Katarzyna Białasiewicz 118, Lightwave Stock Media 105, Marek Cech 104, Michael Simons 65, Mohamad Zaki Mokhtar 107, Nattapol Sritongcom 69, Rawpixel. com 40, Sebnem Ragiboglu 65, Wavebreak Media Ltd 70, ferli 41, nikkytok 69, om12 69, racorn 65, rido 49; **Alamy Stock Photo:** Alex Segre 123, Heritage Image Partnership Ltd 58, Jonathan Goldberg 59, Martin Wierink 19, NG Images 17, Zero Creatives 29, blacksandwhites 93; **Shutterstock.com:** Agnes Kantaruk 69, Aivars Ivbulis 100, Antonio Guillem 64, Christian Vinces 99, Cookie Studio 75, Dean Drobot 25, Dejan Dundjerski 90, Dmytro Gilitukha 93, ESB Professional 52, Elnur 84, F8 Studio 35, FiledIMAGE 99, George Dolgikh 69, Georgejmclittle 88, Gorodenkoff 18, 19, HelloRF Zcool 91, Iakov Filimonov 71, Ilya Osovetskiy 39, John Silver 43, KatieKK 103, KikoStock 47, Kireev Art 83, LightField Studios 15, 43, Look Studio 44, Lopolo 30, 87, MaDOSa 81, Marco Ciccollela 29, Massimo Santi 43, Matej Kastelic 27, Monkey Business Images 32, 77, 95, New Africa 12, Njron Photo 9, Nomad_Soul 33, Phoenixns 99, Photographee.eu 118, Pressmaster 114, RG-vs 94, Rawpixel.com 99, RossHelen 37, Sasa Prudkov 82, Scott E Read 101, Simon Dannhauer 107, Skynavin 107, Stockbakery 76, Tyler Olson 21, VGstockstudios 23, 28, VGtockstudio 9, Vaclab Volrab 69, Victoria Chudinova 10, View Appart 11, Vladimir Melnik 81, Wavebreak Media Ltd 99, aquatarkus 93, cigdem 16, dotshock 20, 59, fizkes 89, kyrien 117, limpido 34, luanateutz 92, markyano 115, stockfour 56, wavebreakmedia 112, 13, zEdward_Indy 9

Cover Image: *Front:* **Getty Images:** Klaus Vedfelt

All other images © Pearson Education

Illustration acknowledgements

Illustrated by Kavel Rafferty (Illustration) p36, p66, p67; Stefanie Clemen (Illustration) p27; Ivan Gillet (NB Illustration) p6, p79.

Every effort has been made to trace the copyright holders and we apologise in advance for any unintentional omissions. We would be pleased to insert the appropriate acknowledgement in any subsequent edition of this publication.

CONTENTS

01 Looking good	LESSONS 1A–1G	4–12
	Unit vocabulary practice	13
	Self-assessment	14
	Self-check	15
02 The digital mind	LESSONS 2A–2G	16–24
	Unit vocabulary practice	25
	Self-assessment	26
	Self-check	27
03 Active and healthy	LESSONS 3A–3G	28–36
	Unit vocabulary practice	37
	Self-assessment	38
	Self-check	39
04 Time to move	LESSONS 4A–4G	40–48
	Unit vocabulary practice	49
	Self-assessment	50
	Self-check	51
05 The next step	LESSONS 5A–5G	52–60
	Unit vocabulary practice	61
	Self-assessment	62
	Self-check	63
06 Do the right thing	LESSONS 6A–6G	64–72
	Unit vocabulary practice	73
	Self-assessment	74
	Self-check	75
07 In the spotlight	LESSONS 7A–7G	76–84
	Unit vocabulary practice	85
	Self-assessment	86
	Self-check	87
08 Consumers' world	LESSONS 8A–8G	88–96
	Unit vocabulary practice	97
	Self-assessment	98
	Self-check	99
09 The power of nature	LESSONS 9A–9G	100–108
	Unit vocabulary practice	109
	Self-assessment	110
	Self-check	111
10 Justice for all	LESSONS 10A–10G	112–120
	Unit vocabulary practice	121
	Self-assessment	122
	Self-check	123

PHRASAL VERBS	124
PREPOSITIONS	125–126
WORD BUILDING	127
PRONUNCIATION TABLE	127
SELF-CHECK ANSWER KEY	128

01 Looking good

1A GRAMMAR AND VOCABULARY

Present Simple and Present Continuous

1 ⭐ **Complete the mini conversations with the verbs from the box.**

feel   have   is enjoying   is getting   need   ~~wear~~

1 **A** I always _wear_ jeans when I'm not at school.

B Me too. I _____ much more relaxed in casual clothes.

2 **A** I really hope Jack _____ his new school.

B I'm not sure. They _____ a uniform and I don't think he likes it!

3 **A** Come shopping with me. I _____ to buy some new T-shirts and shorts.

B Yeah, the weather _____ hotter and I haven't got any light clothes either.

2 ⭐ **Match the beginnings 1–8 with the endings a–h.**

1 ☐ I'm working for a fashion designer for

2 ☐ I change clothes as soon as

3 ☐ Our English classes are getting

4 ☐ My friend thinks the colour blue

5 ☐ I won't be long! I'm getting ready

6 ☐ Clothes prices go up

7 ☐ My eyes look very green

8 ☐ We're thinking about

a very interesting.

b going to the Clothes Show this year.

c a few weeks.

d really suits me.

e when I wear brown clothes.

f every year.

g right now.

h I come home from college.

3 ⭐ **Choose the correct verb forms to complete the conversation.**

Ellie Hi Anna! I **1** _'m loving / love_ your dress! Where **2** _are you going / do you go_? Is there a party I **3** _'m not knowing / don't know_ about?

Anna No! It's my aunt's birthday. Every year we **4** _are going / go_ for a meal at Duke's in the High Street. I **5** _'m walking / walk_ there because my car **6** _isn't running / doesn't run_ at the moment.

Ellie Oh, they **7** _'re serving / serve_ brilliant meals at Duke's. But it **8** _'s getting / gets_ quite expensive these days.

Anna I **9** _'m knowing / know_, but it's not a problem! Dad **10** _is always paying / always pays_ for everyone!

Ellie Cool! Have a great time. **11** _Are you wanting / Do you want_ a lift? You **12** _'re wearing / wear_ high-heeled shoes and they're not very good for walking.

Anna You're a star! Thanks.

4 ⭐⭐ **Choose the correct answers.**

1 What time _____ for work now that he's got a new job?

a is your dad leaving

b does your dad leave

c your dad leaves

2 My sister _____ dressed in the mornings until my mum calls her for the third time!

a doesn't get

b isn't getting

c get

3 _____ here to meet Danny? I think he's still in class.

a Do you wait

b Are you waiting

c Does he wait

4 They _____ an enormous new shopping centre on the edge of town.

a 're building

b building

c build

5 I think everyone _____ a good time at the party. It's a big success!

a has

b is having

c are having

6 Helen _____ good in that smart dress.

a always is looking

b always looks

c looks always

7 My mum _____ with her current job and wants to change.

a get bored

b is getting bored

c gets bored

8 Which car _____ while hers is in the garage?

a do Rose drive

b does Rose drive

c is Rose driving

9 My brother _____ watches DVDs. He prefers reading books.

a always

b hardly

c hardly ever

5 ★★ Complete the voice mail message with the correct Present Simple or Present Continuous forms of the verbs in brackets.

Hi, it's me. I'm at the party, but where are you? I know you **1** _always arrive_ (always/arrive) late, but this is very late and I **2** _____ (get) bored! I **3** _____ (not recognise) anyone here. And I **4** _____ (wear) the wrong clothes! Everyone else is in jeans and tops and I **5** _____ (be) in a dress! I **6** _____ (not usually/wear) dresses but this is a new one. Anyway, I **7** _____ (sit) down and **8** _____ (listen) to rock music. I **9** _____ (hate) rock music and it **10** _____ (get) very loud. Hurry up!

6 ★★ Read the answers and use the prompts to write questions using the Present Simple or the Present Continuous.

1 A What / want / do / when you leave school?
What do you want to do when you leave school?

B I'm hoping to study to be a fashion designer.

2 A you / often / make / your own clothes?
_____

B Yes, it's fun!

3 A you / look for / anything special in this shop?
_____

B Yes, a winter jumper.

4 A your brother / still play / in a band at school?
_____

B Yes, they're really good.

5 A the teachers / have / the same holidays as us?
_____

B No, they're shorter.

7 ★★ Choose the correct verb forms to complete the sentences.

1 I _'m imagining / imagine_ it's difficult to get shoes to fit your brother.

2 _Are you preferring / Do you prefer_ to go to town or for a walk through the park?

3 We _'re staying / stay_ with my grandparents while my grandad is ill.

4 I have to admit that I _'m having / have_ a problem deciding what to wear for the wedding.

5 It _is appearing / appears_ that Tom is doing really well in his new role as a manager.

6 _Is this coat belonging / Does this coat belong_ to someone in this class?

8 ★★★ Complete each pair of sentences with the correct Present Simple or Present Continuous forms of the verb given.

1 have

a I _am having_ dinner with Mark and Lucas at the moment. Can I call you later?

b I sometimes _____ problems buying clothes from this site.

2 think

a _____ you _____ we should go home now? It's getting late.

b The college _____ of starting a fashion design course.

3 look

a The coat in the advert _____ great, but I'm not sure if that colour suits me.

b _____ you _____ at the correct exercise? It's the one at the top of page three.

4 see

a I _____ any difference between the two styles of shoes – they're exactly the same!

b Kyle _____ someone at the moment.

9 ★★★ Complete the conversation with the correct forms of the verbs and phrases from the box.

get go hardly ever wear have improve love make need not fit not know not look forward ~~not seem~~ want

Tom Hi! You **1** _don't seem_ very happy. **2** _____ (you) any problems at school?

Jaz No, it's not that. Everything **3** _____ well at school at the moment. I **4** _____ a lot of progress in Maths and my English marks **5** _____ too. I **6** _____ some extra lessons in French, so I think the exams will be OK. No, it's just that I **7** _____ to the school prom.

Tom Why not? You always **8** _____ parties!

Jaz Yes, I do. But for this you **9** _____ to dress up.

Tom And you enjoy dressing up!

Jaz OK, OK! But I'm taller than I was, and my smart dresses **10** _____ me now. I **11** _____ what to wear!

Tom My sister Katy is about your size. She's got a lot of fantastic dresses and she **12** _____ them. **13** _____ (you) me to ask her to lend you one?

Jaz Tom – you're a star!

10 ON A HIGH NOTE Write a short paragraph about what you are wearing at the moment and what you usually wear to parties.

1B VOCABULARY | Appearance

1 ⭐ Label the clothes and accessories.

1 b<u>ow</u> <u>tie</u>		**7** c_____	
2 s_____		**8** s_____	
3 v_____		**9** h_____	
4 b_____		**10** t_____	
5 t_____		**11** h_____-_____ s_____	
6 s_____ b_____		**12** w_____	

2 ⭐ Find the odd one out in each group.

1 linen / ripped / fur
2 baggy / tight / denim
3 high-heeled / plain / striped
4 narrow / casual / wide
5 faded / shiny / silk
6 matching / nylon / wool

3 Choose the correct words to complete the sentences.

1 I love *nylon / ripped* jeans, but my mother thinks they look terrible.
2 At the weekend I bought new brown leather boots and a *tight / matching* handbag.
3 When it's cold I usually wear my gorgeous fake *fur / bow* jacket.
4 I don't like wearing tight clothes when it's hot, so I usually go for a *faded / loose-fitting* dress.
5 When I was at a gig in the summer, I got a T-shirt with my favourite band's *logo / designer* on it.
6 My brother's got *baggy / shiny* new shoes, but I really don't like them. I prefer casual clothes.
7 I like to carry a *shoulder / matching* bag because then I have both my hands free.
8 My mother has still got a beautiful *loose-fitting / wide* leather belt from when she was a teenager.

4 ⭐⭐ Complete the sentences with the words from the box.

broad clean full heavily tanned thin ~~wavy~~

1 I'd love to have *wavy* hair, but mine's completely straight.
2 My dad needs to order a special size jacket because he's got very _____ shoulders.
3 I don't buy fashion magazines because the models they use are too _____.
4 My family say that I have a _____ figure but I think they're being polite.
5 The advantage of holidaying in Spain is that I'll come back with naturally _____ skin.
6 The man I saw at the bus stop was _____ shaven and quite _____-built.

5 ⭐⭐ Complete the commentary with one word in each gap.

HIGHLIGHTS FROM

ARA Music Awards

All the stars are out this evening for the music awards ceremony and the fashions reflect a whole range of styles!

Pamela Shaw looks very ¹ *glamorous* as usual. She's wearing a stunning ² f_____-l_____ blue dress with shiny ³ h_____-h_____ shoes. The dress shows off her ⁴ p_____ skin to perfection.

Her ⁵ h_____, really attractive husband is with her. He's always well-dressed and tonight he's wearing a grey suit and a black ⁶ b_____-t_____ . His dark, ⁷ c_____ hair is cut short, and the new ⁸ m_____ suits his face much better than the beard last year!

Behind them comes young Parker Barnes, the teenage star of the film. He certainly hasn't dressed up for the occasion and is wearing his trademark T-shirt with the film ⁹ l_____ on it, ¹⁰ f_____ jeans with red trainers and big, dark sunglasses.

Beside him is his girlfriend, Kelly, who has a small part in the film. She's very slim and ¹¹ m_____, which is understandable as she's also a top-class athlete. She's wearing a very expensive red ¹² s_____ dress with ¹³ m_____ shoes. Her ¹⁴ m_____-l_____ hair is blonde today with a streak of red. The older ¹⁵ b_____ man in the loose-fitting, ¹⁶ b_____ black-and-white striped trousers following them is the director.

6 ON A HIGH NOTE **Find a photograph of yourself and your family and/or friends. Write a short description of the photograph, describing everyone's physical appearance and the clothes they are wearing.**

1C LISTENING AND VOCABULARY

1 🔊 *2* You're going to listen to an interview about a man's job as a 'super recogniser'. What do you think he can do? Listen and check your answer.

   a A super recogniser can describe in detail faces he's seen.

   b A super recogniser can remember people he saw once a long time ago.

   c A super recogniser can recognise every face he's ever seen.

2 🔊 *2* Listen again and complete the sentences with one or two words in each gap.

   1 Rob started working with the police *five years* ago.

   2 He and his team study pictures and CCTV _____ and photos to help the police find criminals.

   3 Rob says that super recognisers look at a person's _____ face.

   4 According to Rob, people without this ability can usually recognise about _____ percent of the faces they've seen.

   5 Rob discovered he had this ability when he was watching a news report about a _____ .

   6 Rob adds that a small percentage of people suffer from _____ and have difficulty recognising people that they know well.

3 Decide if statements 1–6 are true (T) or false (F).

   1 ☐ Rob works with the police on his own.

   2 ☐ People can learn the skills of a super recogniser.

   3 ☐ Super recognisers are not cleverer than normal people.

   4 ☐ Rob found he had the ability when he was a child.

   5 ☐ People with problems recognising others use different clues to help them.

   6 ☐ The presenter is surprised by what Rob tells her.

Vocabulary extension

4 Complete the sentences with the words and phrases from the box which you heard in the recording in Exercises 1 and 2.

---
crack down on   down to   have a clue   home in on   ~~make up for~~   pick out   to some degree   track down
---

   1 Sally is going to *make up for* spilling coffee down my shirt by buying me a new shirt.

   2 Can you _____ your friend in this photograph?

   3 I hadn't seen Evan for ten years, but I managed to _____ his brother on social media.

   4 Being a good teacher is all _____ being patient.

   5 I didn't _____ what to revise for the test, so I just read through everything.

   6 Everyone's an artist _____ – it's just that some people have a better eye than others.

   7 My teachers always _____ spelling mistakes in my essay. I'm a terrible speller.

   8 There aren't enough police officers to _____ this problem.

5 ON A HIGH NOTE Would you be a good 'super recogniser'? Write a short paragraph, giving reasons.

Pronunciation

6 🔊 *3* Read the sentences from the recording in Exercises 1 and 2. Underline one word in each sentence which has a silent consonant. Listen and check.

   1 And please tell our listeners what your specific job is.

   2 … super recognisers tend to look at the whole face and not separate features.

   3 They're not focusing on whether someone has narrow eyes, full lips, a big nose … .

   4 Have you always known that you had this ability?

ACTIVE PRONUNCIATION | Silent letters

Silent letters appear in words, but are not heard when those words are spoken, e.g.

- silent **b**: **b**omb
- silent **t**: lis**t**en
- silent **h**: r**h**ythm
- silent **k**: **k**nit
- silent **w**: **w**rinkle

7 🔊 *4* Listen and complete the sentences with the words from the box. Each missing word includes a silent letter. Practise saying the sentences.

~~comb~~   honour   knowledge   subtle
---

   1 You need to *comb* your hair.

   2 There's a _____ difference between the words.

   3 This is a great _____ .

   4 I don't have much _____ of this subject.

8 🔊 *5* Listen and underline the silent letters in the box in Exercise 7. What are the silent letters?

9 Each list contains three words with a silent consonant. Underline one word in each group which does not contain the silent consonant.

1 /b/	climb	debt	stable	plumber
2 /t/	castle	noticed	often	butcher
3 /w/	two	wonder	answer	sword
4 /h/	hour	honest	ghost	honey
5 /k/	killer	knife	knee	knock

10 🔊 *6* Listen and check. Then practise saying the words.

11 🔊 *7* Listen and write the sentences. Which words contain silent letters? Practise saying the sentences.

1D READING AND VOCABULARY

1 Look at the photos and quickly read the first paragraph of the article. What do you think would be the best title for the article?

   a Does it suit you?

   b Why that jacket?

   c Can you afford it?

2 Read the article and choose the correct answers.

   1 The writer thinks that some older people's clothes

     a reflect modern fashion.

     b make them look younger.

     c remind them of their youth.

     d have been kept a long time.

   2 Our parents can influence our choice of clothes because

     a they dressed us in a certain way.

     b they wore clothes that we remember.

     c they advised us what to wear.

     d they liked expensive materials.

   3 The writer thinks that people feel the need to belong because

     a their own families don't help them.

     b they like joining clubs.

     c they get lonely when they're alone.

     d they like the security of a group.

   4 The writer gives 'hippies' as an example to show how

     a fashion changes.

     b clothes can connect people.

     c they influenced other sub-cultures.

     d important the movement was.

   5 Why do some people wear clothes that don't suit them?

     a because they have to

     b because their friends tell them to

     c because they want to look like other people

     d because they want to look different

Vocabulary extension

3 Complete the sentences with the highlighted adjectives in the text.

   1 We often make decisions using our _subconscious_ mind and we aren't really aware of it!

   2 My friends are very _____ and buy the latest fashions.

   3 My parents were _____ when I failed my fashion design exams at college.

   4 It was no accident that Jane spilled orange juice on my new top, it was _____ because she was jealous!

   5 The design is certainly not simple – it's very _____ .

   6 I'm sure there are deep, _____ reasons why some people refuse to wear certain colours.

   7 My gran wears _____ sandals which look terrible, but she says they're comfortable.

   8 Young people are often _____ and wear unusual clothes, just to annoy their parents.

ACTIVE VOCABULARY | Suffix -ical

Some adjectives are formed by adding a suffix to a noun. We can add *-ical* to a noun to form an adjective, e.g. *psychology – psychological*.

Be careful! Sometimes we need to make other changes to the spelling, too.

4 Write the adjective forms of these nouns.

	noun	adjective
1	practice	*practical*
2	theory	
3	geography	
4	critic	
5	history	
6	politics	
7	economy	
8	logic	
9	biology	
10	electricity	

5 Complete the sentences with the adjectives from Exercise 4.

   1 The castle over there has great _historical_ importance. You can read about it in your guide books.

   2 The map will show us the exact _____ location of the lake.

   3 I'm trying to be _____ and adapt these old jeans into shorts!

   4 Unfortunately my new boots aren't very _____ as they let in water!

   5 Our teacher was extremely _____ of my essay and told me that I hadn't checked it carefully.

   6 I'm afraid I'm not interested in _____ programmes – I get bored listening to ministers and journalists talking about the economy or education.

   7 While Jeremy doesn't have much experience in the field, his _____ knowledge of Geology is extensive.

   8 Kristie was adopted but when she grew up she was reunited with her _____ parents.

   9 People who are good at _____ thinking usually like Maths and Science.

   10 It's common now to use windmills to produce _____ energy.

6 ON A HIGH NOTE Write a short paragraph about a sub-culture that you know about and mention the clothes and/or appearance of the people who belong to it and what they believe in.

UNIT VOCABULARY PRACTICE > page 13

You're in a shop and you see a jacket. You think , 'Yes, I'll buy that!'. But have you ever thought about why you want that particular jacket? You may not be aware of it, but the choices you make when buying clothes are quite complicated, and often have their origin in your subconscious mind.

• • •

Experts believe that there are many reasons why we choose certain clothes or a particular 'look' and, like most psychological matters, they say that it all goes back to our childhood! Apparently one reason we go for baggy T-shirts or tight jeans, is that they remind us of a time in our lives when we were happy and secure. We try to recreate that as we grow older. When you see a middle-aged man or woman, you may be able to guess their age because of the style of clothes they're wearing.

Another influence from our childhood is the memory of the clothes we saw around us. It may give us a liking or a preference for a certain type of material – cotton as opposed to nylon, for example. If a father wore silk ties, his son may develop a taste for silk ties when he's older too.

At other times, of course, our clothes decisions are not subconscious, but very deliberate, but the reasons still go back a long way. As children, we may belong to a family which is supportive and approves of what we think and do – it makes us feel safe. As we get older, we look for other groups to belong to – it might be a peer group at school or a rebellious sub-culture like hipsters or Goths. And how do we show that we belong to this group? By wearing a similar style of clothes or changing our appearance in order to fit in with the group.

Have you ever seen pictures of the hippies from the 1960s? The girls were long-haired, they wore full-length, cotton, flowery skirts and loose-fitting tops. They put flowers in their hair. It was their way of identifying with a sub-culture that believed in peace and love. And think about the hipsters. Lots of men wear checked shirts, skinny jeans and have a particular style of beard. It's almost like a uniform and it's a way of showing that you belong.

Undoubtedly advertising and clothes worn by celebrities and friends we admire can also influence our choices. Some of us dress in a particular way, often choosing clothes that don't really suit us, because we want to be like people we admire. Sometimes, it's simply because we don't want to be different – we don't want to stand out from the crowd. This is also a type of belonging, even though there is perhaps no special group that we want to be linked to. Our desire is for people to think we are trendy and not old-fashioned.

So, next time you go clothes shopping, stop and think for a moment about why you're choosing that jacket, that shirt, those shoes. The answer may tell you something interesting about yourself!

1E GRAMMAR

Articles

1 ⭐ Complete the rules with ø (no article), *a/an* or *the*.

1 We use *the* to talk about a specific thing or person, because it is the only one or when it's clear which thing or person we mean.
2 We use _____ with plurals and uncountable nouns to talk about something/someone in general.
3 We use _____ when we mention something/ someone for the first time and _____ when we mention it again.
4 We use _____ with continents, most countries and cities.
5 We use _____ to talk about a singular countable thing/person when it is one of many or one of a group; not the only one.
6 We use _____ with superlatives, ordinal numbers, periods of time and some countries.
7 We use _____ with occupations.

2 ⭐ Match the examples a–g with the rules 1–7 from Exercise 1.

a ☐ Many women like to wear **a hat** to weddings.
b ☐ My cousin is **a fashion designer**.
c ☐ I tried these jeans on in **the changing room**.
d ☐ I bought this handbag in **Milan**.
e ☐ **Plain, white shirts** are always fashionable.
f ☐ I'm going to take you to **the best shoe shop in London**.
g ☐ I wore **a pale silk top** to Andy's party. I spilled some orange juice down **the top** and it's ruined!

3 ⭐ Choose the correct options to complete the sentences.

1 There's *a / ø* new sports shop in *a / the* shopping centre. *An / The* old one closed down a month ago.
2 Unfortunately, *the / ø* high-heeled shoes don't look good on me.
3 My friend usually buys *the / ø* designer clothes online.
4 *A / The* most expensive coffee I've ever bought was in *the / ø* Venice!
5 I'd love to be *a / the* costume designer for *a / ø* theatre company.
6 *The assistant / Assistant* advised me to try on *a / ø* white, linen suit.
7 Sometimes it's *a / the* problem for my brother to find *the / ø* shoes that fit.

4 ⭐⭐ Complete the blog post with ø (no article), *a/an* or *the*.

My Blog

I'm really interested in **1** _ø_ fashion from **2**_____ past. Most of my friends follow **3**_____ latest trends and they all wear **4**_____ same type of **5**_____ jeans, shoes, tops, etc. But my style is different. My gran was young in **6**_____ 1960s and she's kept **7**_____ clothes from back then. Last week she brought down **8**_____ box from **9**_____ attic in her house and I had a great time looking through **10**_____ skirts and dresses in it. I found **11**_____ beautiful long skirt and **12**_____ elegant pair of shoes. I wore **13**_____ outfit to Paul's party and **14**_____ people there loved it!

Be the first to ♡ 🔖 ⬆   next story »

5 ⭐⭐ Underline *the* in the sentences when it is pronounced /ði:/.

1 There was a short fashion show as part of *the* opening of the new shopping centre.
2 The appearance of a famous model from the USA was really unexpected.
3 Unfortunately one of the models nearly fell off the edge of the stage!
4 I had to leave before the end of the show.
5 I really liked one of the experts who talked about the show on TV later.
6 As always, I preferred the expensive suits and shoes!

6 ON A HIGH NOTE Write a short paragraph about a favourite outfit you remember from your past. Write

- a description of the outfit.
- whether you or someone else chose it.
- the reason why you remember it.
- whether you still have the outfit.

1 🔊 *8* Listen and repeat the phrases. How do you say them in your language?

SPEAKING | Participating in conversations

WHEN YOU'RE SPEAKING

CLARIFY YOUR MESSAGE

What I mean is better quality clothes last longer.
The thing is, there are some good value clothes online.
Let me put it another way.

HOLD ATTENTION

Just a second, I haven't finished.
Hold on! Let me finish!

CHECK OTHERS UNDERSTAND

Do you know/see what I mean?
Does that make sense?
Do you get it?

GET OTHERS TO SPEAK

What do you think?
Tell us what you think.
What's your opinion?

WHEN SOMEONE ELSE IS SPEAKING

INTERRUPT POLITELY

Excuse me, can I say something?
That's true/a good point, but you don't get the variety.
Sorry to interrupt, but these clothes don't look cheap at all!

ASK FOR REPETITION

Sorry, I didn't get that. Could you say it again?
I'm sorry, I missed that.

ASK FOR EXPLANATION OR CLARIFICATION

Do you mean we should buy more expensive clothes?
I'm not sure what you mean.
Are you saying that people should have fewer clothes?

CONFIRM YOU UNDERSTAND

Right, I've got that.
Yes, I know/see what you mean.
Ah right! Now I get it.

---

2 Match the beginnings 1–6 with the endings a–f.

1 ☐ Let me put it   **a** make sense?
2 ☐ Just a second,   **b** I say something?
3 ☐ Excuse me, can   **c** another way.
4 ☐ Do you see   **d** what you mean.
5 ☐ I'm not sure   **e** I haven't finished.
6 ☐ Does that   **f** what I mean?

3 Put the words in order to make sentences that are useful for participating in discussions.

1 that / you / again / say / could / ?
   Could you say that again?

2 I / it / now / get
   _____

3 us / you / tell / think / what
   _____

4 missed / I'm / that / I / sorry
   _____

5 I've / that / got / right
   _____

4 🔊 *9* Complete the conversation with the correct phrases from the Speaking box. Then listen and check.

Jess In my opinion, it's much better to spend more money and buy better quality clothes.

Eleni Are ¹*you saying* that people should have fewer clothes?

Jess What ² _____ – better quality clothes last longer, they look better and you don't have to replace them so often.

Eleni Yes, I see ³ _____ mean. But if you do that, you don't get the variety. Let me ⁴ _____. If you haven't got much money and you spend it all on just one or two items, then you don't have a lot of choice about what you wear.

Jess I know that but surely ...

Eleni Hold on! Let ⁵ _____! If you buy cheaper clothes, you can get a lot of different outfits for the same price as just one or two. What ⁶ _____?

Jess That's a ⁷ _____, but I think people always know when you're wearing something cheap.

Eleni Sorry ⁸ _____, but the thing is – there are some really good value clothes online and they don't look cheap at all!

11

Start with a friendly greeting.

Mention your last contact with the other person.

Mention the message you are replying to.

Give a reason for ending your message.

Send greetings or refer to future contact.

Finish with a friendly goodbye.

1_____ Liz,

How's it going? **2**_____! At least three weeks! **3**_____ about the holiday. Are you looking forward to it? I can't wait! It's going to be a lot of fun.

At the moment, I'm thinking about packing, but I really don't know what to take. Have you decided yet? They say it's very hot in Italy right now. So, **4**_____? T-shirts, shorts, sandals? But it's only May so perhaps the evenings are cold. Jumpers, jeans, boots? Oh, I don't know! Help!

Btw, I want to get some books to take with me. **5**_____ with me before we go? And I need sun cream – not coming back from Italy with sunburn! Lol!

Anyway, **6**_____, dinner's ready. It's pizza. Can't wait for the real thing! **7**_____ your mum and dad and **8**_____ about the shopping trip.

Bye 4 now, ·

Amy

---

1 Complete Amy's email with the phrases a–h.

a Long time no see
b give me a call
c Hi there
d Fancy coming shopping
e what do you reckon
f got to go
g Thanks for your message
h Love to

2 Read the email again and tick sentences which describe what you do in an informal email.

1 ☐ Write in a chatty style, similar to the way you speak.
2 ☐ Use long, complex sentences.
3 ☐ Write the full forms of verbs.
4 ☐ Use exclamation marks, emojis and abbreviations.
5 ☐ Use formal language and difficult vocabulary.
6 ☐ Leave out pronouns and the verb to be where possible.

3 WRITING TASK **Write a reply to Amy's email from Exercise 1.**

ACTIVE WRITING | An informal email

1 Plan your reply. Use the ideas below.
- Thank Amy for her email.
- Think about what you want to say about the holiday.
- Respond to Amy's packing suggestions and offer some advice.
- Make some suggestions about what you both need to buy before the holiday.
- Suggest an arrangement for the shopping trip.

2 Write the email.
- Start with a friendly greeting and finish with a friendly goodbye.
- Use a chatty style including short sentences, informal language and punctuation, contractions, emojis and abbreviations.

3 Check your email. Check that:
- all the relevant information is there.
- there are no spelling, grammar or punctuation mistakes.
- there is interesting and relevant topic vocabulary.

1 1A GRAMMAR AND VOCABULARY **Choose the correct words to complete the sentences.**

1 That *good-* / *well-* dressed woman is the new manager.

2 Do you think I'm *overdressed* / *underdressed*? I could change and put on something smarter.

3 My sister hates getting dressed *over* / *up* for family occasions – she prefers jeans and T-shirts.

4 Don't worry! You don't need to get *undressed* / *underdressed* for the medical examination.

5 I always *wear* / *get* dressed before I have breakfast.

6 I feel a bit *overdressed* / *casual* in this suit and tie.

7 It's Paul's party on Friday and everyone's getting dressed up *as* / *for* animals because they're vets!

8 I usually dress *casually* / *casual* at the weekend.

2 1B VOCABULARY **Which word cannot be used with each noun? Find the odd one out in each group.**

1 gold / baggy / high-heeled **shoes**

2 ripped / denim / wool **jeans**

3 bow / silk / tight **tie**

4 narrow / full-length / leather **belt**

5 fake fur / plain / bow **jacket**

3 **Complete the text with one word in each gap.**

Hey Emma,

We're having a great time on holiday. Here's a photo of my family at the beach. Do you remember everyone? My mum is standing behind us. She's got ¹long, straight hair. She's always very ²g_____ with perfect make-up and stays ³s_____ whatever she eats! Next to her is my dad. As you can see, he's a bit different from the rest of the family because he's got dark ⁴c_____ hair. He's ⁵c_____ shaven now, but last year he had a ⁶m_____ - it looked terrible! The boy standing in front of Dad is my brother, Tom. His skin is really ⁷p_____ because he hates going out in the sun. The girl in the middle is my sister, Tara. And of course, the ⁸h_____ boy on the end with short, blonde hair is me, but you know that!

CU soon

Brad

4 1C LISTENING AND VOCABULARY **Complete the sentences with the words from the box.**

bags double eyelashes ~~full~~ shaped smooth wrinkles

1 I'd like to have *full* lips – mine are very thin.

2 My grandmother is very old and her skin has lots of _____.

3 My baby brother's skin is very _____.

4 Denny's really tired – look at the _____ under his eyes.

5 The model has _____ eyebrows and her face is very pretty.

6 Don't look down so much or you'll get a _____ chin!

7 Her eyes are really beautiful – look at these long _____.

5 1D READING AND VOCABULARY **Choose the correct words to complete the sentences.**

1 My dad is a very kind, clever and caring man and I definitely look *on* / *up* to him.

2 I have an aunt who thinks she's very intelligent and looks *down* / *off* on people who aren't.

3 I sometimes try to guess people's nationality from their accents, but I usually get it *bad* / *wrong*!

4 My dad always tries to join *at* / *in* when we play football, but he's getting really slow.

5 It isn't a good time to set *off* / *up* a new business because the economy isn't doing well at the moment.

6 **Rewrite the underlined phrases using compound adjectives. Make any other changes necessary.**

1 My favourite summer dress has short sleeves.
   is short-sleeved

2 People with pale skin shouldn't sit in the sun for long.

   _____

3 My football coach is muscular and has broad shoulders.

   _____

4 We have a new teacher. She's in her middle age.

   _____

5 My brother met a girl with blue eyes and dark hair on holiday.

   _____

6 When I'm an old granny with grey hair, I shall live somewhere warm and peaceful.

   _____

7 ON A HIGH NOTE **Write a short paragraph describing a friend you have known for a long time. Mention how the clothes he/she likes to wear have changed over time.**

1 For each learning objective, write 1–5 to assess your ability.

1 = I don't feel confident. 5 = I feel very confident.

	Learning objective	Course material	How confident I am (1–5)
1A	I can use the Present Simple and the Present Continuous to talk about habits and temporary situations.	Student's Book pp. 4–5	
1B	I can talk about physical appearance and clothes.	Student's Book p. 6	
1C	I can listen effectively and talk about physical appearance.	Student's Book p. 7	
1D	I can understand the main idea and identify specific details in an article and talk about appearance and stereotypes.	Student's Book pp. 8–9	
1E	I can use articles to talk about general and specific things.	Student's Book p. 10	
1F	I can participate in and maintain a discussion effectively.	Student's Book p. 11	
1G	I can write an informal email giving news or opinions.	Student's Book pp. 12–13	

2 Which of the skills above would you like to improve in? How?

Skill I want to improve in	How I can improve

3 What can you remember from this unit?

New words I learned and most want to remember	Expressions and phrases I liked	English I heard or read outside class

GRAMMAR AND VOCABULARY

1 Complete the sentences with the words from the box.

broad-shouldered elegant faded underdressed unshaven

1 The actress looks very _____ in the long, black dress with high heels.

2 In the advert, the football star is _____ and I don't think it suits him.

3 Olly sometimes wears jeans to his work meetings and in my opinion, he's _____.

4 Pete's jacket looks very tight because he's so _____.

5 I've washed these jeans a lot and now they've _____.

_/ 5

2 Complete the sentences with one preposition in each gap.

1 Children often look _____ to celebrities and want to copy their clothes and hair.

2 We're organising a fashion show for charity. Would you like to join _____?

3 I can't wait _____ your fancy dress party on Friday – it's going to be such fun!

4 Hold _____! Let me finish what I'm saying, please!

5 We all got really dressed _____ for the dinner party.

_/ 5

3 Complete the sentences with the correct Present Simple or Present Continuous forms of the verbs in brackets.

1 Is it just me, or _____ (clothes sizes/get) smaller?

2 We hardly ever _____ (have) tests on Monday mornings.

3 These leather handbags _____ (not come) from Italy.

4 Our neighbours _____ (have) a party and it's very noisy!

5 I'm ready to go out now. How _____ (I/look)?

_/ 5

4 Complete the conversation with ø (no article), a/an or the.

Rachel ¹_____ new girl in our class is very fashionable.

Kathy Yeah, I think she'd like to be ²_____ model or an actress! She wears ³_____ great clothes and she's got ⁴_____ very pretty face.

Rachel She's from ⁵_____ USA. I think her clothes are from ⁶_____ expensive designer store. She's living here for six months because of her dad's job. He's ⁷_____ financial expert.

Kathy Ah, I'm sure they're staying in ⁸_____ best part of town!

Rachel Well, she's having party at ⁹_____ weekend for all ¹⁰_____ students in our class. So, we can see!

_/ 5

USE OF ENGLISH

5 Choose the correct answers.

When I was little, clothes were my passion. I dressed up ¹___ princesses, actresses, famous celebrities and so on, and I always hoped to make clothes my career. And I did! I'm now a writer for a fashion magazine and I ²___ visit fashion shows all over the world to write about the new trends. I also work as a costume designer for a local theatre group! That sounds very grand – what I ³___ is, I find the costumes for the plays. Sometimes the plays are about a period in history. Everything has to be correct – even the shoes – and if I ⁴___ it wrong, everybody can see it straight away! A famous actor ⁵___ up the theatre group about ten years ago and it's very successful.

1 **a** for	**b** at	**c** as	**d** by
2 **a** hardly ever	**b** rarely	**c** never	**d** regularly
3 **a** say	**b** mean	**c** think	**d** want
4 **a** make	**b** get	**c** find	**d** take
5 **a** set	**b** did	**c** made	**d** put

_/ 5

6 Complete the second sentence so that it has a similar meaning to the first one. Use between two and five words, including the word in bold.

1 I'm sure we can find an answer to this before tomorrow. **SORT**
I'm sure it will be possible _____ before tomorrow.

2 The class project for our group this week is on fashion. **ARE**
This week _____ class project on fashion.

3 I only occasionally buy something in expensive designer shops. **HARDLY**
I _____ shopping in expensive designer shops.

4 I might take these shoes back to the shop. **THINKING**
I _____ these shoes back to the shop.

5 I've never worn a smart dress like this before. **TIME**
This is the _____ ever worn a smart dress like this.

_/ 5

_/ 30

2A **GRAMMAR AND VOCABULARY**

Present Perfect Simple and Continuous

1 ⭐ **Have these activities finished or are they still continuing? Choose (FA) for Finished Activity or (SC) for Still Continuing.**

1 ☐ I've read four books about the Voyager.
2 ☐ She's been reading all day, she's fed up.
3 ☐ We've been trying to find valuable information about Neptune.
4 ☐ That computer hasn't been working properly.
5 ☐ I think he's found a good website on space travel.
6 ☐ The students have collected a lot of material.
7 ☐ We've studied three units of the book.
8 ☐ Stella has been working on a project about Saturn.

2 ⭐ **Read the sentences and choose the best answers.**

1 The students have studied the movement of the planets.
  a They're going to study something different now.
  b They're going to continue studying the same thing.
2 Kate has been revising for her Physics exam all week.
  a She's still studying.
  b She's finished studying.
3 I haven't been working very hard at school recently.
  a I'm not working hard now.
  b I'm working hard now.
4 The girls have done a project about space travel.
  a The project is not complete.
  b The project is complete.
5 They've been watching a documentary.
  a The documentary is finished.
  b The documentary isn't finished.
6 Mrs Carter has been marking our exam papers.
  a She can give everybody their results.
  b She can't give everybody their results.

3 ⭐ **Choose the correct verb forms to complete the sentences.**

1 Why have you *switched off / been switching off* the computer?
2 I think I've *found / been finding* a good article about space discovery.
3 They've *studied / been studying* the galaxy for six months now.
4 *Have you finished / Have you been finishing* that book about the solar system yet?
5 Scientists *haven't discovered / haven't been discovering* the nature of these satellites yet.
6 Look at Jenny! She's *painted / been painting* and she's covered in paint!
7 Why have you *sat / been sitting* in front of your computer all day?
8 I've *read / been reading* Tim's book about the Voyager space probe; I'll lend it to you when I've finished it.

4 ⭐⭐ **Put the words in order to make sentences.**

1 seen / has / your pictures / Terry
Terry has seen your pictures.
2 sent / has / new information / ? / Voyager
_____
3 have / receiving / not / recently / they / been / news
_____
4 signals / picking up / all day / we / been / have
_____
5 what / investigating / ? / you / been / recently / have
_____
6 any information / collected / have / today / we / not
_____

5 ⭐⭐ **Read the questions and complete the short answers.**

1 Have you done experiments with plants?
Yes, *I have*.
2 Has Jemma followed Gary's research?
No, _____.
3 Have you tried this solution yet?
No, _____.
4 Have they been publishing the results?
Yes, _____.
5 Has the team been working together?
Yes, _____.
6 Has Dr Brown been explaining the process?
No, _____.

6 ⭐⭐ **Complete the sentences with the correct forms of the verbs in brackets.**

1 Scientists *have been studying* (study) the planet for twenty years.
2 What _____ (you/do) since we last met?
3 She _____ (complete) the project, so it's ready for publication.
4 They _____ (not receive) any signals from the space probe yet.
5 _____ (the team/discover) the reason for the radio waves yet?
6 We _____ (not work) on those photos recently, we have other work to do.
7 How much information _____ (Callum/process) so far?
8 I _____ (study) the results for hours, but I still don't understand them.

7 ⭐⭐⭐ **Complete the text with the correct forms of the verbs from the box. Use the Present Perfect Continuous wherever possible.**

have not tire pay study use ~~work~~

Merav Opher **¹***has been working* with the Voyager team since 2001. She is an expert in space physics and computing and **²**_____ her knowledge to make new discoveries about the Sun's behaviour. She **³**_____ different information from both Voyager 1 and Voyager 2. Over the past few years, newspapers **⁴**_____ more and more attention to her work. Opher says she **⁵**_____ lots of funny experiences, including her colleague using a wooden ruler to measure computer charts! She **⁶**_____ of her NASA work yet, and intends to continue.

8 ⭐⭐⭐ **Read the answers and write questions.**

1 *Have you seen the new photos from Voyager yet*?
No, I haven't seen the new photos from Voyager yet.
2 _____?
I've been watching this documentary since I got home.
3 _____?
I've been sleeping all day because I'm tired.
4 _____?
Yes, I've seen the film twice.
5 _____?
No, the information hasn't reached Earth yet.
6 _____?
They have been studying those particles for two years.
7 _____?
Yes, they've managed to fix the spaceship.
8 _____?
No, they haven't launched the space probe yet.

9 ⭐⭐⭐ **Use the prompts to write the interview.**

Journalist **¹**Dr Graham, how long / you / work / for NASA?
Dr Graham, how long have you been working for NASA?
Dr Graham **²**I / work / here / for about ten years
_____
Journalist **³**you / make / any discoveries / yet?
_____
Dr Graham **⁴**No, / I / not / complete / my research / yet
_____
Journalist **⁵**What sort / research / you / be / do / since / you joined NASA?
_____
Dr Graham **⁶**I / study / radio waves
_____

10 ⭐⭐⭐ **Complete the second sentence so that it means the same as the first one. Use no more than three words in each gap.**

1 The astronauts began their journey a week ago.
The astronauts *have been* travelling through space for a week.
2 I haven't received the photos from Gordon yet.
_____ sent me the photos yet.
3 Jerry started work at NASA two years ago.
Jerry _____ at NASA for two years.
4 When did you start studying Physics?
How long have _____ Physics?
5 Sarah is still reading the book.
Sarah _____ the book yet.

11 ON A HIGH NOTE **Think about a project you are working on at the moment or an exam you are preparing for. Write a short paragraph about what you have been doing and what you have done for the project/exam.**

1 Skim the text: look at the photos, the title, and quickly read the headings and the first line of each paragraph to get the general idea of the text. Then answer the questions.

1 Where do you think you would you read this text?

a in a magazine

b in a person's blog

c on a website

2 What is the main idea of the text?

a the science behind micro-chipping humans

b the reasons for and against micro-chipping humans

c the history of micro-chipping humans

2 Read the text again and complete the sentences with one or two words in each gap.

1 In the future, people will have micro-chips in their *bodies*.

2 People have been receiving heart pacemakers since _____.

3 A pet's microchip stores details such as its name _____.

4 Many workers at a _____ get micro-chips in their hands.

5 These micro-chips are unable to read _____.

6 In the future microchips could carry information about our _____ history.

7 One superpower that chips might give us is _____.

8 There are concerns that employers could use chips to follow their workers' _____.

Vocabulary extension

3 Complete the sentences with the highlighted words from the text.

1 My gran's *eyesight* isn't very good and she wears thick glasses.

2 There's a medical _____ that can check for problems inside the stomach.

3 At college there are some _____ about students using smartphones in class.

4 When you get older your _____ can rise.

5 My friend got a tooth _____ and it cost a fortune!

6 Severe depression is a mental _____, but it can be treated with counselling or medication.

7 Technological _____ in the next ten years will solve a lot of health problems.

8 The school keeps _____ of all its students' achievements.

ACTIVE VOCABULARY | Suffixes -ity, -ility, -osity

We can add the suffix -ity, -ility or -osity to some adjectives to create nouns.

- If the adjective ends with a consonant, we add -ity, e.g. *human – humanity*
- If it ends with a consonant and -e, we take off the -e and add -ity, e.g. *secure – security*
- If it ends with -le, we take off the -le and add -ility, e.g. *able – ability*
- If the adjective ends with -ous, we take off the -ous and add -osity, e.g. *curious – curiosity*

4 Read the information above and write the nouns of these adjectives.

	adjectives	nouns
1	moral	*morality*
2	real	
3	creative	
4	electric	
5	public	
6	probable	
7	responsible	
8	generous	

5 Complete the sentences with the nouns from Exercise 4.

1 You need a lot of *creativity* to become a good artist.

2 The actors' wedding got a great deal of _____ in the media.

3 The _____ is that we will all have micro-chip implants in thirty years' time.

4 Organising the music for the party is Aidan's _____ .

5 Sometimes it's difficult to return to _____ after a holiday.

6 We must thank your parents for their _____ in paying for the trip.

7 The house in the country is pretty but it hasn't got _____ !

8 Some people question the _____ of developing AI.

6 ON A HIGH NOTE Write a comment to post after the article, giving your opinion with reasons and examples.

TO CHIP OR *NOT* TO CHIP
That is the question!

THE WAY FORWARD

Smart phones have become part of our daily lives, connecting us with everyone and everything, and the development of smart watches means that we can now have this means of connectivity with us all the time. However, experts believe that soon microchips will move from our phones and watches into our bodies! Man and machine will merge, and we shall become true 'cyborgs'!

NOTHING NEW

The idea of implants – putting electronic devices inside a living body – is not new. It's been happening for a long time. The first electronic heart pacemaker, a device to support the heart, was implanted in 1958 and the first cochlear implant (to help hearing) was in 1982. We have been microchipping pet animals since the 1990s to provide information about the pet's name and owner. But what about implanting humans with information microchips? Well, that's already happening too! A group of people called bio-hackers have been microchipping themselves with chips that can unlock doors or even pay for things with a movement of their hand! Who needs keys or wallets?

WHAT'S HAPPENING NOW?

If you think bio-hackers are an extreme group, then think again. A Swedish company regularly implants its employees with microchips – the size of a grain of rice – under the skin of the hand. They can then open security doors, operate printers and buy things from machines. The technology is similar to that used in contactless credit cards. The chips are 'passive' – that means other devices can read the information on them, but the chips can't read other devices. The employers and the employees appear to be happy with this procedure and they often hold 'implant parties' for workers who are about to get microchipped!

IS THIS PROGRESS?

The main benefit of having an implanted chip is that it makes life easier. It saves time and money and security cards are no longer necessary. In the future, chips could even replace passports. They might improve our health, too. They could store our medical records, with information about our blood type, allergies and so on. They could perform health checks on blood sugar levels and blood pressure, and even release medicines into the blood at the correct times. Looking even further into the future, experts believe that implanted devices could improve our eyesight, prevent brain disorders or possibly even give us super powers such as night vision or the ability to see things over a long distance.

SO, WHAT ARE THE DOWNSIDES?

As with all scientific advances, there are potential dangers. The Swedish company can already find out what their employees do at work, what they buy and what they eat. In the future they may be able to track their exact movements and learn about health problems and other information that the employees might not want to share. If it becomes normal for us all to have chip implants, then these privacy issues will become very important.

However, the most significant change for us will be continual connectivity. We won't be able to take the chips out and leave them on a table like a phone or a watch. We shall never be completely alone again. But perhaps that's what we want? What's your opinion? Click here to send your comments.

This is SO exciting! I can't wait to get one. Excellent! *Evi3*

Sounds horrible! I like to be in control – thank you – not give out all my info to anyone and everyone! So, not in my lifetime please. *Bluesue*

Never in a million years! *Pans1*

2C VOCABULARY | Science, phrases with *think* and *mind*

1 ⭐ **Choose the correct words to complete the sentences.**

1 The *organism* / *gravity* we are studying divides its cells to reproduce.

2 We'd like to do some *radiation* / *research* into these strange waves.

3 The force that keeps us connected to the Earth's surface is *radiation* / *gravity*.

4 Every living organism is made of *pressure* / *cells*.

5 It's best to avoid *cells* / *radiation* because of harmful effects.

6 Water exerts a lot of *pressure* / *gravity* on the things in it.

2 ⭐ **Match the phrases 1–8 with their definitions a–h.**

1 ☐ It blew my mind.
2 ☐ It broadens the mind.
3 ☐ We don't think much of it.
4 ☐ I've changed my mind.
5 ☐ I've made up my mind.
6 ☐ My mind has gone blank.
7 ☐ Think outside the box.
8 ☐ I can't hear myself think!

a We have a negative opinion of it.
b There's too much noise.
c I've made a different decision.
d It was absolutely amazing.
e I can't think.
f It makes you aware of more things.
g I've decided.
h Think in an original way.

3 ⭐⭐ **Complete the sentences with the correct forms of the phrases from Exercise 2.**

1 This article isn't very good – I *don't think much of it*.

2 Jason _____ to study engineering next year.

3 That discovery was incredible – it _____!

4 I'm sorry. I can't think of the correct answer – my _____!

5 Will you turn down the music? I _____!

6 We need more creative ideas – can't you _____ this time?

7 Zoe wanted to study medicine, but she _____ and now she's going to study Physics.

8 You should travel more. It _____ and gives you a very different view of life.

4 ⭐⭐ **Complete the conversation with one word in each gap.**

Anne Have you seen that documentary about pollution? We have to think ¹ s*eriously* about it or things will be much worse in the future.

Vicky I haven't seen it, but I agree. We need to think ² t_____ before building nuclear power stations again!

Anne Well that's true, but there are other problems. We need to think ³ b_____ and look at the whole picture.

Vicky Anne, if you imagine people are going to do that, think ⁴ a_____! Not everyone is interested in environmental problems.

Anne Well, they're wrong. We must think ⁵ a_____ and try to reduce pollution for future generations.

5 ⭐⭐⭐ **Complete the second text with one word in each gap so that it has the same meaning as the original.**

Peter decided to study Biology and began a course, but he wasn't very happy with it, so he made a different choice and decided to do a Chemistry course. The teacher was great, she thought in an original way and she really increased Peter's knowledge of new things. Peter had no experience of Chemistry, so the first experiments he did were really incredible to him. The only problem was the noise from the other students. Sometimes he couldn't concentrate and he was unable to think clearly.

Peter made up his ¹*mind* to study Biology and joined a course, but he didn't think ² _____ of it, so he ³ _____ his mind and decided to do a Chemistry course. The teacher was great, she thought ⁴ _____ the box and she really ⁵ _____ his mind. Peter had no experience of Chemistry, so the first experiments he did ⁶ _____ his mind. The only problem was the noise from the other students. Sometimes he couldn't hear ⁷ _____ think and his mind went ⁸ _____.

6 ON A HIGH NOTE **Write a short paragraph about a situation in which you had to make an important decision. Use at least four of the phrases from the box.**

blow my mind   change my mind   don't think much of
make up my mind   think ahead   think seriously
think twice

_____

2D **GRAMMAR** | Verb patterns

1 ★ **Complete each pair of sentences with the correct forms of the verb given.**

1 steal

   a He has admitted *stealing* Jeff's research results.

   b We didn't mean _____ Jeff's research results.

2 develop

   a She has decided _____ this technology.

   b I hope you keep _____ this technology.

3 insert

   a Please avoid _____ bad codes into the program.

   b The engineer refused _____ bad codes into the program.

4 study

   a I really don't mind _____ this subject.

   b Sorry, but I don't want _____ this subject.

5 learn

   a We really need _____ something about AI.

   b I quite fancy _____ something about AI.

6 code

   a The students practised _____ on their IT course.

   b After a few lessons I managed _____ a new game.

2 ★★ **Complete the sentences with the correct forms of the verbs from the box. There are two extra verbs.**

be discuss interrupt show ~~study~~ talk think work

1 I can't stand *studying* at night – I need to sleep, not revise for exams!

2 This seems _____ a very interesting subject.

3 I can't imagine _____ to a machine!

4 The guide offered _____ us some of the exhibits.

5 Since I've left the project, I miss _____ with the other members of the team.

6 I hate _____ work problems with my family – I like to keep my work and home life separate.

3 ★★★ **Choose the correct verb forms to complete the sentences.**

1 a I have to go home. I forgot *to lock / locking* the door!

   b I forgot *to tell / telling* him the story, so I told it a second time. How embarrassing.

2 a The teacher regretted *to be / being* so hard on the student.

   b We regret *to inform / informing* you that today's lesson is cancelled.

3 a Luckily I remembered *to switch off / switching off* the lights so we didn't have to go back and do it.

   b I remember *to meet / meeting* your cousin very well.

4 a We stopped work *to have / having* a break because we were really tired.

   b A problem occurred so the scientists stopped *working / to work* on that project.

5 a We tried *to add / adding* more information to the program, but it didn't solve the problem.

   b She tried *to explain / explaining* the process but she didn't manage to.

4 ★★★ **Use the prompts to complete the conversation between a student and her teacher.**

Sharon   Mrs Shaw, I have a problem. **¹** I / can / not / understand / the process

I can't understand the process.

Mr Shaw   **²** You / need / study / your notes / again

_____

Sharon   The problem is that **³** I / not / enjoy / study / notes. **⁴** I / love / do / experiments

_____

_____

Mr Shaw   I know, but I can't **⁵** let / you / do / experiments without studying first

_____

Sharon   **⁶** I / like / work / in a lab / one day

_____

Mr Shaw   That's great, but study first! I think it will **⁷** allow / you / achieve / your ambition

_____

Sharon   Thanks, Mr Shaw. Don't worry, I won't **⁸** forget / read over / my notes this evening

_____

5 ON A HIGH NOTE **Write about some things you enjoy or don't enjoy at school and how they might affect your future. Use as many of the words and phrases in the box as possible.**

can't stand decide (don't) enjoy (don't) like
don't mind expect hate hope love refuse want
wouldn't like

2E LISTENING AND VOCABULARY

1 🔊 *10* **Listen to Part 1 of an interview with Deb who is talking about her plans for the future. What is her ambition?**

a to design phone apps
b to develop VR apps
c to develop video games

2 🔊 *11* **Listen to Part 2 of the interview and tick the things Deb mentions.**

1 ☐ video games
2 ☐ sports matches
3 ☐ medical procedures
4 ☐ famous landmarks
5 ☐ the theatre
6 ☐ shops
7 ☐ computer programming

3 🔊 *12* **Listen again to the whole interview and decide if statements 1–6 are true (T) or false (F), or if the information is not given (NG).**

1 ☐ The presenter hasn't met anyone with the same ambition before.
2 ☐ Deb plays video games.
3 ☐ Deb enjoys football.
4 ☐ People can use VR to walk around football matches.
5 ☐ Deb became interested in VR through school lessons.
6 ☐ Deb will begin her career by studying VR development at college.

Vocabulary extension

4 Complete the sentences with the correct prepositions from the box. You need to use some of the prepositions more than once.

---
from   in   of   ~~on~~   through   with
---

1 I've set my heart *on* becoming a pilot.
2 The students will be involved _____ designing the new school IT centre.
3 What did you do _____ History yesterday?
4 I don't remember a lot of things _____ my early Science lessons.
5 Some people learn _____ reading and others by doing things.
6 My friend has an interest _____ music from the 1990s.
7 In this game there's a lot of interaction _____ gamers from other countries.
8 I love the idea _____ getting a VR tour of the shops!

5 ON A HIGH NOTE **Write a short paragraph about a possible use of VR in the future and explain why it could be important.**

Pronunciation

ACTIVE PRONUNCIATION | The letter *o*

The letter *o* can be pronounced in many ways and the spelling of a word is not always a clear guide to its pronunciation. Three common ways of pronouncing *o* are:
• /ɒ/ (e.g. *got*)
• /uː/ (e.g. *do*)
• /əʊ/ (e.g. *go*)

Double *oo* can be pronounced in many ways. Two of the more common are:
• /ʊ/ (e.g. *book*)
• /uː/ (e.g. *moon*)

Be careful! *Blood* and *flood* are pronounced with the /ʌ/ sound.

6 🔊 *13* **Write the words from the box in the correct place in the chart. Listen, check and repeat.**

hope   involved   move

/ɒ/ got	/uː/ do	/əʊ/ go
_____	_____	_____
_____	_____	_____
_____	_____	_____
_____	_____	_____
_____	_____	_____

7 🔊 *14* **Listen to some more words from the interview and add them to the chart.**

8 🔊 *15* **Read the sentences aloud. Can you pronounce the words with the letter *o* correctly? Listen and check. Then practise saying the sentences.**

1 Both the codes for the webpage were wrong, so I didn't post a comment on the show.
2 Most of the clothes cost too much, but I finally chose a loose top with roses on it.
3 Tony lost his keys and couldn't unlock his car, so Sophie drove him home.
4 The notes he wrote prove that the majority of the population don't vote in local elections.

9 🔊 *16* **Write the words from the box in the correct place in the chart. Listen, check and repeat.**

boot   cook   good   hood   look   mood   room   soon   spoon   wood

/uː/ food	/ʊ/ foot
_____	_____
_____	_____
_____	_____
_____	_____
_____	_____

1 🔊 *17* Listen and repeat the phrases. How do you say them in your language?

SPEAKING | Making choices

MAKING SUGGESTIONS

What/How about getting her some books?
What do you think of getting her a new tablet computer?
Why don't we take her to the cinema?
Let's invite her to a restaurant.

EXPRESSING AND JUSTIFYING OPINIONS

You can't go wrong with getting new tech for Gran.
(That) sounds good/like a good idea.
(Personally,) (I think) that's a great idea because she likes reading.
(Personally,) (I think) that's a terrible idea because she hates reading.
It's not a bad idea, but it's not a good one either.
I don't think much of that idea, to be honest.
The main reason is the price.
Another reason is that she hates technology.

COMPARING OPTIONS

It isn't nearly as good/bad as the present I got her last year.
It's almost/It isn't quite as good/bad as getting her a computer game.
That's even better/worse than getting her a science-fiction book.
That's by far the best/worst idea.

REACHING DECISIONS

That's the best idea we've had.
That's the one!
(Let's) go for it!

---

2 🔊 *18* Complete the conversation with the words from the box. Then listen and check.

~~about~~ don't either far for go let's much nearly what

Ben So, it's Gran's birthday next week and we need to get her a present. Any ideas?

Emma How ¹ *about* getting her some books? She loves reading, especially science fiction.

Ben It's not a bad idea, but it's not a good one, ² _____. We don't know which books she's read and which ones she hasn't read! Why ³ _____ we take her to the cinema – she'd love to see the new film about robots!

Emma I don't think ⁴ _____ of that idea, to be honest. She hates the cinema. I think you suggested that because you want to see it!

Ben OK, OK! ⁵ _____ do something else. I know – ⁶ _____ do you think of asking Mum and Dad to get her a new tablet computer? We could add our money to the cost. Gran loves her iPad but it's so heavy. It's like a brick!

Emma Good thinking! You can't ⁷ _____ wrong with getting new tech for Gran. You know – she's amazing. She always emails and browses the internet. She even streams films and things. Yeah, that's by ⁸ _____ the best idea. It'll be expensive, but I'm sure Mum and Dad will agree.

Ben Great! Let's go ⁹ _____ it!

Emma Yes! It's ¹⁰ _____ as good as the present I got her last year.

Ben Oh, you mean when you bought her a computer game because you wanted to borrow it!

3 Choose the correct words or phrases to complete the sentences.

1 That *sounds / appears* like a good idea.
2 I think *that's / there's* a terrible idea.
3 The *another / main* reason I don't want to buy it is the price.
4 It isn't *quite / almost* as good as your last suggestion.
5 That's *quite / even* worse than your first idea!
6 Excellent! That's *the / a* one!

4 ON A HIGH NOTE **Read the following suggestions and write two responses of your own for each, giving reasons. One response should be positive and one negative.**

1 Let's do our Science homework together tonight.
2 Why don't we play your new video game this evening?
3 What do you think of entering the school 'new invention' competition this year?

2G WRITING AND VOCABULARY | A blog post

Mention the key point you want to make. Start with a thought-provoking question, an interesting fact or an inspiring question.

Give one or more arguments supporting your key point.

Mention arguments that don't support your key point.

Sum up your post and finish with something thought-provoking or amusing.

Mark's Blog   12th October

What is it with my mum and dad and technology? I can understand why they have different ideas about stuff like clothes and music. My parents are living in the 1990s as far as music is concerned and they won't even try to listen to the music on my playlist! But as far as tech is concerned I think they should realise how important it is to keep up to date. They're fine with the basics, but if I introduce them to anything new they just don't want to know. Apparently it's all because of something called 'the digital generation gap'!

It's **1**_true_ that some older people aren't comfortable using digital technology because they find it confusing and difficult to use. **2**_____, another reason for the problem is that some older people won't even try! **3**_____ to a recent survey, many older people won't even consider the idea of using VR, or being in a driverless car! What's **4**_____, between seventy and eighty percent of adults think that technology will have a negative effect in the future. It's crazy!

5_____ there are exceptions and some older people are really good at learning new digital skills (like my gran, who's brilliant!), maybe there should be a campaign to try and encourage others at least to try!

To **6**_____ up, the world is changing and new technologies are going to affect everyone – both young and old. We need to accept that, and learn how to function in that world. Be open to change, guys, and you'll be amazed at how your different your life can be!

How about your parents and grandparents? Click here to leave a (polite) comment.

1 Read the blog post and choose the best title.
- **a** Digital generation gap – the truth!
- **b** Changing attitudes
- **c** Can't do it? Won't do it!

2 Read the blog post again and complete it with the words from the box.

according   although   however   more   sum   ~~true~~

3 Tick the comment(s) which would NOT be appropriate to leave in response to the blog post.
- **a** ☐ This is rubbish! Of course older people can use tech! You don't know what you're talking about!
- **b** ☐ I'm not sure this is really true. My parents are very good with new tech.
- **c** ☐ You're right! My parents are scared to try out new tech and I'm often worried that my dad will throw his PC out of the window!

4 Read the writing task and tick the ideas you think you should include in your blog post.
- **1** ☐ lack of time to meet up
- **2** ☐ social media
- **3** ☐ importance of face-to-face conversations
- **4** ☐ easiness of video chats
- **5** ☐ good balance
- **6** ☐ different type of friends today

5 WRITING TASK Write a blog post about this topic: _Is it true that using technology means young people don't interact physically with friends and are becoming isolated?_

ACTIVE WRITING | A blog post

1 Plan your blog post.
- Think of a title which will attract people's attention.
- Plan an interesting introduction with a thought-provoking question or an interesting fact.
- Plan two or three paragraphs with different views.

2 Write your blog post.
- Start with a key point.
- Use chatty, informal language with short sentences.
- Give arguments that support and don't support your key point.
- Give some examples from your personal experience.
- Finish with a conclusion and a request for comments.

3 Check your blog post. Check that:
- there are no mistakes with spelling, grammar and punctuation.
- there is interesting and relevant topic vocabulary.

UNIT VOCABULARY PRACTICE

1 **2A GRAMMAR AND VOCABULARY** Complete the sentences with the words from the box.

constellation galaxy ~~launched~~ moon solar system
spaceship universe voyage

1 When NASA _launched_ the Voyager space probe everyone was very excited.

2 We think there are eight planets in our _____.

3 A group of stars is known as a _____.

4 There are many constellations in one _____.

5 Some planets have more than one _____ orbiting them.

6 It takes a lot of experts to build a _____ capable of carrying astronauts safely.

7 Voyager hasn't finished its _____ and is still travelling.

8 All matter is contained in one _____, but some scientists wonder if there are more.

2 **2B READING AND VOCABULARY** Choose the correct words to complete the sentences.

1 We _require / requirement_ some new information.

2 I'm afraid I _disagree / disagreement_ with your ideas on controlling machines.

3 I was unaware of the _exist / existence_ of this technology.

4 Can you please _identify / identification_ the main worries about AI?

5 I think your discovery was an incredible _achieve / achievement_.

6 Please follow the _proceed / procedure_ carefully.

7 Do you think machines _possess / possession_ emotions?

8 Recent _develop / developments_ in AI are very interesting.

3 **2C VOCABULARY** Complete the conversation with one word in each gap. The first letter is given to help you.

Yuri Eddie, I've made up my **1** m_ind_ about what to do for my Science project. I'm going to do something related to nuclear physics. I read an article recently and it **2** b_____ my mind!

Eddie Nuclear physics? Do you want to do **3** r_____ into nuclear power stations and so on?

Yuri No, I don't mean that. Think **4** a_____, Eddie.

Eddie Sorry, Yuri. My mind has gone **5** b_____. I can't imagine what you mean.

Yuri OK, let me put it another way. In Biology we can study the whole organism and we can also study a single **6** c_____. And then we can look into things which are even smaller.

Eddie Oh, I see. You mean that a nuclear physicist studies the nucleus. Atoms and things like that. I'd never thought about that before. You really broaden my **7** m_____ with your ideas, Yuri. I never think about science.

Yuri You should. It can help you to see things in a different way and to think **8** o_____ the box.

4 **2E LISTENING AND VOCABULARY** Match the words to make collocations.

1 ☐ aerial   **a** delivery
2 ☐ map   **b** filming
3 ☐ weather   **c** enforcement
4 ☐ commercial   **d** making
5 ☐ law   **e** forecasting

5 **2G WRITING AND VOCABULARY** Complete the text with the phrases from the box. There are two extra phrases.

depressed distractions forgetful ~~lack of sleep~~
memory loss multi-tasking sleep disorders stressed

Something that many people suffer from is **1** _lack of sleep_ – just not getting enough of it. The problem is that insomnia (not being able to sleep well) has got many causes. For example, if you are upset or **2** _____ by personal or professional problems, or if you are feeling **3** _____ and generally very down about things, this can lead to not sleeping. The common result of insomnia is **4** _____ . We just can't remember the things we need to – both at home and at work. **5** _____ can interrupt us easily, as we find it hard to concentrate, and we aren't as good at doing lots of things at the same time – what is sometimes known as '**6** _____'.

6 **ON A HIGH NOTE** Write a short paragraph about your sleeping habits and how they affect you.

1 For each learning objective, write 1–5 to assess your ability.

1 = I don't feel confident. 5 = I feel very confident.

	Learning objective	Course material	How confident I am (1–5)
2A	I can distinguish between the Present Perfect Simple and the Present Perfect Continuous to talk about recent finished or unfinished activities.	Student's Book pp. 18–19	
2B	I can understand the main idea and identify specific details in an article and talk about artificial intelligence.	Student's Book pp. 20–21	
2C	I can talk about science.	Student's Book p. 22	
2D	I can use a range of verbs taking the infinitive or the *-ing* form.	Student's Book p. 23	
2E	I can identify the main idea and key details in an interview and talk about technology.	Student's Book p. 24	
2F	I can make suggestions, express opinions, compare options and reach decisions.	Student's Book p. 25	
2G	I can write a blog post.	Student's Book pp. 26–27	

2 Which of the skills above would you like to improve in? How?

Skill I want to improve in	How I can improve

3 What can you remember from this unit?

New words I learned and most want to remember	Expressions and phrases I liked	English I heard or read outside class

GRAMMAR AND VOCABULARY

1 Choose the correct words to complete the sentences.

1 Her main problem was being tired because of *lack of sleep / memory loss*.

2 I think his main *achieve / achievement* was the discovery of a new star.

3 He's *made up / changed* his mind and decided on a different course.

4 The department received a *forecasting / delivery* of some new books.

5 He's an astronomer and loves studying the stars, especially groups of them in *constellations / cells*.

/ 5

2 Complete the sentences with the words from the box. There are two extra words.

ahead broaden changed development law
recognition twice

1 We want to work on the _____ of this new AI technology.

2 Do you think that voice _____ programmes are useful for giving instructions?

3 You need to read more to _____ your mind and learn new ideas.

4 We need to think _____ and plan for the future.

5 Is it against the _____ to send drones over people's gardens?

/ 5

3 Complete the text with the Present Perfect Simple or Present Perfect Continuous forms of the verbs from the box. Sometimes both tenses are correct.

do make not finish not waste work

Our research team **1**_____ on this new development for two years, but we **2**_____ our work yet. What **3**_____ (we) all this time? We **4**_____ time, that's for sure. **5**_____ (we) progress? Absolutely – as we can see from the interest that scientists from all over the world are taking in our project.

/ 5

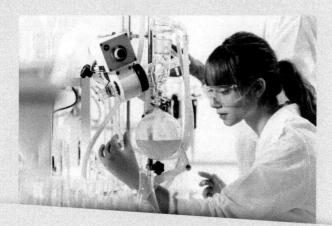

4 Complete the sentences with the correct forms of the verbs in brackets.

1 We recently decided _____ (launch) a new space probe.

2 They've promised _____ (increase) students' knowledge of physics.

3 She says we've met before, but I can't remember _____ (meet) her.

4 You need to stop _____ (do) crossword puzzles all the time and get out more.

5 I'm afraid she's refused _____ (allow) you to do aerial photography over her house.

/ 5

USE OF ENGLISH

5 Complete the text with the correct forms of the words in brackets.

It was very unpleasant when the two scientists had a **1**_____ (DISAGREE) over how to proceed. One of them said the standard **2**_____ (PROCEED) was old-fashioned and wanted to change it. The other said that the **3**_____ (IDENTIFY) of a new one was too difficult – there were too many new **4**_____ (REQUIRE). He rejected his colleague's **5**_____ (PROPOSE) and this offended the colleague.

/ 5

6 Complete the second sentence so that it has a similar meaning to the first one. Use between two and five words, including the word in bold.

1 The Voyagers were launched in 1977. **TRAVELLING**
The Voyagers _____ since 1977.

2 I started this book last week and I haven't finished it yet. **HAVE**
I _____ this book since last week.

3 She said she would never use AI. **REFUSED**
She _____ AI.

4 I'm sure I haven't read that book. **REMEMBER**
I _____ that book.

5 They didn't work on the programme after the disaster. **STOPPED**
They _____ on the programme after the disaster.

/ 5

/ 30

03 *Active and healthy*

3A GRAMMAR AND VOCABULARY

Past Simple, Past Continuous and Past Perfect

1 ★ **Complete the sentences with the correct Past Simple forms of the verbs in brackets.**

1 The viewers ___didn't see___ (not see) the accident because it happened off camera.

2 Where _____ (you / learn) to do those back flips?

3 Martha _____ (not compete) that year because of an injury.

4 The team _____ (take) home seven medals from the championship.

5 How _____ (she / injure) her shoulder?

6 The athlete _____ (try) three times to set a new world record.

7 Maria _____ (start) out as an amateur swimmer but turned professional at the age of eighteen.

8 John was so tired after the race that he _____ (not celebrate) winning the silver medal.

2 ★ **Do these Past Continuous sentences refer to an action interrupted by another action (A), a temporary situation (B), or an action in progress at a precise time in the past (C)?**

1 ☐ At that time, I was staying with my aunt.

2 ☐ My brother was doing his fitness training at four thirty yesterday.

3 ☐ Katie was snowboarding very fast when she crashed.

4 ☐ The team was travelling to the competition when they heard the news.

5 ☐ I was working as a guest coach that summer.

6 ☐ At this time last week I was talking to the doctor about my injury.

3 ★ **Complete the sentences with the correct Past Continuous forms of the verbs from the box.**

do go not concentrate not train ~~sleep~~ stay

1 At six o'clock this morning I ___was sleeping___.

2 Where _____ (you) yesterday morning when I saw you?

3 She _____ hard enough, so her coach gave her more exercises.

4 He _____ with a friend at that time.

5 The athlete _____ during the race so she missed the jump.

6 What _____ (the athletes) when you got to the stadium?

4 ★★ **Choose the correct verb forms to complete the sentences.**

1 Penny *fell / was falling* while she *was running / ran* in the 100-metre race.

2 Their coach *stopped / was stopping* them because they *made / were making* so many mistakes.

3 I *worked / was working* in a sports centre when I *met / was meeting* the paralympic team.

4 Gary *used / was using* crutches until his doctor *suggested / was suggesting* a wheelchair.

5 Jack suddenly *did / was doing* an amazing double back flip as we *watched / were watching* him!

6 Olivia *considered / was considering* giving up sport when she *heard / was hearing* that she had been chosen for the team!

5 ★★ **Use the prompts to complete the sentences. Use the Past Perfect.**

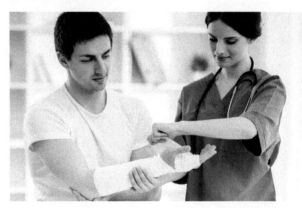

1 At the medical examination Brian discovered ... that he / break / his wrist
   ___that he had broken his wrist.___

2 He got into the team because ... he / not lose / a single match

   _____

3 he / learn / to do back flips ... before he went to Brazil?

   _____

4 The competitor was sure ... she / beat / the world record

   _____

5 the judges / ever / see ... such a brilliant performance before?

   _____

6 She could compete in the Paralympics because ... she / not / become / a professional

   _____

28

6 ⭐⭐ **Complete the sentences with one word in each gap.**

1 Dad had made dinner *by* the time we arrived.

2 We arrived here two days _____.

3 I offered to help, but she had _____ solved the problem.

4 _____ time last week I was running in the park.

5 We called home as _____ as we had heard the news.

6 I went to the cinema _____ Wednesday.

7 I was playing tennis _____ two and three.

8 The match started _____ noon, but all the players had come much earlier.

7 ⭐⭐ **Complete the sentences with the correct Past Simple or Past Perfect forms of the verbs in brackets.**

1 Jack *spent* (spend) six months in hospital after the injury. He _____ (never/spent) so much time in a hospital before.

2 I _____ (not realise) that the Paralympics _____ (be) so spectacular until I _____ (see) the games on TV.

3 Paula _____ (be) an amateur for five years before she _____ (decide) to turn professional.

4 No one _____ (leave) the stadium until the last athlete _____ (complete) the competition.

5 The team _____ (win) easily because they _____ (practise) more than any of their opponents.

8 ⭐⭐⭐ **Complete the sentences with the correct forms of the verbs from the box. Use the Past Simple, the Past Continuous or the Past Perfect.**

be break celebrate feel leave ~~not see~~ run sleep win

1 The children *hadn't seen* a paralympic sport before so they _____ very curious.

2 Martin _____ in a marathon when he suddenly _____ unwell.

3 I can't believe you _____ at eleven o'clock this morning. Why were you still in bed?

4 Clare _____ the team because she _____ her arm.

5 We _____ with a big party when we heard that she _____ the medal.

9 ⭐⭐⭐ **Complete the story with the correct forms of the verbs from the box. Use the Past Simple, the Past Continuous or the Past Perfect.**

give up listen to lose ~~read~~ realise see seem think

One day Rona ¹*was reading* an article about sport, when she ² _____ some information about a local paralympic group. Her brother Tom ³ _____ the use of his right arm three years before in an accident. He ⁴ _____ doing any kind of sport soon after that. Rona called him – he ⁵ _____ music in his room. She showed him the article and asked if he ⁶ _____ about taking part in a sport again. Tom ⁷ _____ very interested – he ⁸ _____ before then that there were local groups like that.

10 ⭐⭐⭐ **Use the prompts to write the interview.**

Journalist ¹ You / become / a paralympic athlete / when / you / be / twenty ² Why / be / that?

You became a paralympic athlete when you were twenty.

_____

Caroline ³ I / lose / the use of my legs / after / I / suffer / a serious injury ⁴ I / be / always / keen on sport / before that

_____

Journalist ⁵ why / you / choose / basketball?

_____

Caroline ⁶ I / watch / TV / one day / when / I / see / a Paralympic match ⁷ I / not see / one / before ⁸ it / inspire / me

_____
_____
_____

11 ON A HIGH NOTE **Write a short paragraph about an athlete or a sportsperson you admire. Describe his/her life story and say why he/she inspires you.**

3B VOCABULARY | Sports, activities, fitness and exercise

1 ⭐ **The words in bold are in the wrong sentences. Write the correct words.**

1 Our coach made us run ten times around the football **room**! _pitch_

2 It's too hot to go to the tennis **pitch** today. _____

3 Julia is taking part in a competition at the swimming **machine**. _____

4 The girls do all kinds of different sports at the leisure **court**. _____

5 The two fighters stepped carefully into the boxing **centre**. _____

6 Can I train on the rowing **track** this evening? _____

7 Let's go and put on our swimsuits in the changing **pool**. _____

8 Training for this year's event will take place at the athletics **ring**. _____

2 ⭐ **Complete the sentences with the words from the box.**

fit get shape ~~unfit~~ weights world

1 I haven't done any exercise for months and I'm really _unfit_!

2 I'd like to get into _____ for my summer beach holiday.

3 You can get stronger by lifting _____, but take care not to injure yourself.

4 I can't believe you _____ out of breath just walking to school! Don't you ever exercise?

5 I want to keep _____ so I can join the volleyball team.

6 This fitness programme is great – it's done me the _____ of good.

3 ⭐ **Choose the correct words to complete the sentences.**

1 Poor Sally has broken _an / her_ arm.

2 Has John hurt _the / his_ back?

3 I think I've pulled _a / my_ muscle.

4 The doctor thinks Bob has dislocated _his / one_ shoulder.

5 Have you banged _the / your_ head?

6 Where did she hurt _her / the_ leg?

4 ⭐⭐ **Complete the sentences with one word in each gap. The first letter is given to help you.**

1 It was very painful when I d_islocated_ my shoulder.

2 George can't walk because he's twisted his a_____.

3 Leo had to stop playing rugby for months after he b_____ his arm.

4 Maya b_____ her head against the door – I think she should sit down for a while.

5 Your wrist isn't broken, but you have s_____ it, which is why it's so painful.

6 He's holding his leg – I think he's pulled a m_____.

5 ⭐⭐ **Complete the text with one word in each gap.**

There are many rules to observe if you are using a tennis or squash ¹_court_ or an athletics ²_____. It is important to stay in your area, or you could bump into another player or athlete. An athlete who falls over during a race risks serious injury – he or she could ³_____ their head against someone or something. Another place with strict rules is the ⁴_____ ring. If a competitor behaves badly, the referee will send him back to the ⁵_____ room.

6 ⭐⭐ **Complete the second text with one word in each gap so that it has the same meaning as the original.**

The other day I was at that place where the kids play football and I was watching a game. Unfortunately, one of the players fell over and didn't get up. I thought he had injured his leg muscle, but after some time they took him to the room where players get changed. The poor boy had broken the part of his body between his leg and his foot. That's worse than twisting it because it takes longer to heal. He'll have to work hard to reach the same level of fitness again.

The other day I was at the football ¹_pitch_ and I was watching a game. Unfortunately, one of the players fell over and didn't get up. I thought he had ²_____ a leg muscle, but after some time they took him back to the ³_____ room. The poor boy had broken his ⁴_____. That's worse than ⁵_____ it because it takes longer to heal. He'll have to work hard to get into ⁶_____ again.

7 ON A HIGH NOTE **Write a short paragraph about a sport you do or would like to do and what risk of injury it involves.**

3C LISTENING AND VOCABULARY

1 🔊 *19* **Listen to six sentences and match them to the functions a–f.**

a ☐ requesting
b ☐ giving opinion
c ☐ explaining
d ☐ complaining
e ☐ advising
f ☐ agreeing

2 🔊 *20* **Listen and choose the correct answers.**

1 You will hear a boy talking about his experience in hospital. What does Josh think of the hospital ward he's in?
  a His treatment would be better in a different ward.
  b He's happy that the staff are so friendly.
  c The atmosphere is helping him to get better.

2 You will hear a girl talking to a friend. Where is the girl?
  a in the hospital café
  b in the hospital garden
  c in the hospital shower room

3 You will hear a boy talking to an ambulance man. What is the boy's main purpose?
  a to explain his dad's medical condition
  b to recommend that others learn first aid
  c to thank the ambulance man for helping his dad

4 You will hear a boy talking to a girl at a party. What is his main purpose?
  a to complain about the A and E department
  b to reassure her that he's not seriously hurt
  c to explain why he is late for the party

5 You will hear a woman talking to a man about visiting a friend in hospital. How was the patient feeling?
  a excited about going home
  b amused by something she'd read
  c bored because she had nothing to do

Vocabulary extension

3 🔊 *21* **Complete the sentences from the recording in Exercise 2 with the words from the box. Then listen and check.**

collapsed infection minor symptoms ~~treatment~~ ward

1 The *treatment* is wonderful all over this hospital.
2 I was so fed up with being on the _____ that I wheeled myself to the café.
3 Congratulations on knowing how to treat your dad when he _____.
4 I know all the _____.
5 Lots of people had cuts and bruises – all _____ injuries, thank goodness.
6 It cheered me up when I was feeling low after a(n) _____ last month.

Pronunciation

4 🔊 *22* **Read some sentences from the listening. Mark where you think the stress is on the highlighted words. Listen and check.**

1 Better than when I came in thanks – I've made a lot of progress, ...
2 Here's a copy of his records and the medicine that he's taking.
3 The doctors and nurses were very busy because of a sudden increase in emergencies.
4 I thought I'd update you on how she's doing.
5 This routine is a real contrast for her.

ACTIVE PRONUNCIATION | Noun and verb syllable stress

There are many two-syllable words in English which have the same noun and verb form. For nouns, we often stress the first syllable and for verbs, we often stress the second syllable, e.g.:
• He's going to re**cord** the interview.
• My mum has an old Beatles **re**cord.

Be careful! Some words, e.g. *answer* have the same stress for both the noun and verb form.

Sometimes moving the stress can change the meaning of a word, e.g.:
• **ob**ject (n) = a thing
• ob**ject** (v) = to disagree with an idea.

5 🔊 *23* **Listen to the words. Circle N for Noun or V for Verb depending on how the speaker pronounces each word.**

1 protest	N / V		**5** reject	N / V
2 upgrade	N / V		**6** contest	N / V
3 insult	N / V		**7** import	N / V
4 refund	N / V		**8** suspect	N / V

6 🔊 *24* **Listen and repeat the two ways of stressing the same words.**

7 🔊 *25* **Read the pairs of sentences aloud. Listen and check. Then practise saying the sentences with the correct syllable stress for the underlined words.**

1 I never refuse an invitation.
The refuse collector takes our bins every Thursday.
2 The teacher was pleased with her students' conduct.
One day my sister would like to conduct an orchestra.
3 It's important to live in the present and not always plan for the future.
My group is going to present our work to the class.
4 It must be exciting to cross the desert in a car.
Don't worry, I'm not going to desert you.
5 This is a strange-looking object.
If you don't object, I'll bring my own lunch.

UNIT VOCABULARY PRACTICE > page 37   31

3D GRAMMAR | Used to and would

1 ★ Complete the sentences with the correct forms of *used to* and the verbs in brackets.

1 ☐ We *used to go* (go) skiing every day during the winter holidays.
2 ☐ They _____ (train) regularly.
3 ☐ _____ (you / eat) a lot of junk food when you were younger?
4 ☐ As children we _____ (not like) getting up early.
5 ☐ People _____ (believe) that smoking isn't bad for you.
6 ☐ _____ (your parents / exercise) more than you when they were children?
7 ☐ I _____ (drink) lots of fizzy drinks when I was younger, but I prefer juice now.
8 ☐ We _____ (love) meeting at the café.

2 ★ Tick the sentences in Exercise 1 where you can replace *used to* with *would*.

3 ★★ Complete the conversation with one word in each gap.

Max   Hey! Do you remember this cartoon?
Peter   Of course I do!
Max   Did you ¹*use* to watch it when you were little?
Peter   Yes, I ² _____ to watch it every day after school!
Max   ³ _____ you have a snack while you were watching it?
Peter   Yes, I ⁴ _____ always make myself a sandwich.
Max   Me too – well. I used ⁵ _____ have a snack. I didn't ⁶ _____ to have a sandwich though. I ⁷ _____ always eat crisps while I was watching TV.
Peter   My mum ⁸ _____ let me eat crisps!

4 ★★ Choose the correct verb forms to complete the sentences.

1 We *never would / never used to* eat meat because my parents are vegetarian.
2 *Did the children use to / Would the children* be well-behaved when they were younger?
3 They didn't *use / used* to have vegan dishes but now there are two on the menu.
4 We *would spend / spent* the yesterday afternoon at the leisure centre – it was great fun!
5 *Did he use to twist / Did he twist* his ankle while he was skiing?
6 Did Sally *used / use* to go to that café when she lived near here?
7 The sports club *would / used* have a party every year.
8 William *pulled / would pull* a muscle in his leg while he was exercising.

5 ★★★ Complete the text with the correct forms of *would* or *used to* and the verbs from the box. Use *would/ wouldn't* wherever possible.

cook ~~eat~~ love order not think watch

Mr and Mrs Jones and their children were a typical family. They ¹*would eat* meat of some sort every day. They ² _____ there was anything wrong with this. Mr and Mrs Jones ³ _____ TV every evening and one evening they saw a documentary about nutrition. They were shocked. Before, they ⁴ _____ burgers every evening. Now they make vegeburgers instead. They've also changed other habits. At restaurants they ⁵ _____ chips with everything. They ⁶ _____ chips more than any other food! Now they prefer salad. Their health has improved a lot since they changed their eating habits!

6 ON A HIGH NOTE Write about how your eating habits have changed since you were a child. Use *would* and *used to*.

3E SPEAKING AND VOCABULARY

1 🔊 *26* **Listen and repeat the phrases. How do you say them in your language?**

SPEAKING | Being polite

DIRECT QUESTIONS

Could you help me?
How much is this?
Will it take long?

INDIRECT QUESTIONS

I wonder if/whether you could help me?
Could you (possibly) tell me how much this is?
Do you think it will take long?

OTHER POLITE PHRASES

I was wondering if you have some time to talk.
I'd like to know if you eat health food.
Have you got any idea how to improve our diet?
Do you (happen to) know where these eggs come from?
Would you mind telling me if this cake contains milk?

REFUSING POLITELY

That's very kind of you, but I'm busy on Sunday.
They look/sound very nice, but I'm afraid they're too expensive.
No, that's alright thanks.
Thanks for the offer, but I can't accept it.
Thank you, but I'm alright.

2 🔊 *27* **Listen to the conversation and choose the correct answers.**

1 Why is the man asking questions?
  a He needs information.
  b He's checking people's health.
2 Who is more polite?
  a the girl
  b the man
3 Do you think the girl eats healthily?
  a yes
  b no

3 **Complete the sentences from the conversation with the words from the box.**

---
afraid   alright   any   could   if   kind   like   mind   ~~wondering~~

---

1 I was *wondering* if you had a few minutes.
2 Would you _____ telling me if you regularly eat health food?
3 Have you _____ idea where the food comes from?
4 Do you know _____ the vegetables are locally grown?
5 _____ you tell me if you ever eat wholemeal bread?
6 I'd also _____ to know if you ever go to specialist health food shops.
7 That's _____.
8 That's very _____ of you, but I've finished.
9 I'm _____ I can't say.

4 **Choose the correct phrases to complete the sentences.**

1 *I was wondering if you could / Would you mind* give me some advice about healthy eating?
2 *Do you know if / Have you any idea* Tony has gone home yet?
3 *I'm afraid / Thanks for the offer*, but I'm a bit busy this afternoon.
4 *I'd like to know what / Could you tell me if* vitamins green vegetables contain.
5 *Do you think / Do you happen to know* when Mr Banks will arrive?
6 *That's alright thanks / I was wondering*, but I've managed to fix the computer myself.

5 ON A HIGH NOTE **Write polite requests and refusals.**
You want …
1 to know what time the health food shop opens.
2 to know if your letter has arrived yet.
3 to say sorry that you can't go to a club meeting.
4 to refuse an invitation to a party.
5 to ask for information about the ingredients of a meal.
6 to find out a friend's phone number.

3F READING AND VOCABULARY

1 **Look at the photos and the title of the blog post. What do you think it will be about?**

   a how chocolate is made

   b the benefits of eating chocolate

   c people's chocolate eating habits

2 **Now read the blog post quickly and decide if statements 1–6 are true (T), false (F), or if the information is not given (NG).**

   1 ☐ The writer believes what the health experts say.

   2 ☐ The writer is concerned about the amount of chocolate he eats.

   3 ☐ The writer's friend has changed recently.

   4 ☐ The writer thinks that all types of chocolate can be good for us.

   5 ☐ According to the writer, chocolate has both mental and physical health benefits.

   6 ☐ The writer has also done some research into junk food.

3 **Read the text again. Match sentences A–H with gaps 1–5 in the blog post. There are three extra sentences.**

   A You have to eat it though, not rub it on your back!

   B But I think it's fair to say that a little of what you like won't harm you.

   C There's no reason to feel guilty about eating a little chocolate.

   D It seems that chocolate can improve our ability to think clearly and to concentrate.

   E Swiss scientists have proved that eating chocolate can have other health benefits.

   F Apparently, they're the same chemicals that are released when we fall in love!

   G She used to eat a well-balanced diet apart from a burger now and then and – unfortunately – quite a lot of chocolate.

   H Of course, eating too much of anything is never a good idea.

Vocabulary extension

4 **Replace the underlined parts with words and phrases a–f from the text.**

   1 I don't mean that you should eat huge quantities.

   2 Watching the documentary made me consider my own lifestyle.

   3 Being heavily overweight can cause heart disease.

   4 Food experts give advice on diets and healthy eating.

   5 Eating a diet which is high in fat can cause serious medical problems.

   6 I used to eat enormous amounts of ice cream.

   a nutritionists

   b binge on

   c obesity

   d lead to

   e I'm not saying that

   f got me thinking about

ACTIVE VOCABULARY | Phrasal verbs

A phrasal verb has a meaning which is different from the original verb, e.g. *look* means to see something with your eyes, but *look up* means to find something in a dictionary.

5 **Match the phrasal verbs 1–6 with their definitions a–f.**

   1 ☐ check out

   2 ☐ cheer up

   3 ☐ cut out

   4 ☐ get over

   5 ☐ lay off

   6 ☐ look into

   a feel/get better (after an illness or injury)

   b stop eating or using something for a short time

   c make someone feel happier

   d try to discover some facts about something

   e look at something (because it might be interesting/ useful)

   f stop eating or drinking something

6 **Complete the sentences with the phrasal verbs from Exercise 5.**

   1 My mum had flu last year and it took her weeks to *get over* it.

   2 If you're not sleeping well you should _____ eating cheese in the evening.

   3 _____ this food website – it's got some interesting information.

   4 Scientists have _____ exactly how chocolate affects brain function.

   5 I know Micky loves coffee but he should _____ it for a while because it gives him headaches.

   6 Let's go and visit Dan in the hospital and try to _____ .

7 ON A HIGH NOTE **Write a short comment about the text you have read on chocolate. Give your reaction to the text and your opinion of what you read.**

| UNIT VOCABULARY PRACTICE > page 37

WELL, THAT'S A NICE SURPRISE ...!

Most people seem to be on some sort of healthy-eating programme these days. There are so many nutritionists, doctors and even celebrities out there, telling us all how to lose weight and live healthy life styles. They make us feel guilty if we even look at a burger or a bar of chocolate! Their statistics and warnings seem convincing, but should we always believe what they tell us?

My friend Evie is a good example. She was a happy, smiley person until … she made up her mind to change her diet. **1**_____ At school, she would eat a bar at break time every morning. So what happened? Well, last year she saw a programme about obesity on TV and she decided to stop eating junk food and sugary snacks, including chocolate. The result? Evie is a little slimmer now, but she's also miserable!

So I did some research into Evie's favourite sugary snack – and I found out some amazing things! If you don't binge on it and only eat the lovely dark stuff, it's actually good for you in lots of ways. Can you believe it? Here's what I discovered …

- First of all, it's good for the brain. **2**_____ In addition, new research from an American university shows that it helps to improve memory too. Many people have problems remembering things and chocolate can help reduce this memory loss. Some studies even claim that chocolate can help people get over minor brain injuries.

- It's good for our hearts, our blood pressure and our digestive systems, too, and it reduces the so-called 'bad' cholesterol in our blood. That's the stuff that affects how the blood moves round our bodies and can lead to heart attacks.

- It's also good for our skin and helps protect it against sun damage! **3**_____

- It can actually help us lose weight. Eating a piece of chocolate tells the brain that we're full and we don't want to eat much more!

- And perhaps most importantly, it improves our mood. It really does make us happier. When we eat chocolate, the brain releases chemicals that relax us and make us feel calm and happy. **4**_____ Isn't that amazing?

Of course, I'm not saying that everyone should become a chocoholic. That would be very irresponsible of me. **5**_____ In fact, it may even do you some good! So, I believe that if Evie eats just a little chocolate, she will feel happier and maybe do better at school, too!

This research has really got me thinking about other foods that are supposed to be unhealthy and I'm going to look into junk food like pizzas, burgers and ice cream next. Then on to sauces like tomato ketchup and salad dressings. Is there a chance that they might be good for us in some way too? Watch this space!!

3G **WRITING** | A short story

Catch the reader's attention with a statement or an interesting detail.

Say where and when the story happened; set the scene.

Use direct speech to add interest.

Use shorter sentences to add drama.

Describe the action using a variety of past tenses.

Use a variety of verbs to report speech.

Finish with how the main character(s) felt and what they learned or a decision they made.

That morning I was really excited – the day had finally come! The sky was clear and blue, but it wasn't hot – perfect weather for the cycle race. Dad drove me and my bike to the start of the race where I waited with the other cyclists.

While we were waiting for the starting gun, I looked through the trees. I had to cycle ten kilometres, but I knew I could win the race. 'We'll wait for you at the finish line!' Dad shouted.

The starting gun sounded. We raced off at top speed. I could hear the spectators shouting, but I just concentrated on cycling. The race went like a dream and soon I was coming into the last 100 metres. I was second in the group of riders! My family were cheering loudly as I passed the leading cyclist. After that, I knew I would win the race. Suddenly, without warning, he moved in front of me. When he banged into my bike, I was thrown into the road and landed heavily on my ankle. I screamed in pain. The other cyclists raced past me. Then I heard my sister yell, 'Come on Davy! You've got to finish!'

Slowly I stood up. I was the only cyclist left on the road. But my sister was right. I had to finish. It took me a long time to walk that last 100 metres, but I did it in the end. The spectators cheered me as I crossed the finish line. My dad was smiling. 'We're proud of you!' he whispered and I felt like a winner.

1 Read the story. What do you think would be the best title?
 a A good race
 b The first and best
 c I lost but I won

2 Write the time linkers next to the correct heading. Then add the highlighted linkers from the story.

after a while   all of a sudden   at first   at the same time
by the time   eventually   finally   from nowhere
in the beginning   just then   later   next

Start the action
at first, _____ , _____
Move the action on

_____ , _____ , _____ , _____ , _____

Introduce a dramatic moment

_____ , _____ , _____ , _____

Describe events that happened at the same time

_____ , _____ , _____

Finish the action

_____ , _____ , _____

3 Look at the pictures A–D at the bottom of the page and make a note of the key words you will need to write this story.

4 WRITING TASK Use the pictures to write a story.

ACTIVE WRITING | A story

1 Plan your story.
 • Look at the pictures and plan what you're going to write in each paragraph.
 • Think of a good title for your story.

2 Write your story.
 • Say where and when the story happened.
 • Use a variety of reporting verbs, interesting adjectives and time linkers.
 • Include some direct speech.
 • Use short sentences to add drama.

3 Check your story. Check that:
 • there are no spelling, grammar or punctuation mistakes.
 • there is interesting and relevant topic vocabulary.

A
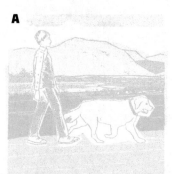

B

C

D

1 **3A GRAMMAR AND VOCABULARY** **Complete the sentences with one word in each gap.**

1 He doesn't compete for money – he's an a*mateur* sportsman.

2 Did you enter the c_____? You have a good chance of winning.

3 I'm sure you can beat the school r_____ because you're so fast.

4 She fell down some stairs and suffered a serious i_____ to her leg.

5 We'd like a p_____ coach who really knows the job.

6 I believe our team will t_____ home a lot of medals.

7 Our football team has q_____ for the finals!

2 **3B VOCABULARY** **Match the beginnings 1–6 with the endings a–f.**

1 ☐ Sally is running around

2 ☐ Stay off the football

3 ☐ You can leave your clothes

4 ☐ I was too scared to go

5 ☐ From the X-ray we can see you've broken

6 ☐ She's in pain because she sprained

a your leg in two places.

b up the rock climbing wall.

c the athletics track.

d her wrist while playing tennis.

e pitch while people are training.

f in the changing room.

3 **Complete the sentences with one preposition in each gap.**

1 I haven't done any sports for a long time. I really need to get *into* shape!

2 I think yoga did my mum the world _____ good! She's not only slimmer now, but also feels more relaxed.

3 My dad is in his sixties, but he never gets _____ of breath!

4 Weightlifting can help you to build _____ your muscles.

5 When my boyfriend and I went walking in the mountains I was so _____ of shape that he had to carry my rucksack for me!

4 **3C LISTENING AND VOCABULARY** **Choose the correct words to complete the sentences.**

1 Emily is *dislocated / unconscious* because she has *fainted / burned*.

2 The man was in *shock / painful* after the car *banged / knocked* him down.

3 A *pain / hurt* in your chest can be a sign of a heart *attack / break*.

4 After the accident she *was bleeding / had a sprain* from the *burns / cuts* on her arm.

5 Some idiot *set fire / reported* to a garage and the owner *bruised / burned* his hands in the fire.

6 I can hear an alarm *ringing / burning* – perhaps we should *report / tell* it to the police?

7 My sister got a nasty *hurt / bruise* when she *banged / shocked* her knee.

5 **3E SPEAKING AND VOCABULARY** **Complete the conversation with the words from the box.**

~~free-range~~ freshly-squeezed locally grown organic wholemeal

Waiter	Hi, can I help you?
Customer	Yes, I'd like to know if your eggs are ¹*free-range*, please.
Waiter	Yes, they are.
Customer	OK, I'd like an omelette. Will it take long?
Waiter	No, just a few minutes. Would you like some ²_____ bread, too?
Customer	That's very kind of you, thanks. About the tomatoes – are they ³_____? I don't want to eat chemicals in my salad!
Waiter	Yes, they are. All the vegetables are also ⁴_____. We buy them from a farmer near here. Anything to drink?
Customer	Would you mind telling me if the orange juice is ⁵_____?
Waiter	Yes, I do it myself to order.

6 **3F READING AND VOCABULARY** **Complete the text with one word in each gap.**

To get into shape, you need to exercise, but you also have to be careful about what you eat – your ¹d*iet* is vital for your health. If your food is high in ²c_____, you'll put on weight. Limit them! Avoid ³j_____ foods from factories and cook your own meals with healthy ⁴i_____. Choose ⁵f_____ fruit and vegetables when possible. Drink water or fruit juice (it's ⁶f_____ of vitamins) and avoid ⁷f_____ drinks full of gas and sugar. And stay away from ⁸f_____ food outlets – they may be cheap but they're very bad for you.

7 **ON A HIGH NOTE** **Write about the kinds of food you eat. Which of them are healthy/unhealthy? Could you do anything to eat a healthier diet?**

1 **For each learning objective, write 1–5 to assess your ability.**

1 = I don't feel confident. 5 = I feel very confident.

	Learning objective	Course material	How confident I am (1–5)
3A	I can use the Past Simple, the Past Continuous and the Past Perfect to talk about past actions.	Student's Book pp. 34–35	
3B	I can talk about sports, activities, fitness and exercise.	Student's Book p. 36	
3C	I can identify the speaker's purpose and specific information in conversations and talk about accidents.	Student's Book p. 37	
3D	I can use *used to* and *would* to talk about past habits and routines.	Student's Book p. 38	
3E	I can use indirect questions to make polite requests or to ask for opinions and information.	Student's Book p. 39	
3F	I can understand the development of ideas in an article and talk about eating habits.	Student's Book pp. 40–41	
3G	I can write a short story.	Student's Book pp. 42–43	

2 **Which of the skills above would you like to improve in? How?**

Skill I want to improve in	How I can improve

3 **What can you remember from this unit?**

New words I learned and most want to remember	Expressions and phrases I liked	English I heard or read outside class

GRAMMAR AND VOCABULARY

1 **Match the words to make collocations.**

1 ☐ football		**a** wrist
2 ☐ squash		**b** fit
3 ☐ world		**c** leg
4 ☐ leisure		**d** court
5 ☐ changing		**e** muscle
6 ☐ sprained		**f** breath
7 ☐ broken		**g** pitch
8 ☐ pulled		**h** room
9 ☐ out of		**i** centre
10 ☐ keep		**j** record

/ 5

2 **Complete the sentences with the words from the box. There are two extra words.**

bruise burn fizzy injury junk organic wholemeal

1 Mike needs to rest after that bad _____.

2 Sue's got a horrible purple _____ where she banged her leg.

3 We prefer to buy _____ fruit and vegetables where possible.

4 I don't think _____ drinks are very good for you.

5 Mark put on weight after eating a lot of _____ food.

/ 5

3 **Complete the sentences with the correct forms of the verbs in brackets. Use the Past Simple, the Past Continuous or the Past Perfect.**

1 We decided to try marathon running while we _____ (watch) one on TV!

2 Josh _____ (not try) snowboarding before and was amazed by how much fun it was.

3 Why _____ (the player/lie) on the pitch when we got there? Was he injured?

4 _____ (you/hear) of the sport of curling before you saw it at the Winter Olympics?

5 The team _____ (not perform) well at that point so the coach changed the players.

/ 5

4 **Choose the correct verb forms to complete the blog post.**

When I was a child I **1** *used to / would* think that fizzy drinks were fantastic. I **2** *didn't know / wasn't knowing* that they were bad for me because they're full of sugar. My mother used to make freshly-squeezed orange juice for me, but I **3** *was always refusing / would always refuse* it! I **4** *didn't used / didn't use* to like the bits in the juice! What else **5** *did I use to / would I* hate as a child? Vegetables! Today I love eating salads and fresh vegetables. But guess what? I still hate fruit juice with bits in it!

/ 5

USE OF ENGLISH

5 **Choose the correct answers.**

Martha **1**_____ never tried squash before because none of her friends **2**_____ play it. When she saw it on TV though, she was fascinated and wanted to try. She found a leisure centre where there was a squash **3**_____ and played her first match. It's a very hard sport, but although Martha was out of **4**_____ by the end, she loved the game. Now she plays all the time and next week she's going to take part in her first **5**_____ – good luck, Martha!

1 **a** hadn't	**b** was	**c** had	**d** would
2 **a** did	**b** use to	**c** would	**d** used
3 **a** court	**b** machine	**c** track	**d** pitch
4 **a** fit	**b** breath	**c** shape	**d** fitness
5 **a** medal	**b** concussion	**c** competition	**d** injury

/ 5

6 **Complete the text with one word in each gap.**

I can't believe what happened last night. I had just fallen asleep when I heard a **1**_____ alarm ringing. I jumped out of bed because I thought a house was burning somewhere. The emergency services arrived quickly – someone **2**_____ called them straight away. I got dressed and went to see if I could help. But there was no emergency. My neighbour, who loves chips, had **3**_____ fire to his kitchen with the chip pan! Luckily he was able to put the fire out by himself, but of course the smoke alarm went off. I'm glad his house didn't burn **4**_____, but by the time I got home I was really tired. I've got sports practice this morning and I'm going to feel exhausted on the football **5**_____.

/ 5

/ 30

Time to move

4A GRAMMAR AND VOCABULARY

Modal and related verbs

1 ⭐ Match the sentences 1–8 with the functions a–h.

1 ☐ You must switch off your smartphones.
2 ☐ You mustn't smoke in this area.
3 ☐ She should be more careful.
4 ☐ Can I take off my seatbelt now?
5 ☐ Could you pass me my bag?
6 ☐ You can get up now.
7 ☐ I can speak four languages because I often travel.
8 ☐ When I was a child I could speak French.

a This is advice.
b This is possible.
c This is a past ability.
d This is necessary.
e This is a present ability.
f This is a request.
g This is not allowed.
h This is for asking permission.

2 ⭐ Choose the correct answers.

1 I'm sorry, but you ____ fold away your tray table now.
 a must **b** has to **c** don't have to
2 During take-off every passenger ____ wear his or her seatbelt.
 a have to **b** has to **c** mustn't
3 You ____ sit down for the entire journey, you can get up.
 a have to **b** mustn't **c** don't have to
4 You ____ go through security, you have no choice.
 a mustn't **b** don't have to **c** must
5 Passengers ____ leave their luggage unattended.
 a have to **b** mustn't **c** don't have to
6 Susie ____ book her flight today, she can do it tomorrow.
 a mustn't **b** has to **c** doesn't have to

3 ⭐ Choose the correct verb forms to complete the sentences.

1 Cabin staff on flights *must / mustn't / don't have to* wear uniforms.
2 Passengers *must / mustn't / don't have to* stay in their seats all the time – they can move about.
3 You *must / mustn't / don't have to* smoke while you are on the plane.
4 You *must / mustn't / don't have to* go through security checks at the airport.
5 You *must / mustn't / don't have to* travel without a valid form of identification.
6 You *must / mustn't / don't have to* put hand luggage in the hold – you can take it with you on the plane.

4 ⭐ Complete the sentences with the verb forms from the box.

didn't have to doesn't have to don't have to had to
has to have to ~~must~~ mustn't

1 You **must** switch your phone to flight mode now.
2 You _____ stand up during take-off or landing.
3 My sister is a flight attendant and she _____ work very long hours.
4 Yesterday we _____ confirm our bookings – otherwise we would lose the holiday.
5 The last time I flew, we _____ wait for very long at our gate.
6 Do I _____ show you my passport?
7 You _____ switch off the reading light – you can use it if you want.
8 Kerry _____ carry a boarding pass – she's downloaded it onto her phone.

5 ⭐ Match the beginnings 1–6 with the endings a–f.

1 ☐ If you hate flying, perhaps
2 ☐ If you have a long journey,
3 ☐ To avoid paying for extra luggage
4 ☐ If you hate hot weather,
5 ☐ When you go through security
6 ☐ As you board the plane

a you ought to avoid hot countries in summer.
b you shouldn't pack too much into your case.
c you shouldn't leave metal objects in your pockets.
d you should think about going by train.
e you ought to have your seat number ready.
f you ought to take some books or something to do.

6 ★ Put the words in order to make sentences.

1 could / help me / you / please / with my case / ?
Could you help me with my case, please?

2 up / passengers / now / can't / stand
_____

3 your seatbelt / off / take / may / now / you
_____

4 use / I / could / the bathroom / please / now / ?
_____

5 me / some water / bring / you / can / ?
_____

6 use / passengers / may / their reading lights
_____

7 ★★ Complete the sentences with *can, can't, could* or *couldn't* and a verb from the box.

fly go pack say ~~speak~~ you/see

1 My aunt *can speak* fluent mandarin Chinese.

2 Sara _____ all her warm clothes into her luggage so she wore them instead.

3 _____ anything out of the plane window? Let me look, too.

4 When I was small, I _____ to bed late during the holidays.

5 Robert _____ many words in German, but he understands a lot.

6 In the past, most people _____ because it was very expensive.

8 ★★ Complete the sentences with the correct forms of *be able to* and the verbs in brackets.

1 *Were you able to book* (book) some cheap flights last summer?

2 _____ (you/ever/travel) without your passport?

3 I'm afraid we _____ (sit) together during the flight tomorrow.

4 Susie _____ (not get) her luggage back yet.

5 They _____ (board) the plane if they don't have their passports.

6 I _____ (not use) the bathroom because there was a long queue.

9 ★★★ Read the answers and write questions.

1 *Do passengers have to go through passport control?*
Yes, passengers have to go through passport control.

2 _____?
No, you don't have to take off your shoes at security.

3 _____?
Sorry, you can't open the window.

4 _____?
Yes, you should ask the flight attendant for assistance.

5 _____?
No, she can't understand Polish.

6 _____?
Yes, you may use the reading light.

10 ★★★ Use the prompts to write questions. Then write short answers.

1 I / should / book / early to get a good price?
Should I to book early to get a good price?
Yes, _____.

2 I / can / choose my seat?
_____
No, _____.

3 I / have to / take / some form of ID?
_____
Yes, _____.

4 I / have to / take / my birth certificate?
_____
No, _____.

5 I / may / do / some shopping at the airport?
_____
Yes, _____.

6 I / should / pack a heavy suitcase?
_____
No, _____.

11 ★★★ Complete the text with one word in each gap.

KARL's TRAVEL
BLOG
Travelling by plane

Because of modern security rules, there are a lot of things to remember when you travel by plane. First of all, of course you **1** *must* take some form of ID with you. You **2** _____ get onto a plane without it! When you go through security, you **3** _____ take any food or drink with you. You **4** _____ take a lot of drink with you to the airport because you'll have to throw it away when you go through security! But don't worry - you **5** _____ buy as much as you want after security. And remember that liquids and creams are not allowed in large quantities - you **6** _____ take big bottles of shampoo but you **7** _____ take small tubes of toothpaste. And you **8** _____ put them into a plastic bag for inspection. Have a good flight!

12 ON A HIGH NOTE Think about the last time you travelled somewhere. Write a short paragraph about what you could, couldn't and had to do during your journey.

UNIT VOCABULARY PRACTICE > page 49   41

4B READING AND VOCABULARY

1 Look at the photos and read the first paragraph of the blog post. Do you think the writer enjoyed his trip?

2 Quickly read the whole text and choose the best title for the blog post.

  a A journey with an unexpected ending

  b A wonderful summer holiday

  c A trip that taught me an important lesson

3 Match the tips about identifying the author's attitude 1–4 with extracts from the reading text a–d.

  1 ☐ Writers use exaggeration to express their attitude.

  2 ☐ Writers express positive, neutral and negative attitudes through their choice of words.

  3 ☐ Writers use comparisons to express their attitude.

  4 ☐ Look at full sentences and follow-up sentences, to identify attitude.

  a Becoming an independent learner sounds <u>more exciting than it actually is</u>.

  b France ... the world-famous food <u>is to die for</u>.

  c The open road – no deadlines – no fixed plans – Heaven! <u>Except that it wasn't</u>.

  d ... we both felt <u>pretty depressed</u> and for the rest of the trip there was a lot of <u>tension</u> in the car.

4 Read the blog post again and choose the correct answers.

  1 Why did the writer want to go on a road trip?

   a He could take a lot of luggage.

   b He could avoid working during the holiday.

   c He could go where he wanted.

   d He could drive a car he liked.

  2 The two men were not suited for the trip because

   a their habits annoyed each other.

   b they reacted differently to disagreements.

   c they both had strong views on politics.

   d they wanted different things from the holiday.

  3 The writer was disappointed because

   a the situation with his friend spoiled the holiday.

   b his friend refused to apologise to him.

   c he didn't enjoy the food he ate.

   d his French wasn't good enough to communicate.

  4 What did the writer enjoy about the holiday?

   a meeting people from a range of countries

   b seeing less well-known places in France

   c finding food he knew he liked

   d having company on some interesting walks

  5 What is the writer's advice for planning a road trip?

   a Only go with your best friend.

   b Take a reliable car.

   c Don't travel with just one person.

   d Have an alternative travel plan.

Vocabulary extension

5 Match the sentences and expressions 1–7 with the highlighted phrases in the text.

  1 ... my advice is ...

   take it from me

  2 You shouldn't misunderstand me ...

   _____

  3 He wouldn't change his behaviour.

   _____

  4 It was actually very different.

   _____

  5 ... is fantastic.

   _____

  6 No way!

   _____

  7 ... chat about unimportant things ...

   _____

ACTIVE VOCABULARY | Compound adjectives

When an adjective has two or more words linked by a hyphen, we call it a compound adjective. Some compound adjectives can be made from:

• numbers, e.g. *a three-month course, a two-year-old girl*

• an adjective or adverb plus a past or present participle, e.g. *slow-moving traffic, a well-known travel website*

6 Use the prompts to form compound adjectives with numbers.

  1 a word with three letters — *a three-letter* word

  2 a boy who's fifteen years old — _____ boy

  3 a street which goes one way — _____ street

  4 a flight of four hours — _____ flight

  5 a bag which weighs three kilos — _____ bag

  6 a holiday for two weeks — _____ holiday

7 Complete the sentences with compound adjectives.

  1 The palace is famous all over the world. It's a *world-famous* palace.

  2 The road trip was for ten days. It was a _____ road trip.

  3 I had to write an essay of 500 words. I had to write a _____ essay.

  4 The guide only worked part-time. He was a _____ guide.

  5 The people in the country speak English. It's an _____ country.

  6 The car had seats for two people. It was a _____ car.

8 ON A HIGH NOTE Write about a road trip that you would like to go on one day. Say who you would like to go with and why.

OK, so a ten-day road trip across France seemed like a great idea at the time. It was the end of my first year at uni and the summer break was coming up fast. Becoming an independent learner sounds more exciting than it actually is and after a year of studying, essay-writing and research, the idea of jumping into a car with just a tent, a few clothes and my guitar sounded like a dream come true. What's not to like? The open road – no deadlines – no fixed plans. Heaven! Except that it wasn't.

A two-seater sports car (a bit old but still a 'sports car') is a cool way to get around, but it's also a bit of a prison if you don't get on with the driver! Don't get me wrong, I didn't start off disliking my travelling companion. Far from it. We were mates – that is, until we had a huge argument somewhere on the south coast of France. I can't even remember what it was about. Knowing Andy, it was probably about politics. Anyway, we said some horrible things to each other. We continued our trip, but you could cut the atmosphere in the car with a knife! I usually get over things quite quickly, but not Andy – he sulked for three, very long days. I tried to make small talk about the weather and the scenery, but he was having none of it. We travelled in silence, put up the tent in silence and slept in silence! If I'd had the money, I would have booked a flight back to the UK, but my bank account was almost empty.

So we carried on through the mountains and past fields of poppies and olive trees. There was a point where we apologised to each other, but we both felt pretty depressed and for the rest of the trip there was a lot of tension in the car. It was such a shame. France is a beautiful country and the world-famous food is to die for. I'm usually a bit conservative about trying new food, but I developed an unexpected liking for garlic snails! When we stopped for camping breaks, Andy would go off on long walks and I would try out the local cafés and chat in my terrible French with the locals. We got lost a couple of times and found ourselves way off the beaten track – but it was good fun. We got to see places that normal tourists would never see. If Andy hadn't been there, it would have been a great holiday.

What are my reflections on the trip? Well, take it from me, a road trip with a friend can be a great adventure, but you must make sure that the friend is someone that you know really well – someone you can rely on and who you trust. You don't have to be best mates, but you need to be able to get on well for long periods. In addition to this, you shouldn't go without some sort of escape route, just in case something goes wrong.

So, would I go on another road trip? I certainly would. You get to learn a lot about a country. Would I do it again with someone like Andy? Not a chance!

4C VOCABULARY | Travel essentials, travel phrases

1 ⭐ **Complete the sentences with the words and phrases from the box.**

ear plugs   first aid kit   insect repellent   ~~sunblock~~
travel adapter   travel pillow

1 I don't want to get sunburn, so I have to take _sunblock_ with me.

2 Remember your _____ in case you get a cut or burn.

3 If it's a long flight, take a(n) _____ so you can sleep comfortably.

4 I need to charge my phone at the hotel, so I have to take a(n) _____.

5 Remember your _____ to block out noise on the plane.

6 There are a lot of mosquitoes at your destination so pack some _____.

2 ⭐ **Complete the sentences with one word in each gap.**

1 If you have a phone, don't forget your c_harger_.

2 A power b_____ is useful for when you can't charge your device.

3 You can listen to music with h_____ so that you don't disturb other people.

4 A p_____ can be useful for cutting things on nature holidays, but you can't take it on the plane.

5 If you're going camping, perhaps you should take a t_____ to see at night.

6 Remember that sometimes there's no internet, so a pocket g_____ book for information is a good idea.

3 ⭐⭐ **Match the beginnings 1–9 with the endings a–i.**

1 ☐ The plane will reach its
2 ☐ They're two hours behind us, so it's 2 p.m. local
3 ☐ I'd like to start early and
4 ☐ It's so busy where I live, I want to escape
5 ☐ We're going to Australia, but we're stopping
6 ☐ I'm not sure if I can find my
7 ☐ Luckily I have no connections, I have a direct
8 ☐ Please call and tell me you've arrived
9 ☐ We're in the centre, within easy

a set off before seven o'clock.
b way around without a map.
c the crowds and the noise.
d safely when you get there.
e time there now.
f off in Singapore for two days.
g reach of shops and museums.
h flight to New York.
i destination on time.

4 ⭐⭐⭐ **Complete the second text so that it means the same as the first. Use between one and three words in each gap.**

SUMMER HOLIDAYS – WHAT *NOT* TO DO!

Traveller magazine recently collected some basic travel mistakes. Here we share them with you to help you prepare for your holiday.

When Mark decided to go camping on a faraway island in Greece it seemed like a great idea – until he realised that travellers to this area should remember to take a spray against insects and basic medical material with them – there are no shops or medical centres nearby. Sadly, after three days of mosquitoes and an infected cut, Mark's holiday was finished.

When Grace booked a holiday in a seaside hotel near shops she didn't ask about the hotel's disco, which she only discovered when she arrived there. Even things to block her ears didn't stop the noise, so she had to change hotel – an expensive mistake!

Jane was thrilled when she left for her stopover in Singapore on the way to Australia. But she forgot to book a flight with no stops for her return journey. Her twelve-hour wait at Singapore airport was exhausting, and she didn't even have a small temporary pillow with her.

Traveller magazine recently collected some basic travel mistakes. Here we share them with you to help you prepare for your holiday.

When Mark decided to go camping on a faraway island in Greece it seemed like a great idea – until he realised that travellers to this area should remember to take ¹_insect repellent_ and a ²_____ with them – there are no shops or medical centres within ³_____. Sadly, after three days of mosquitoes and an infected cut, Mark's holiday was finished.

When Grace booked a holiday in a seaside hotel she didn't ask about the hotel's disco, which she only discovered when she ⁴_____ her destination. Even ⁵_____ didn't stop the noise, so she had to change hotel – an expensive mistake!

Jane was thrilled when she ⁶_____ off in Singapore on the way to Australia. But she forgot to book a ⁷_____ flight for her return journey. Her twelve-hour wait at Singapore airport was exhausting, and she didn't even have a ⁸_____ pillow with her.

5 ON A HIGH NOTE **Write a short paragraph about how to pack the perfect backpack for a one-week camping holiday.**

4D GRAMMAR | Relative clauses

1 ⭐ Circle (D) for defining relative clause or (ND) for non-defining relative clause.

1 The National Park, which is free to enter, closes at 10 p.m. D / ND

2 That's the house where I stay on holiday every summer. D / ND

3 This canyon, which is 446 km long, is in the state of Arizona. D / ND

4 The woman who took this photo of us emailed a copy to me. D / ND

5 Are you the person who has our tickets for the museum? D / ND

6 We asked the guide who took us round to tell us about the mountain. D / ND

7 Nora, whose brother is studying in Canada, is going there next summer. D / ND

8 The weather, which was terrible, prevented us from visiting the wildlife park. D / ND

2 ⭐ Complete the sentences with *which*, *where*, *who* or *whose*.

1 A mountain refuge is a simple place *where* hikers can stay for a night.

2 Can you send me the photo _____ you took of the group?

3 My friend Ruben, _____ mum is from California, told us all about the state.

4 I'd like to see the place _____ this photo was taken.

5 They have to protect this bird, _____ is in danger of extinction.

6 I asked Jason, _____ has already visited Sweden, to give me some advice.

7 The guides _____ pass an exam can become chief guides.

8 Some people _____ car had problems had to stay in our hotel.

3 ⭐⭐ Complete the sentences with *that* where possible, or *who* or *which* if *that* is not possible.

1 I went to see Sarah, _who_ often travels abroad, to ask for some ideas.

2 This is the guide _____ took us round the park.

3 I'd like to see the photos _____ you took on holiday.

4 Holidays by the sea, _____ are very popular in summer, are available at different prices.

5 Brighton, _____ is a popular destination for language students, is on the south coast.

6 She's the travel agent _____ suggested going by train.

4 ⭐⭐⭐ Use the prompts to write sentences with relative clauses. Leave out the relative pronoun where possible.

1 this / guide / show / us / museum
This is the guide who showed us the museum.

2 the house / we / stay in / last summer / be / beautiful
_____

3 my grandmother / be / very active / travel / Canada / last June
_____

4 the video / we / make / on holiday / last / twenty minutes
_____

5 Marion / her brother / work / an airline / get / free tickets
_____

6 the man / we / ask / for directions / be / very helpful
_____

5 ⭐⭐⭐ Rewrite the conversation using relative clauses.

Anna Can I see **1** the pictures? You took them on holiday.
Can I see *the pictures which you took on holiday?*

Karim Sure! This is **2** the flat. We stayed there.
Sure! This is_____

Anna And who's **3** the woman? She's wearing a green dress.
And who's the woman_____

Karim She's my grandmother. My grandfather **4** is next to her. He has got a shop.
She's my grandmother. My grandfather_____

Anna And this? **5** Is this the beach? You spent your days swimming there.
And this? Is this the beach_____

Karim That's right. And this is Naima. **6** Her father runs the beach café.
That's right. And this is Naima_____

6 ON A HIGH NOTE Write a short paragraph about a place you like. Use the words in the box.
_____
where which who whose
_____

4E LISTENING AND VOCABULARY

1 🔊 *28* **Listen to a student talking about how she gets to college every day. How would you describe her attitude?**

a pessimistic about the future reliability of public transport

b glad that she changed her form of travelling

c disappointed that she cannot travel independently

2 🔊 *28* **Listen again and decide if the statements are true (T) or false. (F)**

1 ☐ The speaker chose to attend a good college in spite of the distance from her home.

2 ☐ She often missed the start of lessons because of traffic congestion.

3 ☐ She has been going to this college for six months.

4 ☐ The train is always so full that she doesn't sit down.

5 ☐ The train is sometimes delayed due to weather conditions.

6 ☐ Commuters are warned about cancellations in advance.

3 🔊 *29* **Listen to the radio programme and match the comments with the callers. Write Linzie, Rafal or Marie.**

Which caller mentions ...

1 the size of the platforms. _____

2 air pollution. _____

3 the number of trains. _____

4 how easy it is to find your way. _____

5 commuters being patient. _____

6 the temperatures on trains. _____

7 the number of delays. _____

8 the design of stations. _____

9 the size of the trains. _____

Vocabulary extension

4 **Complete the sentences with the nouns from the box which you heard in the recording.**

action confusion failures nightmare reputation ~~tailbacks~~ variety works

1 There were *tailbacks* for two kilometres on the motorway this morning.

2 Getting to school was a _____ yesterday.

3 The rail company has announced three days of strike _____ in the next month.

4 Road _____ will delay traffic through the town centre for three days.

5 This make of car has a _____ for being unreliable.

6 There's a lot of _____ about which trains will run during the strike.

7 The company has given a _____ of reasons for the recent train delays.

8 Signal _____ caused a lot of delays on the underground last year.

5 ON A HIGH NOTE **Write a short paragraph about your favourite and least favourite forms of public transport, giving reasons for your answer.**

Pronunciation

6 🔊 *30* **Listen to someone reading extracts from the listening. Notice how the ends of some words link to the beginnings of the next.**

1 Commuting to college can be a bit‿of‿a pain.

2 When I started‿out my friend used to give me a lift‿in his car.

3 We didn't get home until‿eight‿o'clock.

ACTIVE PRONUNCIATION | Linking words

English speakers run words together to create a continuous stream of words. This way of linking words together can sometimes be difficult to understand. We can use different ways to link the ending of one word and the beginning of the next. When a word ends with a consonant (e.g. /t/, /d/, /k/ or a consonant sound, e.g. *take*) and the next word starts with a vowel, there is no pause between the words, e.g.

- *I did‿it quickly.*
- *Can you look‿at my work?*
- *Is‿it a boy or‿a girl?*
- How much‿are these‿eggs?

---

7 🔊 *31* **Listen again to the phrases from Exercise 6 and practise saying them.**

8 🔊 *32* **Look at some sentences. Underline the words you think can be linked. Listen and check. Practise saying the sentences.**

1 It's about eighteen miles away from my home.

2 We got a train earlier than we'd expected because it had been delayed.

3 Jim's fed up with all the driving he does on the motorways at the moment.

4 I'm not a fan of motorbikes, but from all these magazines it looks as if Grant is!

5 You keep on making comments about my new hairstyle – please stop it!

9 🔊 *33* **Listen to some more phrases where the words are linked. Write what you think the words are. The number of words in each phrase has been given to help you.**

1 (3 words) *catch up on*

2 (3 words) _____

3 (3 words) _____

4 (3 words) _____

5 (4 words) _____

10 🔊 *34* **Listen to the phrases in context and check your answers from Exercise 9.**

UNIT VOCABULARY PRACTICE > page 49

1 🔊 35 Listen and repeat the phrases. How do you say them in your language?

SPEAKING | Agreeing and disagreeing

AGREEING

You're (absolutely) right.
That's exactly how I feel.
I don't think so either.
That's for sure.
You're not wrong.
I agree with you (100 percent).

PARTLY AGREEING

I agree up to a point.
You've got a point, but what else can they do?
Maybe that's true, but some cars cause more pollution than others.
You might be right, but all cars contribute to the problem.
Yes, but don't you think that it would be enormously expensive to change over to electric cars?
I see what you mean, but the government could help.

DISAGREEING

I'm sorry, but I disagree/don't agree.
You're joking, right?*
You can't be serious.*
Come off it!*
Come on, get real!*
No way!*

* informal, perhaps rude for people you don't know well

2 🔊 36 Read the conversation. Put the words in order to make phrases for agreeing, partly agreeing and disagreeing. You may need to add commas. Listen and check.

Sam There's so much traffic in the city centre. The air quality is terrible. Something's got to change.

Olivia ¹ right / you're / absolutely / It's really polluted.
You're absolutely right.

Sam The council is thinking about banning all cars from the main streets.

Olivia ² joking / right / you're / ? People have to get to work and the shops!
_____

Sam ³ point / but / got / you've / a / what else can they do?
_____

Olivia Well, they could make big cars and lorries pay to come into the centre. That would help.

Sam ⁴ but / think / you / that / yes / don't / all cars contribute to the problem?
_____

Olivia ⁵ true / but / that's / maybe / some cause more pollution than others. How about only letting electric cars into the centre?
_____

Sam ⁶ on / real / come / get / ! It would be enormously expensive for people to change over to electric cars. And anyway, there still aren't enough charging points for electric cars.
_____

Olivia ⁷ you / what / mean / see / I / Perhaps the government could help people pay for new cars.
_____

Sam ⁸ serious / be / can't / you / ! The government's got enough things to spend money on! No, I think a city centre ban is the best option.
_____

Olivia ⁹ I / sorry / disagree / but / I'm / Something has to happen, ¹⁰ for / that's / sure / , but not a complete ban.
_____
_____

3 Which phrases 1–10 from the conversation show that the people know each other well?

4 ON A HIGH NOTE Write three possible reactions to each statement. One should show agreement, one disagreement and one partial agreement. Give a reason for each reaction.

1 The bus company needs to save money. They should cut fifty percent of the buses in the town centre.

2 We need more cycle lanes in the town.

3 I think the age for learning to drive should be lowered.

4G WRITING | A formal email of enquiry

Complete the subject box with your reason for writing.	To: enquiries@summersports527.com Re: sailing opportunity
Start with an appropriate greeting.	Dear [1] *Sir*/Madam,
State clearly why you are writing.	I was looking at your website and read about the week's sailing expedition you are offering this summer. I have a few [2]_____ and I would greatly [3]_____ it if you could answer them.
Use indirect questions to be polite.	You mention that participants do not need a great deal of experience. I learned to sail a few years ago at my local sailing club. [4]_____, since then I have only sailed small boats. Obviously sailing a tall ship would be very different and I [5]_____ whether my experience would be enough.
Signal a new topic using a set phrase.	With [6]_____ to cost, could you [7]_____ how much individual participants would need to contribute financially? You mention part funding by a youth sports charity which is very good, but I would like to know what proportion of the costs they cover.
Conclude your email politely.	I [8]_____ also be interested to know how participants will be selected if there is a large number of applicants.
	This sounds an exciting opportunity to learn how to handle a large ship and to work as part of a team. I am looking [9]_____ to hearing from you.
Close your email appropriately.	Best [10]_____. Ted Danvers

1 Read the email and decide which website advert the writer is enquiring about.

A ☐

> Would you like to spend a week sailing a wonderful tall ship around the south coast this summer? You would be working with a team of young people and learning all about these amazing old ships. You don't need a lot of experience to apply to join the team, and the expedition will be partly funded by a sports charity that offers sporting experiences to young people. The expedition will be from 5th to the 12th August. Email us for further information.

B ☐

> Have you ever wanted to learn to sail, but perhaps live in a city with no opportunities? The youth sports charity Dream Sports is offering several young people a week's residential sailing course at Calthorpe Activity centre near Brighton this summer. The only requirement is that you are able to swim! Contact us for further information.

2 Complete the email with the words from the box.

appreciate confirm forward however queries
regard ~~Sir~~ wonder wishes would

3 Tick (✓) the items which would NOT be appropriate to use in a formal email.

1 ☐ What a brilliant idea!
2 ☐ Concerning the cost of the activity, I …
3 ☐ Therefore I would like you to confirm …
4 ☐ Please write soon.
5 ☐ My plans are a bit up in the air at the moment.
6 ☐ I must close now as I need to do some homework.
7 ☐ How much is it?

4 WRITING TASK Write a formal email asking for further information about the other advertisement in Exercise 1.

ACTIVE WRITING | A formal email of enquiry

1 Plan your email.
- Make a note of the information you want.
- You may wish to ask about clothing/equipment, accommodation, dates, cost.

2 Write your email.
- Divide your points into paragraphs.
- Use appropriate opening and closing phrases.
- Be polite and use indirect questions.
- Use full sentences and avoid contractions and idiomatic language.

3 Check your email. Check that:
- all the relevant information is there.
- there are no mistakes with spelling, grammar and punctuation.

UNIT VOCABULARY PRACTICE

1 **4A GRAMMAR AND VOCABULARY Complete the collocations with one word in each gap.**

1 c<u>hoose</u> an aisle/ window seat
2 go to your g_____ to board the plane
3 don't l_____ your luggage unattended
4 s_____ your phone to flight mode
5 raise your w_____ blind
6 b_____ a flight
7 f_____ your seatbelt
8 p_____ your seat in an upright position
9 put your h_____ luggage in the overhead locker
10 go t_____ security
11 f_____ away your tray table
12 watch the s_____ demonstration

2 **4B READING AND VOCABULARY Complete the sentences with the phrases from the box.**

ask the way   get lost   ~~go off the beaten track~~   hire a car
hit the road   plan the route   turn back

1 We love to *go off the beaten track* and discover unusual places tourists don't go to.
2 It's time to go home. Come on, let's _____.
3 How could you _____? It's only one kilometre away!
4 Sorry, but I think this is the wrong direction. Let's _____.
5 If you need directions, stop and _____.
6 I'd like to look at a map and _____ so we don't waste time.
7 There isn't much public transport so it's a good idea to _____.

3 **4C VOCABULARY Choose the correct words to complete the sentences.**

1 There are lots of flies and mosquitoes, so you'll need a good *penknife / insect repellent*.
2 It's a long journey, so take a *travel pillow / guide book* to help you sleep.
3 Have you got some disinfectant in that *travel adapter / first aid kit*?
4 I don't want to get burned, so I've got my hat and some *insect repellent / sunblock*.
5 The plugs are different in Italy, so don't forget to take a travel *adapter / charger*.
6 If there are lots of passengers, *ear plugs / a power bank* can be a good way to get some peace.
7 A *penknife / pocket guide book* is a good idea to get information if there's no wifi available.
8 Attach some *headphones / torches* to your phone to listen to music without disturbing others.

4 **Match the beginnings 1–6 with the endings a–f.**

1 ☐ Can we stop
2 ☐ I hate connections – I want a direct
3 ☐ Let's leave early, we can set
4 ☐ It's early in New York – only 6 a.m. local
5 ☐ I've got a map to find
6 ☐ Send me a text to say you've arrived

a off at six o'clock and travel before the traffic.
b safely at your hotel.
c my way around the city.
d flight to Vancouver.
e off for a coffee during the journey?
f time over there.

5 **4E LISTENING AND VOCABULARY Read the definitions and write the correct words.**

1 smoke from cars, trucks, etc.
f<u>umes</u>
2 poisonous
t_____
3 the natural world
e_____
4 chemicals that damage air, water and soil
p_____
5 a situation when there is too much traffic
c_____
6 a mix of smoke and other pollutants which makes it difficult to see
s_____
7 a sort of fuel made from petroleum
d_____
8 a wide road with several lanes where cars drive fast
m_____
9 using methods that do not damage the environment
s_____
10 a source of energy which never finishes is this
r_____

6 **ON A HIGH NOTE Write a short paragraph giving some ideas about how a holiday can become sustainable.**

1 **For each learning objective, write 1–5 to assess your ability.**

1 = I don't feel confident. 5 = I feel very confident.

	Learning objective	Course material	How confident I am (1–5)
4A	I can use a variety of modal and related verbs.	Student's Book pp. 48–49	
4B	I can identify the author's attitudes in an article and talk about holidays.	Student's Book pp. 50–51	
4C	I can talk about travelling.	Student's Book p. 52	
4D	I can use defining and non-defining relative clauses.	Student's Book p. 53	
4E	I can identify specific information in a monologue and a radio programme and talk about urban transport and pollution.	Student's Book p. 54	
4F	I can show degrees of agreement using a range of language.	Student's Book p. 55	
4G	I can write a formal email requesting information.	Student's Book pp. 56–57	

2 **Which of the skills above would you like to improve in? How?**

Skill I want to improve in	How I can improve

3 **What can you remember from this unit?**

New words I learned and most want to remember	Expressions and phrases I liked	English I heard or read outside class

GRAMMAR AND VOCABULARY

1 Choose the correct answers.

1 You must never leave your luggage _____.
   a alone **b** unattended **c** upright
   d in a locker

2 We're lost. Let's stop someone and _____.
   a ask the way **b** hit the road **c** hire a car
   d plan the route

3 That's a bad cut on your knee, let's get some disinfectant from the _____.
   a tourist office **b** security **c** first aid kit
   d travel adapter

4 I think we should _____ after breakfast so we arrive in the afternoon.
   a go out **b** reach out **c** set off
   d set up

5 We need to increase the use of solar power and other types of _____ energy.
   a congestion **b** renewable **c** toxic
   d fuel

/ 5

2 Complete the sentences with the words and phrases from the box. There are two extra words.

easy reach got lost hit the road luggage smog toxic travel adapter

1 Please put your _____ in the overhead locker.
2 We wasted a lot of time because we _____ and couldn't find the station.
3 I couldn't use my phone because I hadn't brought a _____ for the plug.
4 It's best to stay in the centre of town, within _____ of all the main shops and attractions.
5 Children in the UK are breathing dangerous levels of _____ air as they walk and cycle to school.

/ 5

3 Choose the correct answers.

Australia – dos and don'ts when entering the country

Please remember when you travel to Australia that you 1_____ follow some basic rules when entering the country. For example, travellers 2_____ bring food or drink into the country. Seeds are also forbidden. If you have any questions you 3_____ check with customs officials. You 4_____ declare jewellery or personal items, but if you are carrying more than 10,000 Australian dollars in cash, you 5_____ declare it.

1 **a** can **b** must **c** ought **d** could
2 **a** shouldn't **b** don't have to **c** mustn't **d** might not
3 **a** had to **b** ought **c** able to **d** should
4 **a** mustn't **b** may not **c** don't have to **d** can't
5 **a** have to **b** don't have to **c** may **d** mustn't

/ 5

4 Complete the sentences with where, which, who or whose.

1 This is the photo _____ I took from the top of the mountain.
2 Do you know the girl _____ cousin lives in Glasgow?
3 A youth hostel, _____ you can stay cheaply, is often a good place to meet people.
4 Diesel, _____ is a fossil fuel, is not environmentally-friendly.
5 Jennifer, _____ cycles through the city every morning, is forced to breathe fumes from traffic.

/ 5

USE OF ENGLISH

5 Complete the sentences with the correct forms of the words in brackets.

1 The traffic _____ is terrible – we can't move! (**CONGEST**)
2 Please watch the cabin crew while they do the safety _____. (**DEMONSTRATE**)
3 The house is in a remote village which is really off the _____ track. (**BEAT**)
4 Are you sure these tomatoes were grown using _____ methods? (**SUSTAIN**)
5 Air and water _____ cause a huge amount of damage to the environment. (**POLLUTE**)

/ 5

6 Read the short texts and choose the correct answers.

1 This road is closed. Please _____ and take the alternative route following the yellow signs.
   a turn back **b** set off **c** hit the road

2 The use of _____ is advised while listening to music to avoid disturbing other passengers.
   a ear plugs **b** insect repellent **c** headphones

3 Need to relax? Want to _____? Quiet cottage by the sea to rent. Call Donna for more information.
   a arrive safely **b** set off early **c** escape the crowds

4 Dear Sir/Madam, I am writing to _____ about your rock climbing course in the Highlands.
   a enquire **b** confirm **c** require

5 Passengers who have purchased QuickBoard _____ wait in the queue. Please proceed directly to your gate.
   a can't **b** don't have to **c** mustn't

/ 5
/ 30

51

05 The next step

5A GRAMMAR AND VOCABULARY

Talking about the future

1 ⭐ Match the sentences 1–8 with the functions a–h.

1 ☐ I might ask my aunt to help me – she's good at Maths.
2 ☐ These questions are so easy! I'm going to pass this exam!
3 ☐ I'll help you with that!
4 ☐ I'm going to study all weekend.
5 ☐ The teacher is nice. I'm sure she'll give us a fair exam.
6 ☐ The exam's about to start and I can't remember anything!
7 ☐ The test starts at ten o'clock.
8 ☐ I'm seeing the manager tomorrow about a summer job.

a a future prediction based on evidence
b a plan, an intention
c an event in the very near future
d an arrangement
e a future prediction based on an opinion or belief
f a timetabled event
g a future possibility
h a decision the speaker has just made

2 ⭐ Choose the correct verb forms to complete the sentences about the future.

1 I can't meet you on Sunday. I *go* / *'m going* to the cinema with Katy.
2 Stop that child! She *is falling off* / *is going to fall off* the wall!
3 I don't like this subject, so I *am getting* / *will get* bored during the lesson tomorrow.
4 I think you *will find* / *are finding* the next week Maths exam easy.
5 You'll be ready in five minutes? OK, I *will wait* / *am waiting* for you outside.
6 He's a sensible person. I'm sure he *will plan* / *plans* his studies for the next month.
7 Sally's overconfident and doesn't study much. She *doesn't pass* / *won't pass* the exam.
8 I'm curious to find out what *is going to happen* / *is happening* in the next episode of the show.

3 ⭐ Match the beginnings 1–6 with the endings a–f.

1 ☐ I'm not sure about this question.
2 ☐ It's an advanced exam.
3 ☐ Please be quiet in the corridor.
4 ☐ You could write to the newspaper editor.
5 ☐ I'm about to finish my homework.
6 ☐ Joanna is very inventive.

a An exam is about to start in here.
b She could have some creative ideas to help.
c I'll help you in two minutes.
d The answer might be 'yes' or 'no'.
e She may offer you a work placement.
f There could be some very difficult questions.

4 ⭐⭐ Complete the sentences about the future with the Present Continuous and the verbs in brackets. If the Present Continuous is not possible, use *be going to*.

1 I *'m spending* (spend) this weekend relaxing and having fun.
2 Look out! Your books _____ (fall off) the table!
3 The film _____ (start) late because of technical problems.
4 Be careful – you _____ (make) a lot of careless mistakes.
5 I've got a DVD. We _____ (watch) it together on Saturday evening.
6 She _____ (pass) the exam easily because she has studied a lot.

5 ★★ Put the words in order to make sentences.

1 you / pass / I / the exam / think / will
I think you will pass the exam.

2 good results / probably / get / will / she
_____

3 study / are / going / we / to / together
_____

4 the lesson / start / to / about / is
_____

5 think / difficult / be / will / don't / it / I
_____

6 understand / not / might / I / everything
_____

7 to the party / Katy / coming / definitely / is
_____

8 probably / Mrs Bennett / us a test / won't / give
_____

6 ★★ Complete the mini-conversations with the words and phrases from the box.

Are you going to begins could be does doesn't think
don't think is about to 'll be might might know
Yes, I am ~~you'll pass~~

1 A Do you think *you'll pass* the exam easily?
B No, I _____ it'll be easy.

2 A What time _____ the revision session start?
B It _____ at four thirty.

3 A I haven't studied much, but I _____ some of the answers.
B You've studied some of the topics though, so you _____ OK.
A Hmm. Let's wait and see.

4 A Hurry up! The train _____ leave!
B Let's run. We _____ get to it just in time.

5 A It's only a mid-year test. Jim _____ it'll be too difficult.
B Is he certain? I'm sure it _____ a challenge.

6 A _____ study over the weekend?
B _____. Would you like to come and study with me?

7 ★★★ Read the answers and write questions.

1 *Are you doing any exams tomorrow*?
No, we aren't doing any exams tomorrow.

2 _____?
Yes, I'm going to study all day!

3 _____?
Yes, of course you'll understand all the questions.

4 _____?
Yes, it's going to rain at the weekend.

5 _____?
Yes, the test is about to start.

6 _____?
No, I'm not about to leave.

8 ★★★ Choose the correct verb forms to complete the conversation.

Ann Ted, would you like to come to my place this evening? **1** I *'m studying / study* French with Matt and Sofie, and we **2** *are going to have / are about to have* pizza, too.

Ted That sounds great! What time **3** *do you start / are you going to start*?

Ann **4** We *might start / are going to start* at six o'clock for sure. Then I think **5** we *will stop / stop* for pizza at about seven thirty. We **6** *probably won't / won't probably* do much studying after that.

Ted Great. I'm not sure, but I **7** *might be / 'm going to be* ten minutes late. Is that a problem? My football training session **8** *finishes / could finish* at five thirty on Saturdays.

Ann No, that's fine, Ted. See you later then.

9 ★★★ Choose the correct answers.

Mum – just a note to say that I **1**_____ for a while, so I **2**_____ at home when you get back. I **3**_____ to Eddie's house to look at some problems I have with Physics. Eddie's really good at Physics and he **4**_____ help me. I don't think I **5**_____ late for dinner. The bus home **6**_____ at five, but if I have a lot of problems I **7**_____ later and catch the six o'clock bus. I **8**_____ you a message and let you know! I have to go – I **9**_____ miss my bus. I **10**_____ you later! Ben

1 a go out
b am going out
c will go out

2 a won't be
b am not about to be
c am not being

3 a will go
b go
c am going

4 a is going to
b might
c is about to

5 a am
b could be
c will be

6 a is going to leave
b is about to leave
c leaves

7 a stay
b am staying
c may stay

8 a am sending
b will send
c am going to send

9 a am about to
b am missing
c won't miss

10 a am seeing
b could see
c will see

10 ON A HIGH NOTE Write a short paragraph about your plans for next week.

• Are you taking any tests or exams?
• Have you got any trips or after-school activities?
• Are you going to spend a lot of time with friends?

5B VOCABULARY | Phrasal verbs related to studying

1 ⭐ Choose a verb from Box A and a word or phrase from Box B to make phrasal verbs that match the definitions.

A catch come drop get go hand ~~put~~

B down to in ~~off~~ out over up on up with

1 to do something later
put off

2 to revise or repeat, so you can learn
_____

3 to do work or study which you have missed
_____

4 to give your work to the teacher
_____

5 to have (an idea)
_____

6 to start a task seriously
_____

7 to leave a course before it finishes
_____

2 ⭐ Complete the sentences with the phrasal verbs from Exercise 1.

1 She managed to *catch up on* the work she had missed by copying her friend's notes.

2 I've got no ideas. Can you _____ some suggestions?

3 I'm really tired, so I think I'll _____ doing this homework until tomorrow.

4 She really hates the drama club; I think she'll probably _____ soon.

5 Remember that we have to _____ our History essays tomorrow morning.

6 I'm not very confident about this topic. I'd like to _____ it again.

7 OK, let's stop chatting and _____ some serious work.

3 ⭐ Complete the sentences with the phrasal verbs from the box.

come up fell behind keep up with picks up
~~pull your socks up~~ put together

1 You haven't studied anything for the exam! You'd better *pull your socks up* or you're going to fail!

2 We need to study this topic – it's definitely going to _____ in the exam.

3 He neglected his studies for weeks and _____ the rest of the class.

4 Are you sure you can _____ the class if you're also doing four activities after school?

5 I need to _____ a plan of my project before class tomorrow.

6 She has a talent for learning, she _____ new information really easily.

4 ⭐⭐ Complete the conversation with one word in each gap.

Mr Tait Simon, are you feeling OK? You seem to be having trouble keeping **1** u__ with the class today.

Simon Actually, I don't feel very well. I can't seem to **2** c_____ up with any of the correct answers.

Mr Tait This isn't normal for you. I never have to tell you to pull your **3** s_____ up.

Simon I just feel really tired and I've got a headache. I can't concentrate. I just can't get **4** d_____ to anything today.

Mr Tait I think I'll ask the secretary to call your parents. Go home. You can **5** h_____ in your work when you feel better. I know you won't **6** p_____ it off without a good reason.

Simon Thanks Mr Tait. I promise to go **7** o_____ today's work when I feel better. I don't want to fall **8** b_____!

5 ⭐⭐⭐ Complete the text with one word in each gap.

I'm not a genius, so I don't **1** *pick* things up as soon as I hear them, but I manage to **2** _____ up with my classwork because I stay organised. I know if I have to go **3** _____ something and I study it again at home. That way I rarely **4** _____ behind. In the past, I used to put **5** _____ exercises or projects that I didn't like, but now I have a new strategy. I **6** _____ down to those tasks first and then I do the things I enjoy. For example, my friend Rob and I are going to put **7** _____ a presentation next week on agriculture, so I'm doing my research first, because I'm not really very interested in the subject. But who knows, I might **8** _____ up with some useful information all the same.

6 ON A HIGH NOTE Write a short paragraph about how you organise and plan your studies so that you can keep up with your school work.

5C GRAMMAR

Future Continuous and Future Perfect

1 ★ **Complete the sentences with one word in each gap.**

1 By the _time_ I'm eighteen, I will have finished school.

2 _____ nine o'clock tomorrow morning I'll be waiting to start my exam.

3 By _____ time next week, all our exams will have finished. Hooray!

4 Will you have returned from your holiday in three days _____ now?

5 _____ the end of this month, I will have saved enough money for a new smartphone.

6 _____ two hours' time, we will have known what our exam results are!

2 ★★ **Complete the sentences with the Future Continuous forms of the verbs in brackets.**

1 At this time tomorrow evening, we _will be watching_ (watch) a film.

2 What _____ (you/do) at this time next week?

3 She _____ (not visit) the college at ten o'clock tomorrow.

4 _____ (you/meet) any other students in the near future?

5 We _____ (not study) Maths this time next year – it isn't part of our course.

6 I really hope that in six months from now, I _____ (attend) a language course abroad.

3 ★★ **Complete the sentences with the Future Perfect forms of the verbs from the box.**

chat form meet not decide ~~return~~ tour

1 By this time tomorrow evening, I _will have returned_ from the university open day.

2 I hope that I _____ a better idea of what I want to study.

3 All the visitors to the university _____ the campus.

4 We _____ to students who are studying at the university now.

5 I _____ lots of new people – maybe some of them will become friends.

6 I _____ if I'm going to choose that college though. I have three more open days to go to!

4 ★★ **Choose the correct verb forms to complete the sentences.**

1 Nigel *won't have solved / won't be solving* these Maths problems before bed time.

2 Do you think Mrs Smith *will have received / will be receiving* our exam results before class?

3 Christina *won't have attended / won't be attending* school tomorrow as she's not well.

4 Where *will you have stayed / will you be staying* when you go to visit the university?

5 If Millie finishes her project on time, she *will have proved / will be proving* how determined she is.

6 After a few days in Spain you *will have picked up / will be picking up* some basic words and phrases.

5 ★★★ **Use the prompts to write sentences. Use the Future Continuous or the Future Perfect.**

1 at / this time / next / week / we / sit / on the beach.
This time next week we will be sitting on the beach.

2 we / not have / lunch / by / one thirty.

_____

3 she / make / a decision / by / next week?

_____

4 I / attend / three / open days / by / next week!

_____

5 what / you / do / by / four o'clock tomorrow?

_____

6 Cheryl / not study / in France next year.

_____

6 ★★★ **Complete the text with the Future Continuous or the Future Perfect forms of the verbs from the box.**

collect enjoy finish not sit see you/decide you/do ~~watch~~

From: Zac
To: Jenny
Subject: Open day

Hi Jenny

I've got the programme for next week's open day at the technical college. It looks good. At nine o'clock, I **1**_will be watching_ a demonstration of pottery making. I **2**_____ in Mr Brown's boring Maths class! Hooray! By lunchtime, I **3**_____ three demonstrations, so I'll be hungry. At one o'clock I **4**_____ a hamburger and chips in a nice warm café. By five o'clock, I think I **5**_____ all the information I want, so I'm planning on going home after that.

What about you? **6**_____ which college you want to go to by tomorrow evening? Or are you still thinking about your choices? By the way, what **7**_____ around eight o'clock tomorrow evening? Why don't you come over to my house if you're not busy. My family and I **8**_____ eating by eight o'clock, so come over anytime after that.

Zac

7 ON A HIGH NOTE **Imagine your life in five years' time. What will you have achieved? What will you be doing? What will you not be doing? Write a short paragraph predicting your future.**

5D SPEAKING

1 🔊 *37* **Listen and repeat the phrases. How do you say them in your language?**

2 **Match the beginnings 1–6 with the endings a–f to make sentences with interview advice.**

You should ...

1 ☐ arrive early so that

2 ☐ turn off your phone so that

3 ☐ wear smart clothes and have a shower so that

4 ☐ only talk about relevant details from your CV so that

5 ☐ point out your strengths and motivation so that

6 ☐ refer to your CV but don't read from it so that

a you are looking up all the time and keep eye contact.

b you can relax and be ready for your interview.

c you look and smell good.

d it doesn't disturb the interview.

e you show why you are right for the job.

f interviewers don't get bored and can see you are focused.

3 🔊 *38* **Listen to an extract from an interview. Lewis is applying for a job teaching English abroad during his gap year. Decide if the statements are true (T) or false (F).**

1 ☐ Lewis's parents have different nationalities.

2 ☐ Lewis's ambition is to be a language teacher.

3 ☐ Lewis hasn't done any teaching before.

4 ☐ Lewis belongs to a tennis club.

5 ☐ Lewis can do several tasks at the same time.

6 ☐ Lewis learns everything very quickly.

7 ☐ Lewis needs to practise his typing.

4 🔊 *39* **Complete the sentences from the interview with one word in each gap. Then listen and check.**

1 Could you please tell us something *about* yourself?

2 I'm self-_____ and that is one reason why I'd like to gain some _____ teaching English abroad.

3 I think I have good communication _____.

4 Do you work well under _____?

5 I manage my _____ carefully.

6 I also think I'm good _____ multi-tasking.

7 I enjoy challenges and _____ problems.

8 I think my biggest _____ is accepting that I can't do everything as fast as I'd like to.

9 I _____ to expect to make quick progress.

10 Also, I'm working _____ my typing skills.

5 **Match the comments 1–5 with the follow-up examples a–e.**

1 ☐ I work well in a team.

2 ☐ I have good organisational skills.

3 ☐ I'm good at meeting deadlines.

4 ☐ I find it difficult to talk to large groups of people.

5 ☐ I'm a fast learner.

a I can remember things easily.

b I get nervous and don't express myself clearly.

c I listen and come up with useful ideas.

d I'm always aware how long I need for my work.

e I plan my work and keep clear records.

6 ON A HIGH NOTE **Imagine you are applying for a summer job. Write a short paragraph about your strengths and weaknesses.**

My strengths are ...

My weaknesses are ...

5E LISTENING AND VOCABULARY

1 🔊 *40* **Listen to an announcement about the 'Young Entrepreneur of the Year' award. Decide if the notes are correct (C) or incorrect (I).**

1 ☐ YEY – every year
2 ☐ regional comps – July; finals – Nov
3 ☐ for people – started business last year
4 ☐ for people – over 13
5 ☐ closing date – 31st March
6 ☐ finals – 15th Nov – Tillings Hotel

2 **Complete the tips about note-taking with the words from the box.**

articles check ~~key~~ similar symbols

1 Only note down the _key_ points.
2 Leave out words such as _____ and auxiliary verbs.
3 Use abbreviations, _____ and numbers.
4 Try not to confuse words which sound _____.
5 _____ anything you're not sure of later.

3 🔊 *41* **Listen to the first part of a radio interview with a young entrepreneur. What is a 'cryptocurrency'?**

a a secret currency
b a currency without cash
c a fictional currency

4 🔊 *42* **Listen to the whole interview and complete the notes with one or two words in each gap.**

1 age Callum set up company _eighteen_
2 completed degree in _____
3 learned coding at _____
4 Bitcoin created in _____
5 not imp. for everyone to have _____
6 young entrepreneurs – have adv. of _____
7 must do something you _____

Vocabulary extension

5 **Complete the sentences with the words from the box which you heard in the recording in Exercises 1–4.**

behind board drop follow ~~name~~ remember

1 My cousin has **made a** _name_ **for himself** in the games industry.
2 I've loved gymnastics **ever since I can** _____.
3 It's good to have some qualifications _____ **you**.
4 Sometimes you don't know the answer, but you just have to _____ **your instinct**.
5 My mum's boss always **takes on** _____ any constructive suggestions my mum makes.
6 Some students _____ **out of** college or university because they can't keep up with the work.

6 ON A HIGH NOTE **Write a short post for a website with the title, 'If you could start your own business in the future, what would it be and why?'**

Pronunciation

7 🔊 *43* **Read some sentences from the listening, paying particular attention to the underlined words which contain the light /l/ sound. Listen and repeat the individual words.**

1 This year the <u>closing</u> date for all entries has been moved from the 31st of March to the 30th of April.
2 The date for the final in <u>London</u> is the <u>eleventh</u> of November.
3 In previous years this has been held at the <u>luxurious Tillings</u> Hotel, but this year it will be at the Royal Trafalgar.
4 I was working and <u>developing</u> my company while I was studying, but now I'm working on it full-time.
5 But that's <u>nearly</u> impossible. There's always going to be competition.

ACTIVE PRONUNCIATION | Dark and light /l/

The /l/ sound can be pronounced in two ways called 'light' and 'dark' /l/.

• We use the light /l/ before a vowel or diphthong, e.g. *London, light, flag, unless, lovely.*
• We use the dark /l/ as the final sound of a syllable, after a vowel or diphthong, e.g. *full, able, will, April.*

Some people confuse the /r/ and the /l/ sounds. When making the /r/ sound the tongue does not touch the roof of the mouth, whereas to make the /l/ sound it does.

8 🔊 *44* **Look at the sentences in Exercise 7 again. Find and underline the words with a dark /l/ in each sentence. Listen, check and repeat.**

9 🔊 *45* **Now practise saying the complete sentences in Exercise 7. Listen and check.**

10 🔊 *46* **Listen and notice how the /l/ sound changes. Practise saying the pairs of words.**

1 gradual gradually
2 final finally
3 feel feeling
4 impossible impossibly
5 eventual eventually
6 school schooling

11 🔊 *47* **Read the sentences aloud. Listen, check and repeat.**

1 Lauren led a rough life.
2 Rachel found the right lights for her room.
3 Olly likes horror films, but Ray likes thrillers.
4 All the latest results were listed online and they revealed excellent progress.
5 There was rain, lightning and deep floods on the country roads and we finally arrived three hours late!

1 Quickly read the article and choose the best title.

   a New technology makes office life easier

   b The changing face of the office

   c Less work and more benefits for office workers

2 Read the article again and answer the questions.

   1 What is missing from modern offices?

   _____

   2 How did people use to dress for work?

   _____

   3 What has caused working styles to change?

   _____

   4 What is affected negatively by remote working?

   _____

   5 Why were open plan offices developed?

   _____

   6 How has 'hot-desking' helped companies?

   _____

   7 What is the main concern of employers today?

   _____

   8 What could make a change to the way people communicate in meetings in the future?

   _____

   9 How might changes at work affect office buildings?

   _____

   10 How many people in 2030 might have responsibilities for elderly family members?

   _____

3 Decide if the statements are true (T) or false (F).

   1 ☐ There used to be a dress code for workers.

   2 ☐ Today teams of workers sometimes travel long distances for meetings.

   3 ☐ Workers today have more choice over their working hours.

   4 ☐ In the future workers will mix work and relaxation within the workplace.

   5 ☐ There will be a reduced workforce by 2030.

4 Complete the chart with the words and phrases from the box.

~~casual dress~~ cubicles face-to-face meetings
flexible hours ~~formal dress~~ laptop mobile phones
landlines nine-to-five open-plan spaces
remote working typewriter work alone work in teams

1950s	Today
formal dress	_casual dress_
_____	_____
_____	_____
_____	_____
_____	_____
_____	_____
_____	_____

Vocabulary extension

5 Complete the sentences with the highlighted words in the text.

   1 My new _ergonomic_ chair really helps my back when I'm sitting at the computer.

   2 Salary increases aren't very high on the _____ at the moment, I'm afraid.

   3 Sometimes I'm working on three different things _____ and I get a bit confused.

   4 The next meeting will be _____ on a video conferencing site.

   5 Because my dad's hours are _____ he can take me to swimming lessons after school.

   6 The school has _____ some money to buying new sports equipment.

ACTIVE VOCABULARY | Nouns with -_sion_ ending

Many verbs ending in -_ide_ (e.g. _divide_) and -_ude_ (e.g. _intrude_) form nouns by changing /d/ to /s/ and adding -_ion_, e.g.

- divide → division
- intrude → intrusion

---

6 Complete the sentences with the noun forms of the verbs in brackets.

   1 We reached the _conclusion_ (conclude) that it would be better to have a face-to-face meeting.

   2 There was a terrible _____ (collide) between a lorry and a car outside our house.

   3 There's a clear _____ (divide) between people who like hot-desking and those who don't.

   4 There isn't any _____ (provide) for people in wheelchairs in our office building.

   5 The _____ (include) of Harry Jones in the football team was very popular with the fans.

   6 Celebrities often complain that reporters taking their photos is an _____ (intrude) of privacy.

   7 Getting the earlier train was a good _____ (decide).

7 ON A HIGH NOTE Write a short paragraph outlining how you think school classrooms will have changed in ten years' time.

If you look at a photo of an office in the 1950s you'll find that it was very different from the offices of today. Gone are the typewriters, the landline phones, the rows of individual office desks and chairs. Imagine an office in twenty years' time and you'll see a completely different picture again. Obviously, we don't know exactly what will have changed, but we can make some pretty good predictions. These are all based on how our working lives are changing and will continue to change.

Our parents and grandparents had a clear division between work and home life. The normal working day was nine to five, and most people didn't take work home with them. They dressed smartly for work and casually at home. When they were at work, they had their own work tasks and their own desks. Meetings were face-to-face and they usually worked on one project at a time.

Today's workers are very different, and this is mainly due to the rapid advances in technology. We work in teams, but the team members might be in different cities, or even different countries, and communication is by video conferencing. We work on many projects simultaneously. We dress more casually. And our hours have become more flexible. With our phones and laptops, we can work anywhere – at home, while commuting, even out shopping. In one way, this can be seen as an intrusion into our private lives, but in another it means that our physical presence at the office is not that important and we can arrive late, leave early or work from home almost as often as we want.

These changes in working style have affected other aspects of our working environment. The physical office has changed. There used to be cubicle offices, where people were separated from each other. Then, in order to encourage collaboration and better communication, the open plan office was born where everyone worked in the same space. After that, we had 'hot-desking' – where people didn't have their own regular workspace, but were allocated an available spot when required. This helped companies to save space and money, but the downside was that it was a bit stressful for employees.

So, what of the future? Employees' health, both physical and mental, is high on the agenda. Stress, back problems and other work-related illnesses cost businesses a lot of money and we are likely to see more done by companies to deal with this. Rows of desks and work spaces will be replaced by office zones with shared spaces for relaxing, working alone or collaboratively, and areas for relaxation. Furniture will be comfortable sofas, or when working, chairs that are ergonomic. Temperature and air quality will be controlled. Meetings, whether face-to-face, video conferences or – as is predicted – conducted using VR, might be held in cleverly-designed fun rooms such as log cabins.

It is predicted that by 2030 a huge twenty percent of the working population in the UK will be mothers, twenty five percent will be single-parent families and close to ten million will need to spend time caring for older relatives. Companies will also be accessing the abilities and talents of disabled people. Remote working and flexible hours will help these people work efficiently and as a result, company buildings may become smaller. All this means that the traditional workplace will have changed forever. Will it lead to healthier lifestyles and increased productivity? We will have to wait and see!

Start with an interesting quote or sentence which catches the reader's attention.	'I regard the theatre as the greatest of all art forms.' This was written by Oscar Wilde, a famous Irish playwright at the end of the nineteenth century and it says exactly how I feel about the theatre. It entertains, it informs and it educates, and **¹that is why** I would like eventually to work in the theatre.
Explain why you're interested in the subject and the course.	The magic of the theatre first captured me when I was only five years old and saw a performance of Snow White in London. **²_____** changed my life. It made me **³_____** that I wanted to help create other amazing experiences for people by bringing plays to life on the stage. The first step in achieving my ambition is to study Drama and Theatre Studies at university.
Mention relevant experience and skills you learned.	With my school drama club, I have taken part in many productions. I love acting, but with my drama club I have also been involved with the lighting, set design and even directed one show myself.
Mention any training that will help in your career.	In addition to this, I have attended several residential weekend courses at a theatre school, where I learned about different aspects of theatrical work. My parents take me regularly to see new productions in London. This **⁴_____** a whole range of different theatrical performances.
Mention any other hobbies connected to the subject.	I am a creative person, with a good imagination, which is very important when working in the theatre. I enjoy writing plays. This hobby **⁵_____** to think about how others behave and react in situations, which is very useful for an actor.
Emphasise your enthusiasm, saying why you deserve a place.	The stage performance is the end result of a lot of **⁶_____** and hard work by many people. I am a hard worker and I **⁷_____** deadlines. I am also a perfectionist and I am passionate about the theatre. Although I haven't yet decided which specific aspect of theatre work I would like to focus on, I am confident that I could learn a lot from this course on Theatre Studies and make a successful career for myself in the future.
Mention longer term ambitions.	

1 Read the personal statement. Why does the writer want to go on this course?

a   to be able to work in some way in theatre
b   to be able to work backstage
c   to become an actor

2 Complete the personal statement with the words and phrases from the box.

dedication   has shown me   has taught me   realise
respect   ~~that is why~~   this experience

3 Decide if the statements about writing a personal statement are true (T) or false (F).

1 ☐ You shouldn't sound too boastful.
2 ☐ Only mention your strong points, not your weaknesses.
3 ☐ Write in an informal, friendly style.
4 ☐ Don't write about things you've done that are not related to the course.
5 ☐ Explain how your experience can help you in the future.

4 WRITING TASK Write a personal statement to accompany an application for one of the following university courses:

- Medicine
- Computer Science
- Law
- Media Studies
- Business Studies
- Sports Science
- Your choice

ACTIVE WRITING | Personal statement

1 Plan your personal statement.
- Make notes on the information you want to include.
- Divide your notes into paragraphs.
- Find an interesting quote or sentence to start with.

2 Write your personal statement.
- Use a formal style.
- Remember to mention any relevant experience, skills or training.

3 Check your personal statement. Check that:
- there are no spelling, grammar or punctuation mistakes.
- the statement is enthusiastic and mentions long term ambitions.

1 5A GRAMMAR AND VOCABULARY **Match the sentences 1–8 with the sentences a–h.**

1 ☐ Thalia is determined to always be first.

2 ☐ The students are curious about new things.

3 ☐ Ollie is really dedicated.

4 ☐ Tamara has real talent.

5 ☐ That's such an original and creative idea.

6 ☐ Jackie is mature for her age.

7 ☐ I know he's sharp.

8 ☐ He always takes great care with his homework.

a She's very gifted.

b He's very responsible about it.

c She's very sensible.

d She's competitive.

e He mustn't become overconfident though.

f They're eager to learn new information.

g You're so inventive!

h He's very hard-working and focused.

2 5B VOCABULARY **Complete the sentences with one preposition in each gap.**

1 I really hate that dance class, so I've decided to drop *out* of it.

2 Come on, concentrate! We have to get _____ to some studying.

3 Because she was ill for two weeks, Christie has fallen _____ with her school work.

4 Have you come _____ with any ideas?

5 When are you going to hand _____ your project?

6 I'm behind in Maths – I'll have to catch _____ on the work I've missed.

7 You're going to have to really pull your socks _____ if you want to pass the exam.

3 **Replace the underlined parts in each sentence with the phrasal verbs from the box.**

come up   go over   ~~keep up with~~   pick up   put off
put together

1 I've got too much work. How will I <u>stay at the same level as</u> my classmates?

keep up with

2 We're going to do some research and <u>create</u> a presentation about tourism.

_____

3 I hope I'll manage to <u>learn</u> a few phrases in German while I'm in Berlin.

_____

4 I have to do this for tomorrow. I can't <u>delay</u> doing the work.

_____

5 Will the topics from Unit 1 <u>appear</u> in the test?

_____

6 I'm not sure I understand this. I'll <u>read</u> the main points <u>again</u> later.

_____

4 5E LISTENING AND VOCABULARY **Complete the sentences with one word in each gap.**

1 My cousin is u<u>nemployed</u> at the moment, so she's looking for a job.

2 I don't really want to work night s_____ – working at night is exhausting!

3 The d_____ for this project is next week, no later.

4 My sister only works p_____ – four hours a day – but my mum works f_____.

5 My work placement is only t_____; it isn't a p_____ job.

6 It's a terrible job with long hours and l_____ w_____. I really want to find something else where I can earn more money.

7 It takes Dad an hour to c_____ to the nearest big city every day. He also does extra work, and when he works o_____ he's often tired at the weekend.

8 Paul is an architect and he's s_____ which means he doesn't have a boss. The idea of f_____ work like that is interesting.

5 5F READING AND VOCABULARY **Complete the text with one word in each gap.**

THE FUTURE OF WORK

It can be difficult to make predictions about how workplaces, working practices and jobs are going to change in the future.

It's possible that the future will bring better career [1]o<u>pportunities</u>, but it's also possible that there will be fewer jobs and more [2]u_____ as people lose their jobs because of advances in technology.

Will job prospects be better for white or blue [3]c_____ workers? Manual jobs may be at [4]r_____ because of automation, but perhaps new technology will [5]g_____ new kinds of work. And what about the economic side of things? Poor working [6]c_____ are hard to accept, but if the [7]s_____ is very low too, then people may refuse to do those jobs. How will they be able to afford to pay their rent, bills, and so on?

[8]R_____ jobs where people do the same thing again and again can affect workers' physical and mental health. People who have to [9]p_____ information all day in front of a computer and have no opportunity to [10]i_____ socially with colleagues will suffer too. So, will the world of work be a positive or negative place in the future? What's your view? Send us your comments.

6 ON A HIGH NOTE **Write a short paragraph about the type of working conditions that you think are ideal for you. Think about hours, salary, type of job, type of employment (freelance or employed by a company).**

1 For each learning objective, write 1–5 to assess your ability.

1 = I don't feel confident. 5 = I feel very confident.

	Learning objective	Course material	How confident I am (1–5)
5A	I can use a variety of forms to talk about future events and situations.	Student's Book pp. 64–65	
5B	I can talk about studying.	Student's Book p. 66	
5C	I can use the Future Continuous and the Future Perfect to talk about future events and situations.	Student's Book p. 67	
5D	I can carry out a simple interview and describe my strengths and weaknesses.	Student's Book p. 68	
5E	I can take effective notes while listening to an interview and talk about jobs.	Student's Book p. 69	
5F	I can identify specific details in an extended text and talk about the future of work.	Student's Book pp. 70–71	
5G	I can write a personal statement as part of a university application.	Student's Book pp. 72–73	

2 Which of the skills above would you like to improve in? How?

Skill I want to improve in	How I can improve

3 What can you remember from this unit?

New words I learned and most want to remember	Expressions and phrases I liked	English I heard or read outside class

GRAMMAR AND VOCABULARY

1 **Choose the correct words to complete the sentences.**

1 He's very *repetitive / hard-working* and spends hours in the library reading and studying.

2 She's very sensible, so I'm sure she'll manage to *fall behind / keep up with* her studies.

3 Clive never enjoyed working for a boss, so now he's *self-employed / part-time* and works from home.

4 My dad wants to find a *temporary / permanent* job which will give him security for the future.

5 I think most people would agree that a good *condition / salary* is important in any job.

/ 5

2 **Complete the sentences with one word in each gap.**

1 Kelly is _____ to learn more about Roman history – she's reading a book about it at the moment.

2 Look – just do the work and stop putting it _____ until tomorrow.

3 You missed a lot of lessons – I want you to _____ up on the notes and exercises by next week.

4 My cousin wants a _____ job in the afternoons so she can study in the mornings.

5 _____ is very high amongst young people – one in four of them don't have a job.

/ 5

3 **Choose the correct answers.**

1 I'm not sure, but I _____ good results in this exam – I've worked hard and I feel quite confident.

a could get

b am going to get

c will get

2 Our first class _____ ten minutes late tomorrow because our teachers have a meeting.

a is starting

b is about to start

c starts

3 _____ me come up with some ideas for my Art project?

a Are you helping

b May you help

c Will you help

4 You're so good at drawing – you _____ any trouble with your Art project.

a won't definitely have

b definitely won't have

c won't have definitely

5 I know we _____ the competition – our project is great!

a are winning

b win

c are going to win

/ 5

4 **Complete the conversation with the Future Continuous or the Future Perfect forms of the verbs in brackets.**

Dad Tom, can you help me with this car engine repair?

Tom Just a moment, Dad. I'm doing a Maths exercise, but I ¹_____ (finish) in ten minutes. OK?

Dad OK. In ten minutes I ²_____ (wait) for you in the garage.

Tom Right, Dad. ³_____ (you / start) the job by the time I arrive?

Dad No, I ⁴_____ (do) anything. I need your help.

Tom So what ⁵_____ (you / do) when I get there then?

Dad Waiting for you! Hurry up!

/ 5

USE OF ENGLISH

5 **Complete the text with the correct forms of the words in brackets.**

What problems do young people face in the world of work today? At the moment, the main problem is that a lot of people are out of work. Others are in boring, ¹_____ (REPEAT) jobs that give no satisfaction. It isn't always easy to stay focused and ²_____ (DETERMINE) and not everyone has a ³_____ (COMPETE) personality. On the other hand, some people can get a little too sure of themselves and become ⁴_____ (CONFIDE), which doesn't help. But these are a minority – most young people in the workplace are realistic and ⁵_____ (SENSE) about their prospects.

/ 5

6 **Complete the second sentence so that it means the same as the first. Use no more than three words.**

1 We intend to prepare a presentation about healthy eating.
We are putting _____ about healthy eating.

2 My appointment with the head teacher is at 10.30 a.m.
I am _____ the head teacher at 10.30 a.m.

3 At this time on Friday, my exam will be in progress.
I _____ my exam at this time on Friday.

4 The train is leaving the station in one minute.
The train _____ to leave the station.

5 I'm sure I'll arrive before tomorrow.
I _____ by tomorrow.

/ 5

/ 30

06 *Do the right thing*

6A GRAMMAR AND VOCABULARY

The first and second conditionals

1 ⭐ Complete the sentences with the first conditional forms of the verbs in brackets.

1 If you *don't tell* (not tell) them the truth, you *will get* (get) into trouble.

2 I _____ (believe) your story if you _____ (give) me some proof.

3 If Sarah _____ (talk) to her parents, they _____ (listen) to her.

4 If they _____ (go) to Paris, they _____ (bring) us a present!

5 I _____ (never / speak) to him again if he _____ (not apologise).

6 We _____ (tell) you the truth if you _____ (promise) not to get angry.

7 Our teacher _____ (be) suspicious if we _____ (not give) her a reason for our absence.

8 If you _____ (come) to the cinema with me tomorrow, I _____ (stay) at home with you tonight.

2 ⭐⭐ Use the prompts to write questions. Use the first conditional.

1 you / go out / if / it / rain / tomorrow?
Will you go out if it rains tomorrow?

2 Joshua / tell / her / the truth / if / she / ask / him to?
_____

3 we / make / something up / if / they / want / an explanation?
_____

4 she / go / to the party / if / Amy / invite / her?
_____

5 if / Noah / stay / at home / you / keep him company?
_____

6 if / your parents / go away / they / let / you stay at home alone?
_____

3 ⭐⭐ Complete the answers to the questions from Exercise 2.

1 No, I *won't go* out if it rains tomorrow.

2 No, he _____ her the truth if she asks him to.

3 No, we _____ anything up if they want an explanation.

4 No, she _____ to the party if Amy invites her.

5 No, I _____ him company if he stays at home.

6 No, they _____ me stay at home alone if they go away.

4 ⭐⭐ Use the prompts to write sentences. Use the second conditional.

1 Sharon / go / to the party if Oliver invited her.
Sharon would go to the party if Oliver invited her.

2 I think Wendy / like / you if you were nicer to her.
_____

3 If I / be / you, I'd talk to your mum about this.
_____

4 If Daniel / buy / the tickets, I'd go with him to the show.
_____

5 Emma / tell / the truth if she weren't so afraid.
_____

6 If we / can live / anywhere, we'd choose Australia.
_____

5 ⭐⭐ Complete the questions with the correct forms of the verbs from the box.

be break you/choose ~~you/go~~ you/talk you/tell

1 Where *would you go* if you could travel anywhere in the world?

2 Would you confess if you _____ your friend's phone?

3 _____ your parents a lie to get what you want?

4 If you had a problem at school, which teacher _____ to?

5 If you _____ an animal, which animal would you be?

6 If you could study just one subject, which one _____?

64

6 ★★ Use the prompts to write sentences. Use the second conditional.

1 I / not live / in New York / if / I / can / choose
I wouldn't live in New York if I could choose.

2 if / she / lie / to him / he / never forgive / her

_____

3 we / not tell / him / the truth / if / he / not promise / to stay calm

_____

4 my teachers / not accept / this excuse / if / my mum / not sign / the letter

_____

5 my parents / not go away / for the weekend / if / I / have / an important concert

_____

6 if / I / not have to / study so much / I / go / to the cinema more often

_____

7 ★★ Read the sentences and choose the correct answers.

1 I'll give you some money if I get paid at the end of the week.
a The speaker will definitely get paid.
b The speaker might get paid.

2 If Yuri asks me to the party, I'll definitely go.
a The speaker is sure Yuri will ask her.
b The speaker is sure she'll accept the invitation.

3 If Zoe and Chris break up, she'll be heartbroken.
a The couple will possibly split up.
b The couple will definitely split up.

4 Come on! We'd have a great time if we went to the party together.
a The friends haven't decided to go together yet.
b The friends are definitely going together.

5 I'd lend you my book if I had it with me.
a The speaker hasn't got his book.
b The speaker has got his book.

6 I'd save a lot of money if I had a job.
a The speaker has got a job.
b The speaker hasn't got a job.

8 ★★ Read the questions and write short answers.

1 Will you invite me if you have a party?
Yes, *I will*.

2 Would you tell me if you knew the answer?
No, _____.

3 Will Samira help me if I ask her?
Yes, _____.

4 If your teacher knew you cheated, would she punish you?
No, _____.

5 If your family wanted to move abroad, would you be happy?
Yes, _____.

6 If Lydia gets some money, will she take us out for a meal?
No, _____.

9 ★★★ Complete the posts on a web forum with the first or second conditional forms of the verbs from the box.

get list never/consider not be say tell ~~you/tell~~

Sam22

When and for what reason **1**_would you tell_ a lie?

Tilda

I **2**_____ false work experience on my CV if I could get a job that way. If I **3**_____ the job, then of course, I'd try to do it properly, so it **4**_____ a really serious lie, would it?

loyalbuddy

I **5**_____ something untrue to a friend if it protected him or if it avoided hurting his feelings. If you ask me what I think of your clothes, I **6**_____ you that you look great – even if you don't! I would never hurt my friend's feelings.

JamieJax

I **7**_____ telling a lie – for any reason whatsoever.

10 ★★★ Use the prompts to complete the conversation.

Alma Simon, **1**if I / ask / you some questions for the school magazine, **2**you / answer / them?
if I ask you ..., will you answer them?

Simon OK, but if it's something personal, **3**I / not / answer.

_____

Alma OK. Nothing personal. First of all, if you could spend a holiday anywhere in the world, **4**where / you / go?

Simon Well, **5**I / not go / to a hot country. I hate hot weather. Scandinavia probably.

Alma OK. And **6**if / your family / move / abroad, where would you like to live permanently?

_____

Simon Let me think. Actually, I think **7**I / choose / a big city, like New York. At the moment, I live in a village, so **8**I / not / go / to another village!

_____

11 ON A HIGH NOTE Write a short paragraph answering these questions.

• Would you be happy if your family decided to live abroad? Why/Why not?
• If you could choose where to live permanently, what place would that be? Why?
• If you moved abroad, what would you miss about your own country?

1 Read the story and answer the question.

What do we learn from the story?

a We need to do exciting things from time to time.

b Our parents sometimes know best.

c Exams aren't the most important thing in the world.

d Different generations like different music.

2 Read the story again. Match sentences A–H with gaps 1–5 in the story. There are three extra sentences.

A Revising for next day's exam was the last thing on their minds.

B She touched an icon and a video clip started playing.

C As well as this they loved the excitement.

D After all, they were going to do some work after the concert.

E That one was their most successful song and always went down very well with the fans.

F As it was, she lingered over each question and the words seemed blurred on the page.

G They were really good ones – right at the front near the stage.

H Later they stopped off for a coffee.

3 Decide if the statements are true (T) or false (F).

1 ☐ Jacky and Mia went to an open-air music concert.

2 ☐ The music concert was at the weekend.

3 ☐ Jacky's mum offered to take her to a concert at another time.

4 ☐ Jacky and Mia went to sleep quickly after the concert because they were tired.

5 ☐ Jacky couldn't concentrate in her exam.

6 ☐ Jacky's mum saw the girls at the concert on TV.

7 ☐ Jacky's mum got very angry and shouted at Jacky.

Vocabulary extension

4 Match the phrases 1–8 from the text with the sentences a–h.

1 ☐ I **dashed off** an email to Eve before I left for work.

2 ☐ I **lingered** over my cup of tea.

3 ☐ My **heart sank** when I read the text.

4 ☐ The photos are **blurred**.

5 ☐ I **walked the exam**.

6 ☐ My dad will **have a fit**.

7 ☐ It was **a dream come true**.

8 ☐ Watching the film was **the last thing on my mind**.

a It was very easy.

b I was really worried about the next day's exams.

c I didn't want to start work.

d I've always wanted to go to a fashion show.

e I didn't have much time.

f It was the worst possible news.

g He never lets me stay out this late!

h I need a new phone.

5 Complete the sentences with the correct forms of the phrases in bold from Exercise 4.

1 All my friends and family think I will _walk the exam_, but I might fail.

2 My mum will _____ if I don't leave the party and get home!

3 Helen was crying and the words in the email _____ on the screen.

4 Meeting the singer was _____ for Tom.

5 Doing her homework was _____.

6 Leo's _____ when he realised he hadn't revised any of the topics on the exam paper.

7 I _____ a note to tell mum we were at the cinema and then ran to catch the bus.

8 I _____ over a cup of coffee for ten minutes because I didn't want to go home.

ACTIVE VOCABULARY | Suffix -y

Many adjectives ending -y (e.g. *healthy*) are formed from nouns of one syllable ending in -*th* or -*lt*, e.g.

• guilt → guilty

• health → healthy

6 Complete the sentences with adjectives formed from the nouns from the box.

fault filth froth ~~guilt~~ health leaf salt wealth worth

1 I felt _guilty_ because I didn't invite James to my party.

2 I think _____ people should give money to charities to help the poor.

3 Our TV wasn't working properly because of a _____ connection.

4 I had to wash my clothes after the football match because they were absolutely _____!

5 I love _____ food, but it isn't really very _____.

6 The best coffee has a _____ top with chocolate sprinkles on it!

7 Martin lives in a large house in a beautiful, _____ part of town.

8 Duncan did a lot of training and was a _____ winner.

7 ON A HIGH NOTE Write a short paragraph giving your opinion of Jacky's behaviour in the story.

A LESSON LEARNED

'If mum and dad knew I was here, they'd have a fit!' Jacky grinned at Mia as the girls followed the queue into the concert hall. Mia rolled her eyes. 'Forget about them. Let's have fun!' she said and pulled Jacky down towards their seats. **1**_____ When the band walked on, they could practically touch their guitars and feel the guys' breath. The audience were immediately on their feet, cheering and singing along to every song. Cameras flashed constantly as the evening was recorded on phones across the concert hall.

This was Jacky's dream come true – her favourite band playing a gig in her hometown! Her heart was beating with excitement, but she was also feeling a little guilty. She remembered telling her parents about the concert a few days ago, with a big smile on her face.

But her mum hadn't smiled. 'No,' she said, frowning. 'You can't go. It's Thursday night – and you've got your last school exam on Friday morning.' Jacky's disappointment was evident. 'Don't worry,' her mum added. 'If you still want to see them, your dad and I will take you to a concert. We're not wealthy, but I'm sure we can afford a night in a good hotel too!'

However, Jacky didn't want to wait. Mia had two tickets and she wanted to be there, on Thursday, with her friend.

On Thursday morning, she had packed a bag, hiding an outfit she'd bought especially for the gig at the bottom. 'I'm staying at Mia's tonight,' she had told her parents. 'We're going to revise for the exam together.' It wasn't really a lie, she thought. **2**_____ So why was she feeling so guilty, standing there, listening to the best band in the world with her best friend? A little voice inside her head was saying, 'This is wrong – and you know it!' But she shivered and pushed the voice away.

All too soon, it was over, and the girls were back in Mia's room. They were too excited by the evening to want to sleep. They spent hours chatting about the band and how electric the atmosphere in the theatre had been. **3**_____ It was three o'clock before they felt sleepy and closed their eyes.

The exam the next day was a total disaster. Jacky was so tired that she couldn't think clearly. Normally, she could have dashed off her answers in super-quick time. **4**_____ Her parents had expected her to walk this exam – everyone had. It wasn't going to happen – and it was all her own fault.

'How did the exam go?' her mum asked when she got home. Jacky lied again. 'It was fine. It went really well!' she murmured, and tried to slip past her mum to shut herself away in her room. Her mum blocked her way. She smiled sadly.

'Well, if you pass, it'll be a miracle,' she said and showed Jacky her phone. **5**_____ Jacky could see a crowd of people moving on the screen and the sound – her heart sank as she recognised the music – music she'd heard less than twenty four hours before. Her mum enlarged the screen and two faces came into focus. Jacky and Mia were waving their hands and grinning in the audience at the gig.

'My friend Gabby was there, too,' Jacky's mum said quietly. 'She had a great time and shared some photos. I hope it was worth it, Jacky.' Jacky felt absolutely terrible. No, she thought, it hadn't been worth it. She'd made her mum unhappy and she was probably going to fail her exam.

It had been a hard lesson, but it was the last time she ever lied to her parents.

1 🔊 *48* **Listen to the first part of a radio interview. What did the special guest on today's show do?**

a He wrote an interesting story for a newspaper.

b He gave some money to help a child.

c He performed a life-changing operation.

2 🔊 *49* **Now listen to the whole interview and choose the correct answers.**

1 Marcus kept what he did a secret because he
   a felt he hadn't done anything special.
   b is a very private person.
   c didn't want to help other people.

2 When the newspapers found out about the story he felt
   a angry because of the unwanted attention.
   b confused by all the interest.
   c proud of what he'd done.

3 Today he is on the show to
   a correct some errors in the story.
   b describe the results of his actions.
   c encourage others to do the same thing.

4 What does he think helped him become successful?
   a He chose a job that paid well.
   b He saved money instead of spending it.
   c He listened to advice about how to make money.

Vocabulary extension

3 🔊 *50* **Complete the sentences with the words from the box which you heard in the interview in Exercises 1 and 2. Listen and check.**

fuss   leak   most   shy   supportive   rainy   raise   ~~treat~~

1 Well, we've got a **special** _treat_ for listeners this morning.

2 His parents were trying to _____ **enough money** to take him to the USA.

3 I don't usually _____ **away from** publicity.

4 I suppose it was inevitable that someone would _____ **the information** to the media.

5 She's very _____ **of** me.

6 I just don't understand **what all the** _____ **is about**.

7 Do I get all fussy about privacy or **make the** _____ **of it** to help others.

8 I have a lot put aside **for a** _____ **day**.

4 **Match the phrases in bold in Exercise 3 with their definitions a–h.**

a ☐ loyal and helpful

b ☐ saved for more difficult times

c ☐ unexpected pleasure

d ☐ avoid something difficult

e ☐ get maximum benefit

f ☐ give information unofficially

g ☐ collect, get donations

h ☐ reaction, unusual interest

Pronunciation

5 🔊 *51* **Read two sentences from the listening. Which tone – rising ↗ or falling ↘ do you think the speaker used for the highlighted words? Listen and check.**

1 I had the money, Jack's parents didn't, so I gave it to them – simple.

2 We're dealt certain cards in this life – some of us are born with intelligence, some with skills and abilities, and some of us are born lucky.

ACTIVE PRONUNCIATION | Rising and falling tones

Often when we are talking about several things consecutively, we use a rising tone to show that we haven't finished, and then a falling tone at the end to show that we have, e.g.

- *I came home, fed the cat, did some homework and then had a rest.*

We also use a rising and falling tone pattern when we offer somebody a choice, e.g.

- *Would you rather take the bus or walk home?*

6 🔊 *52* **Read the sentences aloud. Follow the tone pattern explained in Active Pronunciation. Listen, check and repeat.**

1 This morning I got up, had breakfast, set off for school and then caught the 8.15 bus.

2 We've been given loads of homework – English, Maths, History and French.

3 Before handing in the essay, I checked the spelling, the grammar and the punctuation.

4 I had a superhero fancy dress party for my birthday. There were two Starlords, a Batman, three Thors and a Wonderwoman.

7 🔊 *53* **Look at two sentences from the listening which give alternatives. Do you think the highlighted words have a rising or falling tone? Listen and check.**

1 Do I get all fussy about privacy, or make the most of it to help others?

2 You can let your money sit there doing nothing, or you can help people who need it.

8 🔊 *54* **Read the sentences aloud. Follow the tone pattern explained in Active pronunciation. Listen, check and repeat.**

1 Shall we walk home through the park or along by the river?

2 We've got several fillings for your sandwiches – there's chicken, beef or cheese.

3 My mum could still be at work, or training at the gym.

4 I've got two choices. I can put in some extra time to improve my grades, or I give up the subject.

5 When we went to London we couldn't decide whether to go to Trafalgar Square, the British Museum or the Tate Gallery.

6D GRAMMAR

The zero conditional and alternatives to *if*

1 ⭐ Complete the sentences with the zero conditional forms of the verbs in brackets.

1 If the weather *is* (be) good, Lisa *cycles* (cycle) to school.

4 Everything _____ (get) wet if it _____ (rain).

2 Water _____ (freeze) if you _____ (cool) it to zero degrees.

5 I _____ (take) a cake if I _____ (go) to a party.

3 If you _____ (boil) water, it _____ (become) steam.

6 My mum _____ (listen) if I _____ (talk) to her.

2 ⭐ Match the beginnings 1–6 with the endings a–f.

1 ☐ I don't have parties at my house unless
2 ☐ I always call you as soon as
3 ☐ You can borrow my bike as long as
4 ☐ The singer's husband always waits for her until
5 ☐ Derek helps me with Maths provided that
6 ☐ We always have dinner after

a the show ends.
b it's my birthday.
c we watch the film.
d you bring it back to me.
e I get home – not a minute later!
f I offer him a coffee.

3 ⭐ Choose the correct words to complete the sentences.

1 *Unless / After* she loses her temper, she always apologises.
2 We always travel first class *provided that / unless* we have the money for the tickets.
3 She doesn't get angry *unless / as long as* you really provoke her.
4 I ask people for advice *as soon as / as long as* I trust them.
5 I tend to discuss everything with you *after / as long as* you don't get angry.
6 She can't relax *until / after* she takes off her work clothes and has a cup of tea.
7 I really can't think *after / before* I have my breakfast – give me a few minutes to finish my toast!

4 ⭐⭐ Complete the sentences with one or two words in each gap.

1 She always helps people *if* she realises that they are in trouble.
2 Sorry, but I never go to concerts with Norma _____ she pays for her own ticket.
3 I can talk to people _____ as they are reasonable; if they start insulting others, I leave.
4 You know we always come to your parties _____ that you don't play terrible music!
5 When I'm rude to someone I feel bad _____ I apologise.

5 ⭐⭐ Complete the conversation with the words and phrases from the box. There are two extra options.

after   didn't   don't   long as   make   ~~provided that~~
unless   until   want   when

Miriam Mike, I heard you fell out with Gary again. What happened?
Michael I can tell you ¹*provided that* you promise not to tell anyone else.
Miriam Of course! I mean, ² _____ someone's committed a terrible crime, I keep secrets.
Michael Well, he always borrows my tablet, and he never gives it back ³ _____ he's finished. If you ⁴ _____ a promise, you keep it!
Miriam Perhaps he hasn't finished with it. Would you like me to check? I can ask, as ⁵ _____ you give me permission of course. I never get involved if people ⁶ _____ want me to.
Michael Well, OK, if you ⁷ _____ to help, that's fine by me. Can you call me ⁸ _____ you speak to him?

6 ON A HIGH NOTE How do you usually behave when you meet new people? What do you like and dislike on a first meeting? Write a short paragraph. Use some of the words from the box.

after   as long as   as soon as   before   provided that
unless   until

1 🔊 *55* **Listen and repeat the phrases. How do you say them in your language?**

SPEAKING | Asking for, giving and reacting to advice

ASKING FOR ADVICE

I wonder if you could give me some advice.
What do you think I should/ought to do?
Do you think I need to/should take her out to dinner?
I've got a bit of a problem and I don't know what to do.
I've no idea how/what to do to celebrate her birthday.
I'd really appreciate your advice.
I'm at (a bit of) a loss.

GIVING ADVICE

You could/should(n't)/ought (not) to buy an expensive present.
I (don't) think you should take her to the cinema.
You'd better (not) organise a party.*
It's probably (not) a good idea to organise a picnic.
The first/best thing to do is to prepare some sandwiches.
If I were you, I'd/I wouldn't buy a card.

REACTING TO ADVICE

Thanks. That's really helpful (advice).
You're right, that's good advice, thanks.
I never thought of that, (it's a) good idea.
I don't know if it'll work, but I'll give it a try.
I thought about/of (doing) that but I can't afford it.

* strong advice, similar to *you have to*

---

2 🔊 *56* **Complete the conversation with one word in each gap. Listen and check.**

Angela Hi Kenny, you look really stressed. What's the problem?

Kenny Yeah, I'd really ¹*appreciate* your advice.

Angela Sure, what is it?

Kenny It's Mia's birthday soon, and I'm at a bit of a ²_____ as to how to celebrate it.

Angela Well, you ³_____ take her out to dinner. There's a new restaurant which is supposed to be brilliant.

Kenny The trouble is that it's also really expensive and I'm nearly broke. Do you think I ⁴_____ borrow some money to take her?

Angela It's ⁵_____ not a good idea to borrow money – you'll only get even more stressed trying to pay it back! The best ⁶_____ to do is to find something memorable that doesn't cost much.

Kenny I've no ⁷_____ how to do anything like that!

Angela If I ⁸_____ you, I'd organise a party.

Kenny I thought of ⁹_____ that, but I can't afford it – food, drink ...

Angela No! Listen! Mia loves the countryside. Invite all her friends to a picnic by the river and ask them all to bring a plate of food each!

Kenny Wow! What a great idea!

Angela And you ¹⁰_____ to make it a surprise. Tell her you're going for a walk. You sit down and take out some sandwiches – and she starts getting fed up because it's nothing special. Then one by one your friends come along and join you with their food until you've got a whole big picnic!

Kenny You're a star!

Angela You'd better not forget to invite me!

3 **Choose the correct words to complete the sentences.**

1 I wonder *that / if* you could help me with a problem.
2 What do you think I *should / could* do about getting a job?
3 I don't know *about / if* it will work, but I'll *have / give* it a try.
4 I never thought *on / of* using that excuse!
5 *That's / There's* really helpful advice, thanks.
6 I don't think you *should / better* lie to her.
7 You *ought / should* to discuss it with your parents first.
8 If I *am / were* you, I wouldn't mention it for the moment.
9 I've no idea *what / how* to say to him about it.
10 You *'d better not / wonder if* go on an expensive holiday if you haven't got much money.

4 ON A HIGH NOTE **Read the following problems. For each one, write a request for advice, a response and a reaction to the advice.**

• I've got exams soon and I can't concentrate on revising.
• My younger brother is being bullied at school.

1 ⭐ **Choose the correct words to complete the sentences.**

1 Mel never supports me in any way – she always *lets me down / gets into trouble*.

2 Emma is sick of Alan always *falling out with / cheating on her* with other women.

3 Please calm down – it won't help if you *lose your temper / have a crush on me*.

4 I can't believe he was so cruel as to talk about his friends *at first sight / behind their backs*.

5 If you like Len so much, why don't you *ask him out / hit it off*?

6 When Terry broke up with Sonia, he really *fell out with her / broke her heart*.

2 ⭐ **Match the beginnings 1–6 with the endings a–f.**

1 ☐ I was sorry to hear that Ava and Ron had split

2 ☐ She really hit it

3 ☐ Irma always goes red when Tim arrives, I think

4 ☐ You should talk directly to Ned and

5 ☐ I was really angry to hear that you made

6 ☐ They were right to break

a she has a crush on him.

b fun of my sister.

c up – they weren't good together.

d up – they seemed so happy.

e not behind his back!

f off with her cousins' friends.

3 ⭐ **Complete the sentences with one word in each gap.**

1 Chris asked Stefania out the day he met her – it was love at first s*ight*.

2 Nathan was so angry – he really lost his t_____.

3 I'm sorry to hear that you and Josie have fallen o_____ – are you sure you can't talk about it?

4 I think my brother has f_____ in love – he can't eat or sleep.

5 Why do you p_____ up with his bad temper?

6 I've tried so often to talk to you and you just insult me – sorry but I'm t_____ with you.

4 ⭐ **Complete the sentences with the words from the box. There are two extra words.**

behind boss crazy crush fun heartbroken ~~serious~~ trouble

1 My cousin and her boyfriend are in a *serious* relationship; I think they'll get married soon.

2 Kerry was _____ when her boyfriend left her for another girl.

3 Don't post insults to people on social networks – you'll get into _____.

4 My parents don't listen to me – they just _____ me around.

5 Jonas is _____ about a girl in his class called Elizabeth.

6 Why do you make _____ of people? It's not nice.

5 ⭐⭐ **Complete the text with one word in each gap.**

Teresa

I'm writing you this message to tell you to be careful about Ellen. You seem really friendly and I'm worried you don't know that she always lets people **1** *down*. Every time she makes a new friend, she starts laughing at them **2** _____ their back, and she **3** _____ them – saying really nasty things. She likes to make **4** _____ of people. No one else will **5** _____ up with her anymore, so be careful. I know you think that the two of you have hit it **6** _____, but she's always like that with new people and then … just wait and see!

Sue

6 ⭐⭐⭐ **Complete the second text so that it means the same as the first one. Use between one and three words in each gap.**

My friend Seb was really depressed when he discovered that Gillian was going out with another boy behind his back. He decided to end their relationship. He felt really disappointed in her because when they met he really liked her – there was an instant attraction. Anyway, he decided not to do anything without her knowledge, so he asked her what the situation was. And here's the surprise! Gillian said she was really in love with him, and she wasn't seeing any other boy. The boy was her cousin Tommy, and they were planning a surprise birthday party for Seb!

My friend Seb was **1** h*eartbroken* when he discovered that Gillian was **2** c_____. He decided to **3** b_____ with her. He felt really **4** l_____ by her because when they met they really **5** h_____ – it was love **6** a_____. Anyway, he decided not to do anything **7** b_____, so he asked her what the situation was. And here's the surprise! Gillian said she was really **8** c_____ about him, and she wasn't going **9** o_____ any other boy. The boy was her cousin Tommy, and they were planning a surprise birthday party for Seb!

7 ON A HIGH NOTE **What would you do if your friend was not loyal to you? Write a short paragraph.**

6G **WRITING** | A for-and-against essay

Begin with a general statement.

End first paragraph with a statement or a question mentioning both sides.

Give several arguments for the issue.

Give examples, or explain your points.

Give arguments against the issue, with examples and reasons.

Summarise the debate briefly.

Add your own opinion.

Should parents help their children with homework?

Children and teenagers today are given a lot of homework to do every evening. This is sometimes very difficult and they ask their parents for help. But should the parents say 'no' or should they help?

1_One_ reason that parents often give for helping their children is that they are sharing their knowledge and therefore continuing their child's education. They believe that the child can learn more when the parent helps. **2**_____ argument for helping with homework is to encourage and motivate the child. For **3**_____, if the parents know something about the topic they can share this interest with the child, who will then become more excited by the subject.

4_____, not everyone agrees that helping their children is good. Many people consider that a child needs to learn to work on his or her own and develop self-discipline. Homework is often given by the teacher to encourage good working habits and independent learning. **5**_____ is more, if the parents help too much, the teacher cannot assess the child's needs very well. She will not know who answered the questions – the child or the parent – and she will therefore not know how to help that child in the best way.

In **6**_____, I must say that there are good reasons both for and against the idea of parents helping their children with homework. On the one hand children can learn from their parents, but on the **7**_____ hand parents can do too much. In my **8**_____, I feel that it is more important for the teacher to be able to assess the child's work well and that this is in the best interests of the child.

---

1 **Read the essay and choose the correct answer.**
The writer thinks that
- **a** parents should help their children.
- **b** parents shouldn't help their children.
- **c** parents should sometimes help their children.

2 **Complete the essay with the words from the box.**

another   conclusion   however   instance   ~~one~~
opinion   other   what

3 **Complete the sentences with one word in each gap.**
1 To begin w_ith_, I'd like to point out the benefits of working in a team.
2 A_____ to some experts, teenagers need more sleep than older people.
3 H_____ said that, there are a lot of people who disagree.
4 In s_____, we need to look at both sides of the question again carefully.
5 U_____, lying to a friend can never be the right thing to do.
6 M_____ of us agree that lying is wrong.
7 Having pocket money allows children to learn the value of money. F_____, it gives them some independence.

4 **Complete the lists with linking words and phrases from Exercise 3.**
- **Introducing new arguments**
  First of all; Secondly; Finally; _To begin with_; _____, _____
- **Giving examples and support**
  For example; for this reason; such as; _____
- **Introducing a contrast**
  Although; Nevertheless; _____
- **Introducing a conclusion**
  To conclude; _____
- **Introducing your own opinion**
  Personally; I believe; _____

5 WRITING TASK **Write an essay entitled _Should parents limit the time children spend in front of a screen?_**

ACTIVE WRITING | A for-and-against essay

1 Plan your essay.
- Make a list of points for and against the issue.
- Think of some examples to illustrate your points.

2 Write your essay.
- Write an introduction that mentions both sides.
- Use linking words and phrases to connect your ideas.
- Summarise the arguments in your conclusion.

3 Check your essay. Check that:
- you gave your personal opinion at the end.
- there are no spelling, grammar and punctuation mistakes.

1 **6A GRAMMAR AND VOCABULARY** Complete the sentences with the phrases from the box.

cover for   fall for   fool   make something up
saw right through   ~~through my teeth~~

1 I told them complete nonsense! I just invented a story and lied *through my teeth*!

2 He believes everything you tell him – he'll _____ any crazy story!

3 I don't think you can _____ Julia about this – she knows the situation.

4 They didn't believe a word of your story – they _____ you.

5 If Olivia asks questions, can you _____ me and tell her I'm at Kate's house?

6 I don't know what to say. I suppose I'll just _____ if they ask why I'm late.

2 **6B READING AND VOCABULARY** Match the beginnings 1–8 with the endings a–h.

1 ☐ Pola hugged her children and
2 ☐ The walkers stood gazing at
3 ☐ Tom is so happy – look at him
4 ☐ She didn't want anyone to hear,
5 ☐ Meghan groaned in pain as she
6 ☐ Give me a suggestion! Don't just
7 ☐ I think he knows the answer – he
8 ☐ Eryk's clothes were wet and he

a the beautiful view of the mountains.
b winked at me when they asked the question.
c tried to stand on her injured leg.
d was shivering with cold.
e shrug your shoulders.
f kissed them goodbye.
g so she whispered into my ear.
h grinning at everyone!

3 **6C LISTENING AND VOCABULARY** Complete the sentences with the correct noun forms of the adjectives from the box.

disappointed   embarrassed   envious   excited
lonely   ~~sad~~   sympathetic

1 A feeling of *sadness* filled her heart as her family got into the car and drove away.

2 I'm sorry, but I've got no _____ for you – this situation is your own fault!

3 If you expect too much from your friends, you may experience some _____.

4 I'm afraid all that _____ was too tiring for my grandmother – she's having a rest.

5 The problem of _____ is very common among older people who have no family or close friends.

6 I know you feel _____ because he won the prize, but he really deserved it.

7 It was a huge _____ for the organisers when she won the prize and refused to collect it.

4 **6F VOCABULARY** Complete the text with one word in each gap.

When you fall **1** o*ut* with a friend it can be for many reasons. The friend might have let you **2** d_____ by talking about you behind your **3** b_____. Or perhaps he or she made **4** f_____ of something you said or wore, or behaved badly by bossing you **5** a_____. Unfortunately these things happen, and they hurt, so our advice is: talk! Don't put **6** u_____ with bad behaviour or with silence. Ask for an explanation and listen without losing your **7** t_____. Perhaps you can save your friendship and end up hitting it **8** o_____ better than ever!

5 Complete the conversation with one word in each gap.

Martin   Yolanda, what's wrong? You look terrible!

Yolanda   I feel awful, Martin. I just broke up **1** *with* Ian. I'm afraid we're **2** _____ with each other.

Martin   You're joking! Why? Did he **3** _____ on you? He'll get into **4** _____ from me if he did that!

Yolanda   No, it isn't that. We had an argument and he lost his **5** _____. He says he doesn't want to be in a **6** _____ relationship right now.

Martin   I'm really sorry. You've been going **7** _____ with him for a year. I thought he was **8** _____ about you.

6 Complete the sentences with the phrases from the box.

ask her out   ~~break his heart~~   fall in love
has a crush on her   heartbroken   love at first sight

1 Julie, don't cheat on Dan! You'll *break his heart*!

2 I don't want to watch one of those boring romantic comedies where two people _____.

3 If you like Lorna so much, why don't you _____ on a date?

4 Eddie and Kate liked each other immediately – it was _____.

5 I think Piet really likes Emma. I'm sure he _____.

6 Jill and Mike broke up – they're both really sad and _____ at the moment.

7 **ON A HIGH NOTE** Write a short paragraph about the types of behaviour that you can put up with and those that make you lose your temper. Are there any special situations when you will accept bad behaviour from someone?

1 For each learning objective, write 1–5 to assess your ability.

1 = I don't feel confident. 5 = I feel very confident.

	Learning objective	Course material	How confident I am (1–5)
6A	I can use the first or second conditional to talk about possible or hypothetical situations.	Student's Book pp. 78–79	
6B	I can understand the development of ideas in a short story and talk about being honest.	Student's Book pp. 80–81	
6C	I can identify specific details in a radio programme and talk about winning a lottery.	Student's Book p. 82	
6D	I can use the zero conditional to talk about real situations that are always true.	Student's Book p. 83	
6E	I can ask for, give and react to advice on a wide range of subjects.	Student's Book p. 84	
6F	I can talk about relationships, conflicts and problems.	Student's Book p. 85	
6G	I can write a for-and-against essay.	Student's Book pp. 86–87	

2 Which of the skills above would you like to improve in? How?

Skill I want to improve in	How I can improve

3 What can you remember from this unit?

New words I learned and most want to remember	Expressions and phrases I liked	English I heard or read outside class

Self-check

GRAMMAR AND VOCABULARY

1 Choose the correct words to complete the sentences.

1 I was sorry to hear that you broke *down / in / up* with Tom.
2 She's really angry with Ben. I think she's *through / cheated / lost* with him.
3 He just *winked / frowned / glanced* at my work and walked away – he wasn't interested at all.
4 I think his mother has lost her patience – she just rolled her *mouth / eyes / expression*.
5 Having no friends and experiencing *envy / excitement / loneliness* is very difficult.

/ 5

2 Choose the correct answers.

1 If I can't find a good excuse, I'll just _____.
 a cover for you **b** make something up
 c see through you
2 She looked really sad, _____ and walked away.
 a hugged **b** grinned
 c sighed
3 It's no use feeling _____ because of other people's success – you should focus on achieving your own goals.
 a envy **b** sympathy
 c disappointment
4 They _____ the very first time they met and have been friends ever since.
 a lost their tempers **b** hit it off
 c let each other down
5 Stop telling everyone what to do and _____!
 a insulting them **b** cheating on them
 c bossing people around

/ 5

3 Complete the sentences with the first or second conditional forms of the verbs in brackets.

1 If Tom asks for the truth, I _____ (tell/him) what happened.
2 If I were you, I _____ (not trust) Bill.
3 What _____ (you/do) if your best friend let you down?
4 I _____ (not get) angry if you explain what happened truthfully.
5 If I could have a holiday, I _____ (go) to Paris.

/ 5

4 Complete the conversation with the words and phrases from the box. There are two extra options.

as long as as soon as finish get provided unless
will finish

Jake Katie, can you help me? I don't understand this homework.
Katie Sure, I can help you [1]_____ it's French – I hate French.
Jake No, it's not French.
Katie That's what I have to do for homework.
Jake I can help you with French [2]_____ that you help me with Maths.
Katie OK. It's a deal. I'm always depressed when I [3]_____ my French homework back. It's nearly always wrong.
Jake Fine – we can look at your French after we [4]_____ my Maths.
Katie OK, [5]_____ we complete the Maths, we can do my French exercise and then we can watch a film!

/ 5

USE OF ENGLISH

5 Choose the correct answers.

Sarah is a very kind person and she has a lot of [1]_____ for people who are sad, so she often gets asked for advice. If people ask her for help, she usually [2]_____ to them – [3]_____ that they don't lose their temper of course. She always says that she doesn't like bad-tempered people or loud voices. If someone got angry, she [4]_____ up and walk away, so people have to keep calm [5]_____ they want her to leave.

1 a jealousy	**b** sympathy	**c** loneliness	**d** happiness
2 a listens	**b** would listen	**c** will listen	**d** is listening
3 a as long as	**b** until	**c** provided	**d** after
4 a gets	**b** will get	**c** got	**d** would get
5 a unless	**b** when	**c** before	**d** as soon as

/ 5

6 Complete the text message with one word in each gap.

That's it. I'm [1]_____ with him. I never want to see him again. If he tries to call me, I [2]_____ answer. Sorry, but if people [3]_____ fun of me, they lose my friendship. I [4]_____ listen to him if I thought he had an excuse, but he hasn't. He lied through his [5]_____ about me and laughed at me. So goodbye!

/ 5

/ 30

In the spotlight

7A GRAMMAR AND VOCABULARY

Reported speech

1 ⭐ Complete the sentences using reported speech.

1 Andy: 'I always watch the news.'
   Andy said he always **_watched_** the news.
2 Emma: 'They're interviewing my teacher on TV!'
   Emma said they _____ her teacher on TV.
3 Noah: 'I don't like the journalist.'
   Noah complained that he _____ the journalist.
4 Abigail: 'This trend isn't growing fast.'
   Abigail explained that that trend _____ fast.
5 Liam: 'It's a very silly idea.'
   Liam warned that it _____ a very silly idea.
6 Charlotte: 'The students are sleeping in class!'
   Charlotte confessed that the students _____ in class.

2 ⭐ Match the expressions 1–8 with the reported expressions a–h.

1 ☐ these   **a** the day after/the next day
2 ☐ a few days ago   **b** those
3 ☐ we   **c** there
4 ☐ here   **d** then/at that time
5 ☐ tomorrow   **e** the day before/the previous day
6 ☐ yesterday   **f** a few days before
7 ☐ I   **g** they
8 ☐ now   **h** he/she

3 ⭐⭐ Choose the correct verb forms to complete the sentences in direct speech.

1 Nathan said that he had seen the programme about surfing dogs several times.
   Nathan: 'I *saw / have seen* the programme about surfing dogs several times.'
2 Olivia said they had gone to the cinema the day before.
   Olivia: 'We *went / have been* to the cinema yesterday.'
3 Carrie said that she hadn't been to the TV studio the day before.
   Carrie: 'I *didn't go / haven't been* to the TV studio yesterday.'
4 Matt explained that he hadn't finished the article yet.
   Matt: 'I *didn't finish / haven't finished* the article yet.'
5 Mia complained that the journalist hadn't talked to her during the interview.
   Mia: 'The journalist *didn't talk / hasn't talked* to me during the interview.'

4 ⭐⭐ Complete the sentences using reported speech.

1 Sally: 'I'll help you!'
   Sally said that _she would help_ me.
2 James: 'We'll watch the film together.'
   James said that _____ the film together.
3 Mike: 'I'm going to try this new idea tomorrow.'
   Mike said that _____ that new idea the next day.
4 Nora: 'My mum's going to take me shopping.'
   Nora explained that _____ take her shopping.
5 Mark: 'My teacher isn't going to like this.'
   Mark complained that _____ like that.
6 Isa: 'I'll finish this job next week.'
   Isa promised that _____ that job the next week.

5 ⭐⭐ Match the reporting verbs from the box with their definitions.

add agree complain confess ~~explain~~ promise reply warn

1 to say how or why something happened _explain_
2 to tell someone of a negative possibility _____
3 to give a second piece of information _____
4 to answer _____
5 to admit that you did something, usually negative _____
6 to talk about something which annoys you _____
7 to have the same opinion _____
8 to say that you will definitely do something _____

6 ★★ Complete the sentences with the reporting verbs from the box.

admitted claimed complained ~~pointed out~~
predicted warned

1 Jamie _pointed out_ that Bella had made a mistake.
2 The woman _____ that she was a famous actress, but we didn't believe her.
3 The newsreader _____ that the strong studio lights made her look old.
4 He _____ me not to go into the studio because they were still filming.
5 He _____ that it would rain and he was right!
6 The man _____ that he had stolen some equipment from the studio.

7 ★★ Complete the sentences with the correct reported forms of the verbs in brackets.

1 Maria promised that she _would read_ (will read) the article the next day.
2 Tommy said he _____ (can't give) us any more information.
3 Vicky confessed that she _____ (wouldn't work) with Gary because she didn't like him.
4 Teresa told Jack he _____ (should see) his teacher.
5 The journalist said she _____ (might interview) some of us.
6 Mr Dawkins told the class they _____ (must hand in) the project by Friday.
7 My dad said he _____ (might not watch) the news.

8 ★★ Complete the sentences with the correct reported forms of the verbs from the box.

not be ~~not forget~~ not touch read tell

1 His colleague told him _not to forget_ his glasses.
2 The director asked her _____ the news more slowly.
3 The cameramen asked his colleagues _____ his camera while he was away.
4 We asked the journalist _____ us what she knew.
5 His boss told him _____ late.

9 ★★★ Complete the sentences using reported speech.

1 'Go away now!' Gary shouted at us.
Gary _shouted at us to go away then_.
2 'Find a better news programme,' Jake told Eddie.
Jake _____.
3 'Don't make fun of me,' Mandy told Anna.
Mandy _____.
4 'Don't drink that water,' Den advised his colleague.
Den _____.
5 'Give the prize to this dog,' the judge told the organiser.
The judge _____.
6 'Don't watch this programme,' Dad told Shaun.
Dad _____.

10 ★★★ Complete the conversation so that it means the same as the text. Use between one and two words in each gap.

> Gina told Will to listen. She said a journalist had fallen off her chair on TV the day before. Will answered that his mum had told him about it. He said he might have a picture and told Gina to look. Gina said it was going to be difficult for her on TV that evening. Will said he thought she would take the day off.

Gina Will, **1**_listen_ to this! A journalist **2**_____ off her chair on TV **3**_____!
Will Yes, my mum **4**_____ me about it. I **5**_____ a picture. **6**_____!
Gina It **7**_____ be difficult for her on TV **8**_____ evening!
Will I **9**_____ she **10**_____ the day off!

11 ★★★ Complete the reported conversation.

Dave I've heard some amazing news!
Chloe Tell me about it.
Dave Some journalists came to the school yesterday. They interviewed my teacher.
Chloe I imagine it was about your teacher's new book.
Dave I can't believe my teacher wrote a book!
Chloe She'll be famous!

1 Dave told Chloe that _he had heard some amazing news_.
2 Chloe _____.
3 Dave _____
_____.
4 Chloe _____
_____.
5 Dave _____.
6 Chloe _____.

12 ON A HIGH NOTE Think of a recent, brief conversation you have had, and report it in a short text.

1 ★ Complete the sentences with the words and phrases from the box.

binge-watching ~~episode~~ on-demand content
screen time series spoilers
subscription streaming service viewers

1 When this _episode_ finishes, I'm going to watch the next one right away.
2 The content is getting boring, so _____ are starting to watch different series.
3 We try to limit our _____ to a few hours per day.
4 My brother is terrible for _____ – he can watch an entire series in two days!
5 I think this _____ is really great. I'm happy to pay for it and avoid national TV channels.
6 Don't read Matt's blog – it's full of _____. He keeps writing about how films and episodes end.
7 My parents didn't have _____ when they were young; they had to watch whatever was on TV that evening.
8 My mum has been watching this _____ for years.

2 Match the beginnings 1–8 with the endings a–h.

1 ☐ You should put a spoiler alert on your messages –
2 ☐ Their screen time is limited
3 ☐ We need to think of some interesting new ideas
4 ☐ I can't wait for the last episode
5 ☐ If there's never anything you like on TV,
6 ☐ On-demand content means that people can choose
7 ☐ I think binge-watching is a big problem with some people –
8 ☐ Have you watched Season 2

a to get more viewers to watch us.
b to see how the story ends.
c of the series?
d you keep telling us how our favourite series end!
e they just sit in front of the screen watching episode after episode of TV series.
f if they want more sport, films or cartoons.
g as their parents keep the TV off and confiscate their phones.
h why not pay for a subscription streaming service so you can choose what to watch?

3 ★★ Choose the correct words to complete the sentences.

1 I don't understand the _trailers / credits / dialogue_. Can we watch the film in another language, please?
2 I like watching films in other languages, but I put the _trailers / subtitles / credits_ in English.
3 My uncle works for a TV station and I sometimes see his name in the _seasons / credits / dialogue_.
4 I think the producers plan to make six _seasons / title sequences / subtitles_ of this show.
5 Sometimes I watch _trailers / dialogues / seasons_ to decide if I want to watch a film or not.
6 After I've seen it twice, I go past the _credits / trailer / title sequence_ to the start of the episode.

4 ★ Match the beginnings 1–6 with the endings a–f.

1 ☐ None of my friends have heard of this little-
2 ☐ He's a really talented, award-
3 ☐ I heard they're going to make a feature-
4 ☐ Fans will be happy to hear that the eagerly-
5 ☐ The series talks about difficult issues – it's very thought-
6 ☐ The book was well-

a awaited new season starts next month.
b known Belgian science fiction film.
c provoking and intelligent.
d reviewed and it soon became a bestseller.
e winning young actor.
f length film version of this series.

5 ★★★ Complete the second sentence so that it means the same as the first one.

1 This film has won a lot of awards.
This is an _award-winning_ film.
2 Lots of people are waiting eagerly for the new series.
The series is _____.
3 Not many people know about this actress.
This actress is _____.
4 They are going to make a long film out of this series.
They are going to make a _____ film out of this series.
5 This episode really makes you think.
This episode is _____.
6 This series got good reviews.
This is a _____ series.

6 ★★★ Complete the text with one or two words in each gap.

We realised that our new series was good because parents complained their children were [1]_binge-watching_ it from Saturday until Sunday evening! It was really popular. Then we were given a prize. We became a(n) [2]_____ TV series, and passed from anonymous, [3]_____ producers to being internationally famous. We are making a second [4]_____ next year and we admit that it's still fantastic to see our names in the final [5]_____. Of course the problem with our teenage [6]_____ sitting watching for hours made us think. The parents' complaints were very [7]_____. So we also decided to start a campaign to raise awareness and convince teenagers to watch our series, but cut down their daily [8]_____ to a couple of hours: fewer episodes over more days.

7 ON A HIGH NOTE Write a short paragraph about the sort of TV programmes which you enjoy/don't enjoy watching. Think about how and when you watch them and why you like/don't like them. Write about: _on-demand content, binge-watching, series and seasons, subtitles and languages, friends or alone._

7C LISTENING AND VOCABULARY

1 🔊 *57* **Listen to the interview and match the speakers with their concerns. Write: Sadie, Russ, Monty or Beth.**

1 producing a reaction

2 pleasing the critics

3 getting small details right

4 avoiding problems that could spoil the show

2 🔊 *57* **Listen again and choose the correct answers.**

1 What did Sadie do in this production?

A 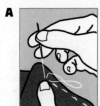 B  C

2 Where did Russ get his idea for his set design?

A  B  C

3 What was Monty's first experience with lighting?

A  B  C

4 Which play did Beth win an award for?

A  B  C

Vocabulary extension

3 **Complete the sentences with the words and phrases from the box which you heard in the interview in Exercises 1 and 2.**

a far cry from   down to   make a come-back
make a living   put on   ~~was plain sailing~~

1 The play was a great success – it *was plain sailing*.

2 The set looked great – it was all _____ good planning.

3 This production was expensive – it was _____ the cheap shows we did five years ago.

4 We _____ at least two shows a year.

5 It's sometimes difficult for an actor to _____.

6 This is Greg's first play for ten years. It's good to see him _____.

Pronunciation

ACTIVE PRONUNCIATION | /v/ /f/ and /w/ sounds

/v/ and /f/ are similar sounds in English, but /f/ is not voiced.

• /v/ is voiced at the end of the word:
  leave /liːv/   leaf /liːf/

• When we use *have to* for obligation, *have* is pronounced /ˈhæf tə/:
  I have a dog. /hæv/
  I have to go. /ˈhæf tə/

Sometimes /v/ and /w/ are confused at the beginning of a word (e.g. in the word *very*) Remember that your teeth touch your bottom lip to make the /v/ sound, but they don't touch your lip to make the /w/ sound.

4 🔊 *58* **Listen to these pairs of words. Tick the word you hear first.**

1 ☐ lift   ☐ lived

2 ☐ thief's   ☐ thieves

3 ☐ ferry   ☐ very

4 ☐ fine   ☐ vine

5 ☐ safer   ☐ saver

6 ☐ half   ☐ halve

7 ☐ offer   ☐ over

8 ☐ fan   ☐ van

9 ☐ refuse   ☐ reviews

5 🔊 *59* **How is *v* pronounced in the word *have* in these sentences? Listen, check and practise saying the sentences.**

1 I have two dogs, called Mandy and Blake. They both have black faces.

2 Where do we have to meet at the theatre?

3 I wish we didn't have a test tomorrow. I'll have to revise all evening!

4 I usually have two showers every day. I have to have one after football because I get so dirty!

5 Have you got a dictionary? I have to look up some words for the essay.

6 🔊 *60* **Complete the sentences with the words you hear.**

1 Our cat was ill so we took him to the *vet*.

2 My uncle lives to the _____ of London.

3 The _____ of the play was very good.

4 A _____ was seen swimming along the River Thames last month.

5 Mark is repairing the car _____ after a minor accident.

7 🔊 *61* **Practise saying these sentences. Listen and check.**

1 I'm worrying about what to wear for work.

2 Val visited various villages on her vacation.

3 Your vote is very valuable and everyone has a voice.

4 It's vital that we wait for Wendy and Vicky before we watch the video.

7D READING AND VOCABULARY

1 Read the title of the article. What do you think ephemeral art is?

  a artworks that have been restored to their original form

  b artworks that don't last very long

  c artworks that are often moved to different locations

2 Look and the photos and read the article. In which paragraphs can you read about each of the photos?

3 Read the article again. Match the headings A–E with paragraphs 1–5.

  A It's been done before

  B A lesson to be learned

  C Everything ends

  D A moment for the senses

  E An interesting question

4 Choose the correct answers.

  1 The writer mentions a mayfly in Paragraph 1 in order to

    a describe the beauty of an insect.

    b give a typical example of an art form.

    c help explain the meaning of a word.

    d show us the joys of looking at nature.

  2 Some people think that ephemeral art tries to

    a make us think about the importance of living well.

    b teach us about nature.

    c show us that art should not be enclosed in galleries.

    d point out the shortness of life.

  3 In Paragraph 3 the writer suggests that ephemeral art

    a is sometimes destroyed because it's in a public place.

    b sometimes communicates a different idea than the artist intended.

    c can last for many years longer than planned.

    d is made with environmentally-friendly materials.

  4 Why does the writer give the example of Milde's 'Cloud'?

    a because it was very difficult to create

    b because it was captured on a photograph

    c because it gave the spectators more than a beautiful image

    d because it had a philosophical message

  5 The writer believes that ephemeral art

    a is typical of modern society.

    b should have a real home.

    c has many different functions.

    d is something all of us can do.

5 Correct the information in the statements.

  1 A mayfly lives for only ~~one week~~ _one day_.

  2 Tibetan monks create mandalas in a few days.

  3 Andy Goldsworthy used poppies in a creation in 2005.

  4 'Cloud' was created in London in 2012.

  5 Pavement art first appeared in the twentieth century.

Vocabulary extension

6 Complete the sentences with the words from the box which appeared in the text.

> fleeting   prominence   promoted   provoked   ~~roused~~   smudged

  1 The article about the death of the painter definitely _roused_ my curiosity.

  2 I made a pencil drawing and _____ the lines to add some shadow.

  3 The artist's new art installation _____ a lot of different reactions from the art critics.

  4 I'm sure I saw a _____ smile on my teacher's face. She's usually very serious!

  5 The documentary _____ awareness of how much plastic we throw into the sea.

  6 The artist first came to _____ when he won the Turner prize a few years ago.

ACTIVE VOCABULARY | Suffix -less

We can add the suffix -_less_ to a word to make a negative adjective meaning 'without', e.g.

- nameless = without a name
- careless = without care

---

7 Complete the sentences with adjectives formed from the nouns from the box.

> age   cord   end   fear   ~~help~~   name

  1 The performance was so funny that I was _helpless_ with laughter.

  2 Explorers need to be _____ to go to places that nobody else has ever been to.

  3 A(n) _____ government minister leaked the story to the newspapers.

  4 Parents have to answer _____ questions from their children when they're growing up.

  5 Some art is _____ and could have been created at any time in history.

  6 When _____ phones first became popular, my grandparents couldn't understand how they worked!

8 ON A HIGH NOTE Write a short post for a website describing a piece of ephemeral art you have seen and how you reacted to it. If you want, you can use some of the examples and ideas from the reading text.

Ephemeral Art
Here today, gone tomorrow

1 ☐

What does 'ephemeral' mean? I looked it up in a dictionary and discovered that it is used to describe something that only lasts for a short time. You know, like a mayfly, the insect that lives for one day, or a pleasure that you experience, but which passes. I was amazed to find that it is also used to describe a genre of art. OK, you may ask – how can you study or debate the value of art that is here today and gone tomorrow? Good question. It roused my curiosity!

2 ☐

Ephemeral art is not about pictures, statues or art installations that can be kept in a gallery. It's a term that came to prominence in the 1950s. That was a time when artists were experimenting with different types of art and debates about the nature of art were common. At that time, it was used to describe any type of fleeting event such as a performance or a lighting display. One interpretation of ephemeral art is that it promotes awareness of how quickly life changes. It tries to bring us closer to nature and understanding that nothing lasts forever. Tibetan monks spend weeks creating spectacular, colourful patterns in sand (mandalas) that are blown away in days. They want to create a symbol to remind us that life passes quickly.

3 ☐

Some artists create ephemeral art using materials that will self-destruct. In 1984, Andy Goldsworthy created a ribbon of poppy petals held together by saliva, which quickly fell apart when it dried. And in 2014, Brazilian artist Néle Azevedo made 5,000 tiny figures out of ice which sat on some public steps in Birmingham until they melted. The project was a memorial to the nameless men and women who died in WW1. Her melting men ice sculptures have been placed in public squares all round the world since 2005. Originally her idea was to protest against the big bronze statues and monuments to heroes. However, her art has taken on a new life. People now see it as symbolic of the melting ice caps and consider it a comment on the dangers of climate change.

4 ☐

Many ephemeral artists explore profound ideas in their work, but others are more concerned with producing unique experiences that cannot be truly documented. In 2012, Dutch artist Smilde created a perfect cloud in the hallway of a building in New York. He used water, temperature and smoke to make the cloud. It lasted a few seconds. The cloud was photographed, so we can see what he created, but we cannot feel the humidity or breathe in the smoke, which was an important part of the experience.

5 ☐

Ephemeral art is not a new idea. Street artists have been drawing with coloured chalk on pavements since the sixteenth century. More recently, starting in the twentieth century, spectacular 3D pavement art has shown how the genre is progressing. And photography allows the artists to record their work before it is washed away by the rain or smudged by the feet of careless pedestrians. The development of another traditional type of ephemeral art is seen in sand sculpture. It has progressed from simple children's castles made on holiday to complex and stunningly beautiful creations produced by specialist artists today; still waiting, however, for nature to take back the sand. And then we have that other, controversial street art – graffiti. This is ephemeral, not because it will quickly be washed away or self-destruct, but because it is unprotected and can be painted over, cleaned off or added to.

Some people might say that in our modern, consumer society, ephemeral art has found a proper home. In my opinion, it is just another example of human beings' ability to adapt and create wonderful things that can provoke reactions, raise awareness or simply give us pleasure.

7E **GRAMMAR**

Reported questions

1 ⭐ Choose the correct words to complete the sentences.

1 Julian: 'Do you know the presenter?'
Julian asked *if / how / do* I knew the presenter.

2 Belinda: 'Why do you enjoy singing, Zac?'
Belinda asked Zac *if / why / how* he enjoyed singing.

3 Rob: 'Where did they film the show?'
Rob asked *where / whether / why* they had filmed the show.

4 Katie: 'When do you use the green screen?'
Katie asked *whether / why / when* we used the green screen.

5 Clive: 'Has it all gone well today?'
Clive asked *had / if / when* it had all gone well that day.

6 Becky: 'Can you help me?'
Becky asked me *whether / why / where* I could help her.

2 ⭐ Read the reported questions and rewrite them in direct speech.

1 Gabriel asked me if I was from London.
'*Are you* from London?' asked Gabriel.

2 William asked whether the singer was nervous.
'_____ nervous?' asked William.

3 Olivia wanted to know whether I needed anything.
'_____ anything?' asked Olivia.

4 Sam asked Julia if she was preparing her song.
'_____ your song?' asked Sam.

5 The woman asked us if we had auditioned before.
'_____ before?' asked the woman.

6 The judge asked whether we were going to perform an original song.
'_____ an original song?' asked the judge.

3 ⭐⭐ Complete the sentences using reported speech.

1 Jon asked Mike: 'Where are you from?'
John asked Mike *where he was* from.

2 The judge asked Sarah: 'Why did you choose this song?'
The judge asked Sarah _____ that song.

3 Charlie asked Liam: 'How are you travelling there?'
Charlie asked Liam _____ there.

4 Eva asked Marie: 'What instrument can you play?'
Eva asked Marie _____.

5 Gina asked Henry: 'When will the show start?'
Gina asked Henry _____.

6 Danny asked Andrew: 'Which performer do you like best?'
Danny asked Andrew _____ best.

7 Sue asked Catherine: 'Have you learnt any new songs?'
Sue asked Catherine _____ any new songs.

4 ⭐⭐⭐ Complete the text so that it means the same as the conversation.

Organiser	Hi, what's your name and where are you from?
Dylan	My name's Dylan and I'm from Liverpool. Can I start?
Organiser	Just a moment, Dylan. Have you practised your song today?
Dylan	All day. Should I tell the judges that?
Organiser	No, don't worry. How many times did you audition to get here?
Dylan	Four times. Where can I get a sandwich, please?
Organiser	Over there. Would you prefer cheese or ham?
Dylan	Cheese, thanks.

The talent show organiser greeted the boy. She asked him **1** *what his name was* and **2** _____ . He replied that his name was Dylan and he was from Liverpool. He asked **3** _____ . The organiser told him to wait a moment. She asked him **4** _____ . Dylan replied he had practised all day and asked **5** _____ .
The organiser told him not to worry and asked him **6** _____ to get there. Dylan said he had auditioned four times and asked **7** _____ a sandwich. The organiser said he could get it over there and asked **8** _____ cheese or ham. Dylan answered 'cheese' and thanked her.

5 ON A HIGH NOTE Can you think of some surprising, difficult or irritating questions people have asked you? Can you report three or four questions and how you felt about them?

7F SPEAKING

1
🔊 *62* **Listen and repeat the phrases. How do you say them in your language?**

SPEAKING | Describing a personal experience

SAY WHEN AND WHERE IT TOOK PLACE

Have I ever told you about that time when I was taking part in a rock concert?
You won't believe what happened last night!
It happened a few weeks ago/last year.
It was maybe a year ago.
I was appearing in a talent show/play.

CONNECT THE DIFFERENT PARTS OF YOUR STORY

At first, everything went really well, **but then** something awful happened.
The next thing I know is that the curtains suddenly opened.
Suddenly, I noticed the table had disappeared.
As soon as I stood up I realised I had lost a shoe.
Immediately after I'd appeared on stage, the lights went off.
We'd just moved all the furniture off the stage **when** we realised it should have stayed there.
On the first day, /The following night,/In the end, we had some problems with the props.
Although we were tired, we were also really happy.
We had to cancel the performance **because** the actress was ill.
Despite his lack of experience, he was brilliant on stage!
The audience was a bit bored, **so** he decided to sing some more cheerful songs.

SAY HOW YOU FELT

I couldn't believe it.
I felt like crying.
I just felt really/so silly/embarrassed!
I was so nervous/embarrassed!
It was really/so embarrassing!
We were so relieved.

USE DIRECT SPEECH AND REPORTED SPEECH

He said, 'Yes, this role requires you to shave your head.'
He said that role required me to shave my head.

2
Complete the story with the words and phrases from the box.

because believe first happened ~~have~~ panic
relieved said soon was when whispered

¹*Have* I ever told you about a really embarrassing moment ² _____ I was appearing in a play called *The Ghost Train*? This ³_____ in my last year before college and I was playing a passenger in the waiting room at the station. At ⁴_____, everything went really well, but then something dreadful happened! I had to fall down on the floor, and the other passengers put me on a bench. So I was lying down and one of the other actors/passengers said that he ⁵_____ a doctor.

'Let me check her over,' he ⁶_____ and he bent down to listen to my heart. You won't ⁷_____ what happened next! As ⁸_____ as he started to stand up, we realised that some of my hair had wrapped round the button on his jacket! I started to ⁹_____. If he stood up, he would pull me up with him! He whispered in my ear, 'What are we going to do?' and I ¹⁰_____ back, 'Just pull!' So he pulled and I kept my head flat. It was really painful ¹¹_____ he pulled out a lot of my hair! For the rest of the scene he walked around with a piece of my hair hanging from his button! I was so ¹²_____ when the play was over!

3
Put the sentences in order to complete the stories.

A

☐ I was in a group of twenty. ☐ The introductory music stopped and the curtains began to open. ☐ The curtains stuck half open. ☑ This happened when I was singing in a concert. ☐ There were only a few metres in the middle, so we all tried to squeeze into the space to sing. ☐ Then, I couldn't believe it.

B

☐ Luckily, someone rushed on to stop it. ☑ On the first night I had a near disaster. ☐ Usually, the stage crew put blocks behind the wheels to stop them moving. ☐ It frightened the life out of me! ☐ I had to stand on a desk which had wheels on it. ☐ I was so relieved! ☐ That night they forgot and immediately after I'd climbed on to it, it started to roll across the stage!

C

☐ Everyone was waiting for me to speak. ☐ I was so upset afterwards that I felt like crying. ☐ Finally, someone whispered my next line to me and I remembered. ☑ At first, the play went well, but suddenly I completely forgot my lines!

4
ON A HIGH NOTE **Write a short paragraph starting with the words: *Last week I saw something really funny ...***

Start with an interesting opening sentence to attract your reader's attention.

Give key information about the play.

Mention the characters and the plot.

Give your opinion on aspects of the performance.

Summarise your opinions.

Make a recommendation.

SHADOWLANDS

If you go to see *Shadowlands* at the Royal Theatre this week, take a box of tissues! It's really moving and last night the cast had the whole audience in tears. It **¹** *stars / uses* Liam Nelson and Karen Edwards and has won several awards.

The play is about the relationship between C. S. Lewis, the author of the Narnia books, and an American poet, Joy Gresham. The ending is very sad, but I'm not going to give any spoilers! It is set mainly in Lewis's house in Oxford in the 1930s and also **²** *plays / features* a really great child actor, Peter Carter, as Joy's son.

The actors are incredibly **³** *talented / breathtaking* and their performances are **⁴** *slightly / utterly* convincing. The play is well written and has some **⁵** *totally / witty* dialogue, and the combination of humour and sadness works very well. The set is **⁶** *quite / thoroughly* basic and the lighting simple, but because the power of the acting is **⁷** *so / such* strong it doesn't need a lot of special effects.

There have been a large number of good theatre productions this year, but for me this **⁸** *makes / stands* head and shoulders above the rest. The audience loved the performance and at the end they stood up and cheered. I can't **⁹** *advise / recommend* it highly enough. Try to get tickets for the remaining shows. You may be lucky!

1 Read the review and choose the correct answer.

The writer thinks that
 a there may not be any tickets left for the play.
 b the play is too sad for a lot of people.
 c you will enjoy the special effects.

2 Choose the correct words to complete the review.

3 Complete the comments with the adjectives from the box.

dramatic entertaining forgettable impressive terrifying ~~witty~~

 1 Some of the lines in the play are really *witty* – they made everyone laugh.
 2 The play was completely _____ – I wouldn't recommend it to anyone.
 3 The plot was _____ – there were three murders!
 4 The last scene was _____ – the loud music shocked everyone.
 5 The costumes were _____ – someone spent a long time creating the queen's dresses.
 6 It was a very _____ show – the music and the dancing were excellent and we loved it.

4 Put the words in brackets in the correct position in the sentences.

 1 I enjoyed the film because it was funny! (so)
 2 It was a ridiculous story. (completely)
 3 We left early because it was a boring film. (such)
 4 It was a long show but very interesting. (quite)
 5 It was a simple set but it worked well. (slightly)
 6 I had a good view of the stage. (particularly)

5 WRITING TASK Write a review of a play you've seen recently.

ACTIVE WRITING | A review of a play

1 Plan your review.
 • Think about different aspects of the play: characters, plot, actors, set, lighting, etc.
 • Make some notes and divide them into four main paragraphs.
2 Write your review.
 • Start with an interesting opening sentence.
 • Use a variety of adjectives and modifying adverbs.
 • Give your opinion on different aspects of the play.
 • End with a recommendation.
3 Check your review. Check that:
 • there are no spelling, grammar or punctuation mistakes.
 • there is interesting and relevant topic vocabulary.

UNIT VOCABULARY PRACTICE

1 **7A GRAMMAR AND VOCABULARY** Match the beginnings 1–7 with the endings a–g.

1 ☐ When I haven't got much time, I don't read the whole article,

2 ☐ I heard a very funny news

3 ☐ Apparently, there have been reports

4 ☐ My parents like to sit on the sofa and watch a few TV

5 ☐ I couldn't believe my eyes at the breaking

6 ☐ My favourite newsreader

7 ☐ I really enjoy human

a coming in about a bad accident.

b interest stories more than economics.

c item about a dog that could ski.

d news from the centre of Birmingham!

e news programmes with a cup of tea.

f I just glance at the headlines.

g has got a wonderful voice.

2 **7B VOCABULARY** Complete the sentences with the words from the box.

binge watching credits eagerly-awaited
little-known season spoilers subtitles ~~viewers~~

1 I can't believe ten million *viewers* watched the programme!

2 Don't tell me how the series ends – I hate _____!

3 Frances says that the next _____ of *Doctors at War* has already come out in America.

4 Could you put on the _____? I can't hear the dialogue very well.

5 I want to wait for the _____ to see what the actor's name is.

6 She's a(n) _____ actress who is just beginning her career.

7 I feel exhausted because I was up all night _____ the last season of *Pretty Little Liars*.

8 Tomorrow night, fans can watch the _____ first episode of the new season.

3 Complete the sentences with one word in each gap.

1 The *title* sequence at the start of each episode in this series is amazing – I never miss it!

2 We only watch o_____ content, so we can choose the programmes we watch.

3 Can I see the t_____ for that new spy film? I want to see if it's any good.

4 There's a brilliant, a_____ film on this evening – it got the Oscar for best picture.

5 It's a th_____ programme which really makes you think about things in a different way.

6 I'm really sorry that this is the last episode in the s_____.

7 I prefer watching f_____ films than TV series.

4 **7C LISTENING AND VOCABULARY** Complete the sentences with the words and phrases from the box.

back to square one best-seller bit of a setback
got my first break ~~huge flop~~ really took off sell-out
they came to nothing

1 Unfortunately, the new film was a catastrophe – a *huge flop*.

2 We had a lot of hopes about making the film, but in the end _____.

3 I was eighteen when I had my first opportunity and _____ in the movies.

4 I wasn't sure if the play would go well, but people loved it and it _____.

5 I had a great part, but I broke a leg, which was a _____.

6 Her new book has sold a huge number of copies and is a national _____.

7 We had to start again and go _____.

8 There are no tickets left, the play is a _____.

5 **7D READING AND VOCABULARY** Complete the conversation with one adjective in each gap.

Peter Emma, how was the show last night? I heard that it's ¹u*nique* – nobody has ever seen anything like it.

Emma Yes, it was absolutely ²b_____ – I mean, literally, I couldn't breathe! The lights and music were ³s_____ – amazing colours and the volume – incredible!

Peter So I imagine with all those strange effects it was really ⁴a_____. Not like our ordinary world at all.

Emma It was all like a fantasy world. It wasn't ⁵r_____ at all. And the actors were really good at communicating their feelings – very ⁶e_____. And the dialogue was very deep and ⁷p_____. Actually, I couldn't understand some of it! It was confusing.

Peter Yes, I've heard that some of the ideas and the plot are a bit ⁸p_____.

6 **7G WRITING AND VOCABULARY** Complete the text with one word in each gap.

An actor must first ¹*audition* for a part. When the ²_____ is chosen – I mean all the actors – they can start work. This usually means ³_____ for weeks, so that the actors can learn their parts. The technicians have to design the ⁴_____ with different colours illuminating the stage. At the same time, other people are making ⁵_____ for every actor to wear. If the actor's hair isn't right, he or she might have to wear a ⁶_____ and put a lot of ⁷_____ on his or her face to change it. Another part of the job is learning to use ⁸_____ – the different objects the actor has to carry on and off the stage.

7 **ON A HIGH NOTE** Have you ever taken part in a school play or a play with a drama group? If you have, write a short paragraph about your experience. If you haven't, imagine you have and invent any necessary details. Describe your role, your costume and your lines, the rehearsals, the show and how you felt at the performance.

1 For each learning objective, write 1–5 to assess your ability.

1 = I don't feel confident. 5 = I feel very confident.

	Learning objective	Course material	How confident I am (1–5)
7A	I can use reporting verbs to report stories.	Student's Book pp. 94–95	
7B	I can talk about viewing habits.	Student's Book p. 96	
7C	I can specific details in a radio programme and talk about artists and performers on social media.	Student's Book p. 97	
7D	I can identify specific details in an article and talk about art.	Student's Book pp. 98–99	
7E	I can use reported questions to talk about what someone else said.	Student's Book p. 100	
7F	I can describe a personal experience.	Student's Book p. 101	
7G	I can write a review of a play.	Student's Book pp. 102–103	

2 Which of the skills above would you like to improve in? How?

Skill I want to improve in	How I can improve

3 What can you remember from this unit?

New words I learned and most want to remember	Expressions and phrases I liked	English I heard or read outside class

GRAMMAR AND VOCABULARY

1 Match the words 1–10 with their definitions a–j.

1 ☐ breaking news
2 ☐ subtitles
3 ☐ abstract
4 ☐ audition
5 ☐ stage
6 ☐ newsreader
7 ☐ flop
8 ☐ unique
9 ☐ puzzling
10 ☐ rehearsal

a a person who reads the news
b the space where actors perform
c which is not like anything else
d very recent news heard for the first time
e confusing, difficult to understand
f dialogue written on a screen
g perform in order to get a part
h practise for a performance
i not obvious, concrete or realistic
j film, series, etc. which is not a success

/ 5

2 Choose the correct words to complete the sentences.

1 You can choose what you want to watch with *seasons / breaking news / on-demand content*.

2 The band's new video was an instant success and went *setback / viral / to square one* in a few hours.

3 The play wasn't very easy to understand – it was really *sophisticated / realistic / breathtaking*.

4 We loved the *lighting / rehearsal / set design* – it looked like a fairy castle!

5 Her third film was very popular and since then she's never *made a name for herself / looked back / looked forward*.

/ 5

3 Complete the sentences using reported speech.

1 Jamie: 'I didn't want to watch that.'
Jamie said he _____ to watch that.

2 Dawn: 'I've chosen my programme.'
Dawn said she _____ her programme.

3 Penny: 'My mum told me not to switch on the TV.'
Penny said her mum had told her _____ the TV.

4 George: 'Did you audition for the part?'
George asked me _____ for the part.

5 Zac: 'Where did you learn to sing?'
Zac asked me _____ to sing.

/ 5

4 Complete the text so that it means the same as the conversation.

Anne   Are you going to be in the show?
Kerry Yes, I am. Who did you hear that from?
Anne   My teacher. She thinks you're very good.
Kerry Buy a ticket!
Anne   Don't worry.

Anne asked Kerry [1]_____ in the show. Kerry answered that she was and asked Anne who [2]_____ from. Anne said her teacher and, that her teacher [3]_____ very good. Kerry told Anne [4]_____. Anne told Kerry [5]_____.

/ 5

USE OF ENGLISH

5 Complete the text with the correct forms of the words in brackets.

I wanted to buy a [1]_____ (SUBSCRIBE) streaming service, so that I could watch my favourite series. I had to be careful though because my friends were always sending me messages with [2]_____ (SPOIL) in them! So I had to tell them to stop! The point is to be surprised! My favourite series is really [3]_____ (ATMOSPHERE) with brilliant [4]_____ (LIGHT) effects. It's set in a fantasy land. My mum hates it – she says the violence is [5]_____ (SHOCK) and refuses to watch it.

/ 5

6 Read the short texts and choose the correct answers.

1 Silence please in this area: actors _____.

a in a huge flop   b in rehearsal   c are looking back

2 For those with hearing problems, the _____ in several different languages on the menu.

a subtitles can be set   b credits are at the end
c title sequence is

3 Save the date – 10th March is the première of Episode 1 of the _____ of *Lowlanders' Revenge*.

a breathtaking actor   b eagerly-awaited new season
c best-selling novel

4 I was about thirty and had worked hard before I finally had some success and started to _____.

a go viral   b go back to square one
c make a name for myself

5 I think that play was really deep and profound and _____.

a not at all expressive   b not very unique
c very meaningful

/ 5

/ 30

08 Consumers' world

8A GRAMMAR AND VOCABULARY

The passive

1 ⭐ **Underline the passive forms in these sentences.**

1 The new phone will be delivered tomorrow.
2 Her new designs have been presented.
3 That advert was filmed in the street outside my house.
4 The plans are secret and can't be revealed.
5 Our new design is being discussed.
6 These cars are produced in Korea.
7 The company's image was being damaged by negative publicity.

2 ⭐ **Match the tenses a–g with the sentences 1–7 in Exercise 1.**

a ☐ Present Perfect   e ☐ Present Continuous
b ☐ future with *will*   f ☐ modal verb
c ☐ Present Simple   g ☐ Past Simple
d ☐ Past Continuous

3 ⭐⭐ **Complete the second sentence in each pair using the passive so that it means the same as the first sentence.**

1 Advertising influences my sister.
My sister *is influenced* by advertising.
2 We sell over twenty of these rucksacks every week.
Over twenty of these rucksacks _____ every week.
3 We are testing the new product now.
The new product _____ now.
4 They aren't considering my idea.
My idea _____.
5 They are signing a contract.
A contract _____.

4 ⭐⭐ **Complete the sentences with the correct Past Simple passive forms of the verbs in brackets.**

1 The new campaign *was announced* (announce) yesterday.
2 The shoes _____ (not advertise) very well.
3 The contract _____ (sign) by our boss.
4 Unfortunately, no offers _____ (make) for the product.
5 The proposals _____ (not accept).
6 Mr Carter _____ (inform) of the problem.
7 I couldn't use the library because it _____ (close) for repairs.
8 The bathroom _____ (not repaint) in time for the start of term.

5 ⭐⭐ **Complete the sentences with the correct Past Continuous passive forms of the verbs from the box.**

create   explain   install   offer   ~~promote~~   show

1 The products *were being promoted* in schools and colleges.
2 When Mark finally got to the meeting his idea for the project _____.
3 We heard that free meals _____ in return for advertising space.
4 When the new teacher entered the school building a huge wall painting _____ by pupils from Year 9.
5 The children _____ around the school by the older pupils.
6 An interactive white board _____ in our classroom when we arrived for class.

6 ⭐⭐ **Choose the correct answers.**

1 The winning design has been _____ at last.
   a chose   b chosen
2 Free goods _____ in return for advertising space.
   a has been offered   b have been offered
3 I'm sorry, but your proposal _____ been accepted.
   a hasn't   b isn't
4 The new advert hasn't _____ yet.
   a been shown   b being shown
5 _____ abandoned or are we still considering it?
   a The idea has been   b Has the idea been
6 _____ about the new changes?
   a Have you been informed   b Have you informed

7 ⭐⭐ **Use the prompts to write sentences. Use the future passive with *will*.**

1 new jobs / will / create / here soon
New jobs will be created here soon.

2 the adverts / will / remove / as soon as possible
_____

3 people / will / not tell / about the problem
_____

4 money / will not / give / in exchange for this publicity
_____

5 new products / will / offer / by the company
_____

6 consumers / will / not convince / by this excuse
_____

8 ⭐⭐ **Complete the sentences with the modal verbs in brackets and the correct form of the verbs from the box.**

find   include   inform   ~~install~~   remove   stop

1 A new drinks machine *might be installed* (might) in the corridor soon.

2 This product _____ (can) in all major department stores.

3 This irresponsible advertising _____ (must) immediately.

4 I think consumers _____ (should) that there's a problem with this product.

5 The idea _____ (may not) in the project – we're not sure yet.

6 The advert _____ (could not) for legal reasons so it had to stay there.

9 ⭐⭐⭐ **Use the prompts to write questions in the passive.**

1 the candidates / interview / right now?
Are the candidates being interviewed right now?

2 the logo / redesign / Artur / yet?
_____
_____

3 the billboards / remove / yesterday afternoon?
_____
_____

4 how / could / the advertising slogan / improve / the copywriter?
_____
_____

5 a jingle / play / at the beginning / of every programme?
_____
_____

6 all the spam emails / remove / if I click this icon?
_____
_____

7 why / those posters / take down / when we arrived at school?
_____
_____

10 ⭐⭐⭐ **Complete the text with one word in each gap.**

Last month, our head teacher **1**_was_ offered ten free computers if he agreed to make students wear the computer company's T-shirts. The offer **2**_____ accepted, because the head teacher said it wasn't ethical. He said students couldn't **3**_____ made into walking billboards! Everybody was sorry that the computers **4**_____ accepted, but we agreed with his decision. He told us that other ways to raise money for the school were **5**_____ investigated. He also explained that a more interesting offer has **6**_____ received from a different company. They will give us new computers in return for a short article on the school website saying that the donation **7**_____ been made. We think the offer **8**_____ be accepted soon by the head teacher because it seems reasonable.

11 ⭐⭐⭐ **Complete the second text so that it means the same as the first. Use between two and four words in each gap.**

Important school rules

- *We don't permit smoking in any area of the school. The school will punish students that it catches smoking!*
- *Please wear correct school uniform at all times. Do not wear clothes with obvious logos and brand names. If you ignore this rule, we will ask you to change. We have asked students to change in the past!*

Important school rules

- Smoking **1**_isn't permitted_ in any area of the school. Students who **2**_____ smoking **3**_____!
- Correct school uniform must **4**_____ at all times. Clothes with obvious logos and brand names should **5**_____. If you ignore this rule, you **6**_____ to change. Students **7**_____ to change in the past!

12 ON A HIGH NOTE **Write a short paragraph about an advert you were influenced by while buying a product.**

8B LISTENING AND VOCABULARY

1 🔊 *63* **Listen to five people talking about their attitudes to money when they were young children. Which of the topics 1–7 are mentioned?**

1 ☐ earning money
2 ☐ selling things
3 ☐ receiving pocket money
4 ☐ taking money that is not theirs
5 ☐ buying presents
6 ☐ borrowing money
7 ☐ hiding money

2 🔊 *63* **Listen again and for speakers 1–5 choose from the list (a–f) what each person says about their attitude to money as a child. There is one extra option.**

Speaker 1 ☐   Speaker 4 ☐
Speaker 2 ☐   Speaker 5 ☐
Speaker 3 ☐

a He/She didn't get the money they felt they deserved.
b He/She spent money more easily than a close relative.
c He/She thought their parents spent too much money.
d He/She wanted to help a family member with a money problem.
e He/She enjoyed saving money but not spending it.
f He/She learned that some things were worth waiting for.

Vocabulary extension

3 **Complete the sentences with the words from the box which you heard in the recording in Exercises 1 and 2.**

granted   helped   miser   ~~penny~~   pocket   price   rate

1 I work hard at my weekend job and I earn every *penny*.
2 Dad gives me £8 for cleaning his car; I give my brother £2 for helping me and _____ the rest.
3 I got these jeans for a very good _____ in the market – they were a real bargain.
4 My sister's a bit of a _____ and always lets other people pay for her.
5 The going _____ for walking someone's dog is £10 an hour.
6 The thief waited until the assistant left the counter and then _____ himself to the money in the cash register.
7 You should never take money for _____; just because you're earning a lot now, it doesn't mean that you always will.

4 ON A HIGH NOTE **Write a short paragraph about the money you were (or weren't) given as a child. Is giving pocket money a good thing for parents to do?**

Pronunciation

5 🔊 *64* **Read some sentences from the listening. How are the highlighted words pronounced? Listen and check.**

1 Although I always spent the full amount, my brother used to spend about one pound.
2 When we had enough to buy something we'd planned, we definitely valued it a lot more.
3 They taught me that nothing in life is free.
4 It was a way of teaching us about money I suppose, through a game.
5 I guess he had a good laugh later!

ACTIVE PRONUNCIATION | Words with *gh*

Words with *gh* can sometimes cause problems for pronunciation. There are several different ways *gh* can be pronounced:

- The letters *gh* are not pronounced after *ei*, (e.g. *weigh*) or the letter *i* (e.g. *sigh*). They are also silent in words ending in *-ght* (e.g. *bought*, *taught*).
- *gh* is sometimes used at the beginning of words and then has the /g/ sound (e.g. *ghost* or *ghastly*).
- The letters *gh* can also be pronounced /f/ (e.g. *cough*, *laugh*).

---

6 🔊 *65* **Match the words 1–8 with the words from the box which they rhyme with. You can use the words from the box more than once. Listen, check and repeat.**

off   owl   sort   stuff

1 caught   **4** cough   **7** bought
2 rough   **5** plough
3 thought   **6** tough

7 🔊 *66* **Read the sentences aloud. Can you pronounce the words with *-gh* correctly? Listen and check. Then practise saying the sentences.**

1 I **thought** my **daughter's** **weight** **ought** to be **roughly** the same as mine.
2 **Although** the children had **enough** toys each, they **fought** over the toy **plough** for their mini farm.
3 I **caught** a bug on holiday and I had a bad **cough**.
4 It was **tough** climbing the **high** hill in the snow, but it was a **laugh** to **sleigh** down the other side!

UNIT VOCABULARY PRACTICE > page 97

8C VOCABULARY | Money

1 ⭐ **Choose the correct words to complete the sentences.**

1 You should save some money and stop spending it like *water / wine*.

2 My friend keeps asking me for a loan – he must think I'm *full / made* of money.

3 My uncle made a lot of money with his business – he's *lying / rolling* in it!

4 She's so rich that I think she's got money to *burn / throw*.

5 I can't go out – I've run *out of / away from* money.

6 Could you lend me £10? I'm a bit *not with / short of* cash at the moment.

7 They offer discounts on Sundays – we could go then and get our money's *value / worth*.

8 Have you got any cash *on / in* you? I've only got a credit card.

2 ⭐ **Complete the sentences with the words from the box. There are two extra words.**

broke   debt   in the red   loan   loose change   ~~mean~~
poverty   sense

1 Alex is so *mean* that he never offers to buy me a coffee.

2 They spent too much and ended up with huge _____ to pay back.

3 Have you got any _____ for the coffee machine?

4 I've got no money left – I'm completely _____.

5 My parents wanted to renovate our house so they asked for a _____ from the bank.

6 It's terrible how many people have nothing and live in _____.

3 ⭐ **Complete the sentences with one word in each gap. The first letter is given to help you.**

1 He never spends money unless he has to; he's really c*areful* with his money.

2 My bank account is empty and I'm in the r_____.

3 She buys such stupid things – she has more money than s_____!

4 My class is organising a charity concert to r_____ money for the animal shelter.

5 That's too expensive – I can't possibly a_____ it!

6 We decided to ask contributions using social media – c_____ is a popular way to collect money.

4 ⭐⭐⭐ **Complete the second conversation so that it has the same meaning as the first. Use one or two words in each gap.**

Mark   Karen, could you lend me some money? I haven't got any.

Karen   As usual. You spend too much. What's it for?

Mark   It's for my bus pass. I've got a few coins, but not nearly enough for a pass. I can't pay for it.

Karen   So why did you buy that new T-shirt yesterday? Honestly, you seem to think you can just waste your money.

Mark   It's just a bad moment. I haven't got much money right now.

Karen   Oh, all right. But it's temporary, OK? I want it back tomorrow!

Mark   Karen, could you lend me some money? I'm ¹*broke*.

Karen   As usual. You spend money ² _____. What's it for?

Mark   It's for my bus pass. I've got some ³ _____, but not nearly enough for a pass. I can't ⁴ _____ it.

Karen   So why did you buy that new T-shirt yesterday? Honestly, you seem to think you've got money to ⁵ _____.

Mark   It's just a bad moment. I'm a bit ⁶ _____ money right now.

Karen   Oh, all right. But it's a ⁷ _____, OK? I want it back tomorrow!

5 ⭐⭐⭐ **Complete the text with one word in each gap.**

Julia and her brother Eddie couldn't be more different. Julia spends money like ¹*water*. She seems to think she's ² _____ in money and buys anything she wants. Then she asks her parents for more because she thinks they're ³ _____ of money. And they aren't – they're paying back a bank ⁴ _____ every month. Eddie on the other hand is really ⁵ _____ with his money. He's never ⁶ _____ – he's always got something saved. I think he does a few extra jobs to earn it, so he only buys what he can ⁷ _____ and doesn't spend too much. Julia rarely has any money ⁸ _____ her when it's time for her to buy somebody a coffee!

6 ON A HIGH NOTE **Write a short paragraph about your spending habits. Do you spend money like water or are you careful? Have you got a friend or relative who is the opposite to you? How? What differences are there between you?**

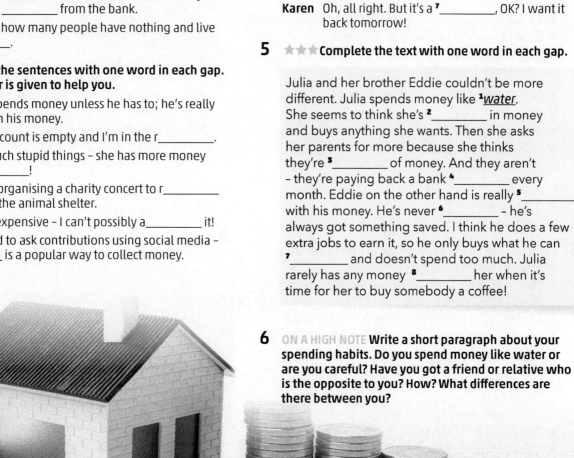

8D READING AND VOCABULARY

1 Look at the photo and the title of the article. What do you think a 'hoarder' is?

   a a person who finds and sells rare things

   b a person who likes collecting rare things

   c a person who doesn't throw things away

2 Read the article and check your answer to Exercise 1.

3 Read the article again and complete gaps 1–6 in the text with sentences A–G. There is one extra sentence.

   A I have to admit though, his story does make me wonder about what happened to that old coin collection of mine.

   B However, all that had changed, and I have to say it was a bit of a shock.

   C That's maybe where his love of books comes from.

   D However, part of him was aware that this behaviour wasn't normal.

   E For example people like this also feel comfort surrounded by all their treasures.

   F That's when the collecting fever set in.

   G This can involve swapping things with others or going online and checking out websites.

Vocabulary extension

4 Match the highlighted words and phrases 1–8 from the article with their meanings a–h.

   1 ☐ addictive   **5** ☐ tumble

   2 ☐ autographs   **6** ☐ first edition

   3 ☐ initial   **7** ☐ monetary

   4 ☐ give someone   **8** ☐ only kidding
        a hand

   a (usually valuable) first printing of a book

   b just joking

   c first, at the beginning

   d financial, related to money

   e signatures (usually of famous people)

   f so enjoyable you can't stop

   g help someone

   h fall down

5 Complete the sentences with the correct forms of the words and phrases 1–8 from Exercise 4.

   1 My sister got her favourite singer's _autograph_ when he played at a local gig.

   2 Can you _____ with moving this desk please?

   3 A _____ of a Harry Potter book will be worth a fortune!

   4 My _____ reaction was to say that I couldn't do it, but then I changed my mind.

   5 These comics are of no _____ value, but I'll never throw them away.

   6 That T-shirt looks terrible! _____ – it's amazing!

   7 Computer gaming is _____ – some kids play for hours.

   8 I slipped and _____ down the stairs.

ACTIVE VOCABULARY | Suffix -ive

Some adjectives can be formed by adding -ive to a verb. If the verb finishes with e, we cut e before adding the ending.

- obsess → obsessive
- create → creative

Sometimes if the verb ends in -d or -de we remove the -d/-de and add –sive, e.g.

- defend → defensive
- decide → decisive

6 Write the adjective form of the words given.

   1 addict   _addictive_

   2 conclude   _____

   3 defend   _____

   4 decide   _____

   5 explode   _____

   6 express   _____

   7 possess   _____

   8 select   _____

7 Complete the sentences with the adjectives from Exercise 6.

   1 The politician was very _defensive_ about his decisions; it seemed as if he had something to hide.

   2 Drinking coffee can be as _____ as eating chocolate.

   3 I'm not very _____! I like other people to make decisions for me.

   4 My sister has a very _____ face and we always know when she's upset.

   5 Linda is very _____ about what she eats and refuses anything that looks unusual.

   6 Some people are very _____ about their books and won't let them out of their sight.

   7 The plot of the film is very fast and it has a(n) _____ ending.

   8 I'm afraid that the police have _____ evidence that Jones is a thief.

8 ON A HIGH NOTE Write a short paragraph about someone you know who can't throw things away.

COLLECTOR or HOARDER

Most people do some form of collecting when they're children. Sometimes it can be things like stamps or coins, shells or comic books. There's something addictive about having a collection of objects and adding to it. There's also a certain thrill that goes with finding just the right item you want or need. **1** ☐ My dad collected autographs of famous people and my mum had a postcard collection. I remember collecting coins from different countries but, like a lot of people, I lost interest after a while and forgot all about it.

However, I was reminded the other day of how addictive that initial collecting fever can be. We have a neighbour who has lived in our street for as long as I can remember. He's a lovely man and he was always very kind to me when I was growing up – lending me books and even giving me a hand with homework. I think he used to be an English teacher. **2** ☐ He really encouraged me to read and introduced me to some of the greatest writers in the world.

Last month he stopped me on my way home from college. I hadn't seen him for ages and it was good to chat. Then he asked me if I might help him with something. He showed me inside and upstairs to his study where we used to talk about books together. It used to be a neat, tidy area with all his books carefully placed on bookshelves. **3** ☐ There were enormous piles of books all over the floor with no space to walk between and you couldn't even see the bookcases. When he opened the door, it knocked against one pile of books that threatened to tumble over.

He explained; apparently, he'd developed an obsession with collecting first editions of books. It all began when he found a first edition of a classic crime novel in a second-hand book shop and he bought it for 50p. Someone later told him that it might be worth some money, so he went online and discovered it was valued at £50! **4** ☐ To begin with, he browsed online auction sites to find bargains. Then he started to buy up boxes of books from second-hand stores – which cost next to nothing – just in case

there might be a valuable book somewhere in amongst them. He kept them all because he didn't know which might become valuable in the future, and he didn't sell the ones he knew were worth a lot, in case their values increased still further. The piles of books got higher and higher.

That's the point at which I think he stopped being a collector and became an obsessive hoarder, unable to throw anything away. **5** ☐ He knew that he needed to get a proper focus back in his life and he couldn't do it on his own. When he saw me passing, he decided that being an old friend I wouldn't judge him and asked me for help. So, now I have an after-college job. Every week I spend some time in Mr Peters' study going through his piles of books. We box up the ones that have no real monetary value and we take them to charity shops or give them to hospitals.

At last we are beginning to see some carpet in the study! I think Mr Peters was lucky and asked for help before the hoarding became a big problem. **6** ☐ Might it be worth much money today …? Only kidding!

8E SPEAKING

1 🔊 *67* **Listen and repeat the phrases. How do you say them in your language?**

2 🔊 *68* **Complete the mini conversations with the words from the box. Listen and check.**

> entirely   make   offer   return   sorry   sorted   ~~wonder~~
> would

A **Tomek**   I ¹*wonder* if you could help me? I'd like to ²_____ this shirt. It's too small. It says 'medium' on it, but it's clearly an extra small.

Assistant   I see. Yes, that's ³_____ our fault. We had a batch of shirts in that were wrongly labelled. I can ⁴_____ you a refund or ⁵_____ you like store credit?

Tomek   A refund please.

B **Gizela**   Excuse me. I'd like to ⁶_____ a complaint. I ordered three vinyl albums last week in store. I paid you to deliver them to my uncle for his birthday, but they never arrived.

Assistant   I'm so ⁷_____ about that. We had a problem with deliveries last week, but we've ⁸_____ it out. It will go out tomorrow.

Gizela   It's a bit late for his birthday though, isn't it?

3 🔊 *69* **Listen to a phone conversation between a customer and an assistant. Decide if the statements are true (T) or false (F). Correct the false statements.**

1 ☐ Danny wants to book some driving lessons.
_____

2 ☐ He is free on Friday afternoons.
_____

3 ☐ He wants lessons at 4.30 on Friday.
_____

4 ☐ The woman can offer him lessons at 4.30 on another day.
_____

5 ☐ Danny wants to talk to the manager.
_____

4 🔊 *69* **Complete the conversation with the correct words and phrases from the Speaking box. Listen again and check.**

Michelle   Good morning. This is Michelle.

Danny   I'm sorry to ¹*bother you*, but I wonder if you ²_____ me? I've got a ³_____ with a booking.

Michelle   Certainly. Is this for lessons you've already booked or want to book?

Danny   Already booked. I booked a series of driving lessons over the next two months. They're for 4.30 on Friday afternoons when my college class finishes. You emailed me the details, but the time on your booking sheet is 3.30. I'll still be in class then.

Michelle   Oh, I'm ⁴_____ that. Let me check. Can ⁵_____ your name and booking reference?

Danny   Danny Saunders. Ref number: 2010365477.

Michelle   Thank you, Danny. Let me put you on hold for a moment. Hello caller? Sorry. There was a problem with our website, but we've ⁶_____ now. Yes, you're booked in for lessons at 3.30 on Friday afternoons, starting this coming Friday.

Danny   Excuse me ... Could you please check if the 4.30 slot is free?

Michelle   I'm afraid the 4.30 slot is ⁷_____ all week for the next month. I ⁸_____ you 2.00 on Fridays if you like.

Danny   No! I'm at college – as I've just explained to you. This is ridiculous. You originally agreed to 4.30.

Michelle   I'm sorry, there's ⁹_____ do about it.

Danny   I'm ¹⁰_____ about this.

Michelle   I see you've already paid for ten lessons. Would you like a refund?

Danny   No, I want my driving lessons. When is your manager back? I want to make ¹¹_____!

5 ON A HIGH NOTE **Think of a complaint you've made recently and write the conversation. If you can't remember one, invent a situation.**

have/get something done

1 ⭐ Choose the answer, a or b, which means the same as the first sentence.

1 We had our accounts managed by a professional.
  a A professional managed our accounts.
  b We managed our accounts by ourselves.

2 I got my work checked.
  a I asked someone to check my work.
  b I checked through my work.

3 She made a lovely dress for herself.
  a She got a dress made for her.
  b She sewed the dress.

4 When she was ill she had someone walk her dog for her.
  a She asked someone to take her dog out.
  b She made an effort to go out with her dog.

5 We're repairing my bike this afternoon.
  a I'm asking a mechanic to repair my bike.
  b My friends and I are going to repair my bike.

6 He gets his shopping delivered to his home.
  a The supermarket sends the shopping to his home.
  b He goes to the supermarket to do his shopping.

2 ⭐⭐⭐ Use the prompts to write sentences.

1 Ivan / get / his car / service / yesterday
Ivan got his car serviced yesterday.

2 we / have / our shopping / bring / to our house / every Saturday
_____

3 the girls are at the hairdresser, they / have / their hair / style
_____

4 Mick / get / his homework / correct / later today
_____

5 the shop / have / its sign / paint / last month
_____

6 I / get / my computer / scan / for viruses / once a week
_____

3 ⭐⭐⭐ Use the prompts and the correct forms of the verbs from the box to write sentences.

cut   make   manage   paint   ~~repair~~   service

1 yesterday / Jenny / have / her broken phone
Yesterday Jenny had her broken phone repaired.

2 last week / my dad / get / his car
_____

3 my parents / have / their accounts
_____

4 at the moment / my cousin / get / her wedding dress
_____

5 my room looks great / because / last week / I / have / it
_____

6 that's the hairdresser / where / I / get / my hair
_____

4 ⭐⭐⭐ Complete the second conversation so that it means the same as the first. Use between one and four words in each gap.

Journalist	Can I ask you a few questions for an article?
Mrs Watson	Of course. Will you put my picture in the newspaper?
Journalist	Perhaps. Can I ask, do you do your own shopping or do you ask someone to deliver it?
Mrs Watson	I do it myself. But if I'm not well, I order online and ask someone to bring it to my house.
Journalist	And what about repairs? Do you repair broken things or ask someone to repair them for you?
Mrs Watson	That depends. I always ask the plumber to repair my pipes.
Journalist	And your car?
Mrs Watson	For safety I always pay a mechanic to check it.

● ● ●

Journalist	Can I ask you a few questions for an article?
Mrs Watson	Of course. Will I **¹*have my picture put*** in the newspaper?
Journalist	Perhaps. Can I ask, do you do your own shopping or do you **²_____**?
Mrs Watson	I do it myself. But if I'm not well, I order online and **³_____** to my house.
Journalist	And what about repairs? Do you repair broken things or **⁴_____** for you?
Mrs Watson	That depends. I always **⁵_____** by the plumber.
Journalist	And your car?
Mrs Watson	For safety I always **⁶_____** by a mechanic.

5 ON A HIGH NOTE **What do you think people should pay for and what should they do by themselves? Write a short paragraph. Use *have/get something done*.**

8G WRITING | An opinion essay

Restate the question in your own words.	**IS IT NECESSARY TO SPEND A LOT OF MONEY TO ENJOY A HOLIDAY?**

Everyone needs a holiday, but the problem is usually the cost, especially if you're a student who's short of money. However, <u>as far as I'm concerned</u> it needn't cost a fortune to have a good time.

Give your overall opinion for the first time.

My first reason for saying this is that enjoying a holiday really depends on who you're with. <u>In other words</u>, you can be on an expensive holiday, but if you don't get on with the people you're with, you won't enjoy it. I remember an expensive school trip I went on to Switzerland, but I argued with my friend and had a miserable time. Then I went camping with my sister, which cost very little, and we had a great time.

State your first point.

Give a supporting argument and a personal example.

<u>Another reason</u> I don't think a holiday needs to be expensive is because there are a lot of good deals these days. If you really want to go somewhere different and maybe stay in a hotel, then wait until the last moment and you can pay very little. My parents went to Florida last summer and they found a very cheap offer two days before they went. It was a bargain!

State your second point.

Give a supporting argument and a personal example.

<u>Some people do not agree and feel that</u> you should save up all year and spend all your savings on a special holiday. But cost isn't a guarantee of a good holiday. I know people who've spent a lot of money, only to be really disappointed with the hotels, had terrible problems with flights or become ill while they've been away.

Give an opposing point of view.

Say why you disagree.

To sum up, I would say that a holiday is what you make it. Go with someone you like and look around for good deals. Most importantly, don't end up with a huge debt for a holiday which you might not enjoy anyway.

Summarise your opinion.

Finish with a point to consider.

1 Read the essay. What is the author's answer to the title question? What are his two arguments?

2 Complete the examples with the words from the box.

~~argue~~ firm first put true while worth

Phrases to give your overall opinion
This essay will **1** <u>argue</u> that …
It is my **2**_____ belief that …
a _____

Phrases to add further support
My **3**_____ reason for this opinion is …
It is also **4**_____ pointing out that …
My final point is …
b _____

Phrases to emphasise your opinion by repeating it
To **5**_____ it another way, …
c _____

Phrases to introduce an opposing opinion
It is **6**_____ that …
7_____ some people say that …
d _____

3 Add the underlined phrases in the essay to the correct sections a–d in Exercise 2.

4 WRITING TASK Write an essay entitled *Is it necessary to spend a lot of money on clothes to look good?*

ACTIVE WRITING | An opinion essay

1 Plan your essay. Make notes on the paragraphs in the plan.
  1 Introduction _____
  2 First main point _____
     Supporting argument _____
     Personal example _____
  3 Second main point _____
     Supporting argument _____
     Personal example _____
  4 Opposing point of view _____
     Reason to disagree _____
  5 Conclusion _____

2 Write your essay.
  • Develop each point in your plan.
  • Remember to use a variety of phrases expressing and emphasising opinion.

3 Check your essay. Check that:
  • there are no spelling, grammar or punctuation mistakes.
  • there is interesting and relevant topic vocabulary.

UNIT VOCABULARY PRACTICE

1 8A GRAMMAR AND VOCABULARY **Match the beginnings 1–9 with the endings a–i.**

1 ☐ A poster is a
2 ☐ We find billboards
3 ☐ You can hear a jingle
4 ☐ Companies put logos
5 ☐ A TV commercial
6 ☐ Adverts
7 ☐ Children often repeat
8 ☐ You can have a folder
9 ☐ Pop up ads suddenly

a on radio or TV adverts; it's musical.
b advertising slogans they hear on TV.
c large piece of paper to put on a wall.
d appear on your screen.
e in your email account for spam emails.
f on all their products and on their shopping bags.
g usually lasts for no more than thirty seconds.
h in the streets, on walls and buildings and along roads.
i usually try to be memorable to sell products.

2 8B LISTENING AND VOCABULARY **Complete the sentences with the phrases from the box.**

a good deal   a rip off   bargain hunting
for the price of one   next to nothing   on special offer
spent a fortune   waste of money

1 These jumpers are half price; that's two _for the price of one_.
2 This cost a lot – I really _____ on it!
3 Paying for bad products is a _____ .
4 Can you believe how cheap those shoes are? They cost _____.
5 I got a great new phone. It had a discount because it was _____.
6 They're asking lots of money for this tiny hamburger. What _____!
7 I've saved some money. Let's go _____ in the sales.
8 It's a good shop – honestly – and I think I got _____.

3 8C VOCABULARY **Complete the sentences with one word in each gap.**

1 She wastes so much money – she really has money to b_urn_!
2 I can't pay for this coffee because I've r_____ out of money.
3 My parents are good at shopping around and getting their money's w_____.
4 You spend money like w_____! Where do you get it from?
5 I'm broke – have you got any money o_____ you?
6 You seem to think your dad is m_____ of money.
7 They must be r_____ in money – look at their new car!
8 I'm not going out this evening because I'm a bit s_____ of money.

4 **Choose the correct answers.**

1 I think he's careful with money because he's got debts – that's not _____.
   a living in poverty   b the same as being mean
2 We need to raise money for the youth club, so let's try crowdfunding since we can't _____.
   a take out a loan   b be in the red
3 She's gone clothes shopping again. She really _____.
   a has got loose change   b has more money than sense
4 I have to pay at the car park machine. Have you got any _____?
   a crowdfunding   b loose change
5 We're not going abroad on holiday because we can't _____. We're broke!
   a live in poverty   b afford it
6 I can't believe it – you're _____ and you're buying designer clothes?
   a in the red   b careful with money

5 8D READING AND VOCABULARY **Complete the sentences with one word in each gap.**

1 I don't have a credit card, so I have to pay for everything in c_ash_.
2 I've only got a banknote. Have you got any small c_____ for the drinks machine?
3 My dad always puts his banknotes in his w_____.
4 Can you lend me some change for this v_____ machine?
5 I need to find an A_____ to get some money.
6 If you're travelling, a bank c_____ is safer than carrying a lot of cash.

6 **Choose the correct words to complete the sentences.**

1 I need to go to a _transaction / exchange / cashpoint_ and get some money out.
2 Have you got your own bank _account / purchase / wallet_ for your pocket money?
3 My new prepaid credit card is _rate / currency / contactless_ so I don't need to remember my PIN.
4 Don't forget that bank _credits / purchases / transactions_ aren't free – there's a charge for each one.
5 You can pay for your _account / purchase / charge_ in our shop in cash or by credit card.
6 There's a good exchange _rate / currency / transaction_ at the moment if you want to change your dollars.
7 Can I _withdraw / exchange / purchase_ some money from my account, please?
8 If you go abroad, a prepaid credit card is a good idea, but take a little foreign _exchange / currency / charges_ to pay for coffees and bus tickets.

7 ON A HIGH NOTE **Write a short paragraph about how you pay for things. Do you always use cash or do you have a prepaid credit card? What do you think is the best way to pay for services?**

1 **For each learning objective, write 1–5 to assess your ability.**

1 = I don't feel confident. 5 = I feel very confident.

	Learning objective	Course material	How confident I am (1–5)
8A	I can use the passive to talk about different actions.	Student's Book pp. 108–109	
8B	I can identify specific details in a podcast and talk about spending habits.	Student's Book p. 110	
8C	I can talk about money.	Student's Book p. 11	
8D	I can understand links and identify specific details in a text and talk about money.	Student's Book pp. 112–113	
8E	I can make and respond to complaints.	Student's Book p. 114	
8F	I can use *have/get something done* to talk about services.	Student's Book p. 115	
8G	I can write an opinion essay.	Student's Book pp. 116–117	

2 **Which of the skills above would you like to improve in? How?**

Skill I want to improve in	How I can improve

3 **What can you remember from this unit?**

New words I learned and most want to remember	Expressions and phrases I liked	English I heard or read outside class

GRAMMAR AND VOCABULARY

1 Complete the sentences with one word in each gap.

1 I hate that advert's _____ – don't sing it!
2 The coat was really expensive; he spent a _____!
3 Is that all you paid? You really got _____ for money with that purchase.
4 The band decided to pay for their new CD recording with _____ from their fans.
5 Don't change any money today – the exchange _____ is terrible. It might improve tomorrow.

/ 5

2 Match the beginnings 1–5 with the endings a–e.

1 ☐ They print their
2 ☐ What a waste of money – it's
3 ☐ She thinks I'm
4 ☐ Here are few coins if
5 ☐ Is there a bank with a

a made of money.
b cashpoint near here?
c logos on everything.
d a rip off if you ask me.
e you need some loose change.

/ 5

3 Choose the correct verb forms to complete the sentences.

1 These dolls are *made / making* in Peru.

2 Lots of photos *been taken / were taken* by the fans during the festival.

3 More skateboards have *being bought / been bought* online than in shops.

4 The design is *been / being* considered by the experts.

5 I'm sure these shoes will be *sell out / sold out* by tomorrow.

/ 5

4 Use the prompts to write sentences and complete the text.

Our new survey shows an increase in online shopping for all sorts of products. At present more people **1***have / their purchases / deliver* to their homes than ever before. Young people increasingly **2***get / items / pay for* by their parents with a credit card from specialised websites. Another change is in the number of services customers **3***get / renew* online. Travel passes are an example. And concert-goers seems to prefer to **4***get / their tickets / book* through an online ticket seller. Some language learners even **5***have / their lessons / teach* online by teachers who are thousands of miles away!

1 _____
2 _____
3 _____
4 _____
5 _____

/ 5

USE OF ENGLISH

5 Complete the second sentence so that it means the same as the first. Use no more than three words.

1 The company was advertising their new product on TV.
   The company's product _____ on TV.
2 They didn't realise that the government had banned the game.
   They didn't realise that the game had _____ the government.
3 Susie's at the hairdresser's at the moment – they're cutting her hair short!
   Susie's at the hairdresser's at the moment – she _____ hair cut short!
4 He didn't ask the mechanic to repair the car – it wasn't worth it.
   He _____ the car repaired – it wasn't worth it.
5 That rucksack is a real waste of money if you ask me.
   That rucksack _____ off if you ask me.

/ 5

6 Complete the text with one word in each gap.

When you travel abroad, always check the **1**_____ rate a few days before. If the country uses a different **2**_____ to your own, it might be better to change money at home rather than abroad. A **3**_____ credit card is a good idea – if it **4**_____ stolen you can cancel it, and you know you loss will be limited. Remember that most small transactions must **5**_____ paid for in cash, so keep a little money for that.

/ 5

/ 30

The power of nature

9A GRAMMAR AND VOCABULARY

The third conditional

1 ★ **Choose the answer, a or b, which means the same as the first sentence.**

1 If you had asked me, I would have helped you.
   a You asked me for help.
   b You didn't ask me for help.

2 If Sam hadn't pulled the girl out of the water, she could have been in serious danger.
   a Sam pulled the girl out of the water.
   b Sam didn't pull the girl out of the water.

3 That old building would have fallen down if the wind had been stronger.
   a The wind was very strong.
   b The wind wasn't so strong.

4 If we hadn't watched the news, we wouldn't have known about the tsunami.
   a We watched the news.
   b We didn't watch the news.

5 They couldn't have saved the woman from the water if there hadn't been a roof nearby.
   a There was a roof nearby.
   b There wasn't a roof nearby.

6 If the coastguard hadn't sent the boat home, it would have got into trouble.
   a The coastguard didn't send the boat home.
   b The coastguard sent the boat home.

2 ★ **Match the beginnings 1–6 with the endings a–f.**

1 ☐ If we hadn't known about the risk of tsunamis, we
2 ☐ If the wind had been stronger, many buildings
3 ☐ If she hadn't climbed onto a roof during the flood, rescuers
4 ☐ If more people had helped in the search, the lost boys
5 ☐ If they had gone into that cave with a guide, they
6 ☐ If you had understood the local weather better, you

a would have been found sooner.
b wouldn't have got lost in it.
c might have gone to that coast on holiday.
d might not have seen her.
e would have realised this is the stormy season.
f would have collapsed.

3 ★★ **Choose the correct verb form to complete the second sentence so that it means the same as the first sentence.**

1 If you hadn't rescued that family, they would have risked their lives.
   You rescued that family and so they *risked / didn't risk* their lives.

2 If they hadn't gone into the caves, they wouldn't have got lost.
   They went into the caves and *got / didn't get* lost.

3 If Mandy hadn't climbed the tree, she might have drowned.
   Mandy climbed the tree and so she *drowned / didn't drown*.

4 We wouldn't have realised you were lost in the wood if we hadn't found your bike.
   We found your bike and *realised / didn't realise* you were lost in the wood.

5 If I hadn't seen the weather forecast, we could have got lost in the storm.
   We saw the weather forecast and so we *got lost / didn't get lost* in the storm.

6 We might have taken the dangerous path if they hadn't warned us against it.
   They warned us against it so we *took / didn't take* the dangerous path.

4 ★★ **Complete the sentences with the correct forms of the verbs in brackets.**

1 If you ___*hadn't called*___ (not call) the emergency services immediately, they wouldn't have arrived so quickly.

2 If Maria _____ (study) the walking guidebook, she would have known it was a dangerous area.

3 The guide would have gone with the group if they _____ (ask) him.

4 More tourists might have lost their lives if the local people _____ (not help) them.

5 If the weather forecasters _____ (not predict) the storm, a lot of fishermen would have got into trouble out at sea.

6 More people would have been hurt if the storm _____ (happen) in the morning.

5 ★★ Choose the correct answers.

1 If they hadn't trusted their guide, they _____ followed her.

a wouldn't have

b could have

c would have

2 If you hadn't learned to swim with diving equipment, you _____ got out of the cave.

a would have

b might have

c wouldn't have

3 They _____ realised a storm was coming if they had studied the weather.

a would have

b might not have

c wouldn't have

4 If she had been in the forest during the storm, she _____ killed.

a might not have been

b could have been

c couldn't have been

5 They _____ injured if they'd been on the beach during the tsunami.

a wouldn't have been

b couldn't have been

c might have been

6 If we hadn't got help from a local person, we _____ got lost.

a would have

b wouldn't have

c couldn't have

6 ★★★ Use the prompts to write sentences. Use the third conditional.

1 if / you / ask / me / for advice, / I / tell / you / stay at home

If you had asked me for advice, I would have told you to stay at home.

2 if / they / be / more careful, / they / not / get / into trouble

_____

_____

3 they / not / drown / if / the waves / not / be / so big

_____

_____

4 they / might / not / get lost / if / they / take / a map

_____

_____

5 we / can / not / find / you / if / you / not / light / a fire

_____

_____

6 if / she / listen to / their advice, / she / not / go / sailing / in that weather

_____

_____

7 ★★★ Use the prompts to write questions. Then write short answers.

1 if / you / go / into the caves, / you / ask / a guide / to go with you?

If you had gone into the caves, would you have asked a guide to go with you?

Yes, *I would*.

2 if / she / study / the map, / could / she / find / her way / out of the mountains?

_____

No, _____.

3 you / have / call / for help / if / you / be / near the tsunami?

_____

Yes, _____.

4 if / the rescuers / arrive / late, / you / try / to help / the trapped people?

_____

Yes, _____.

5 if / they / not / climb / onto a roof, / people / see / them?

_____

No, _____.

8 ★★★ Complete the text with one word or contraction in each gap.

Sarah Tyndale had walked many times in her favourite park in Colorado, but this was the first time she had left the trail. If she **1**_hadn't_ enjoyed many danger-free walks before she might **2**_____ have felt the same sense of security. And **3**_____ she had listened to the warnings, she **4**_____ have stayed on the path. But on that day, she decided to wander into the forest, where she met … a rare mountain lion! She immediately grabbed a stick. 'If I **5**_____ waved the stick at the mountain lion, it would **6**_____ attacked me straight away,' she explained. What else could she do? She decided to make a noise – by singing! Sarah is an excellent opera singer. 'If I **7**_____ sung opera songs, the animal **8**_____ have been so surprised,' said Sarah. Eventually it walked away, confused by the noise and the movement.

9 ON A HIGH NOTE Write a short paragraph about how your life would or could have been different because of one decision you made in the past.

9B LISTENING AND VOCABULARY

1 🔊 *70* **Listen to a radio interview with an actor. How many films are mentioned?**

2 🔊 *71* **Listen to the first part of the interview again and complete the notes with one or two words in each gap.**

   1 People can see Jake's film from *15ᵗʰ September*.

   2 The first showing was in _____ last month.

   3 The name of the new film is _____.

   4 The film is located in the _____ of England.

   5 The time period covered in the film is _____.

   6 Jake had to spend a long time in _____.

3 🔊 *72* **Listen to the second part of the interview again and choose the correct answers.**

   1 Jake thinks that people like disaster movies because

     a they teach them what to do in a disaster.

     b they happen in different countries.

     c they show things they haven't experienced.

   2 According to Jake, how are modern survival films different from big disaster movies?

     a They are cleverer and more creative.

     b They concentrate on a small number of people.

     c They feature real people as well as actors.

   3 In *Touching the Void* the two men

     a ignored the possibility of bad weather.

     b helped each other down the mountain to safety.

     c were trapped in a snowstorm at the top of the mountain.

   4 What is true about the story of *The Revenant*?

     a It was inspired by a book written by a real survivor.

     b It is probably an exaggerated version of a true story.

     c It was imagined by the script writer.

   5 How does Jake feel about the film he's in compared to *The Revenant*?

     a He regrets it didn't have the same financial support.

     b He hopes to win an award for his performance too.

     c He would have preferred to act with DiCaprio.

Vocabulary extension

4 **Complete the sentences with the words and phrases from the box which you heard in the recording.**

> bitter cold   blizzard   burst   courageous   ~~eruption~~
> far-fetched   hit   struggle

   1 The *eruption* of Mount Vesuvius happened in 79 AD.

   2 After their island was struck by a huge earthquake, the residents faced a _____ to survive.

   3 A _____ local farmer risked his life to help an injured climber down the mountain.

   4 The story seemed so _____ that at first I didn't believe it, but it's actually true.

   5 A devastating hurricane _____ the island.

   6 We couldn't see even a metre in front of us as we tried to make our way through the _____.

   7 The river is about to _____ its banks.

   8 Despite the _____, we put on our boots and coats and set off across the ice.

Pronunciation

ACTIVE PRONUNCIATION | Emphatic stress

Sometimes we stress a particular word in a sentence to give it more meaning. We may make this word a little louder, longer or higher than the others. We can use emphasis:

- when we give new information or add details, e.g.
  *My friend lives in a **flat**. It's a **big** flat.*
- to point out important words; these can change depending on the context, e.g.
  ***Sarah** (not Jack) is going to **college** (not university) in **September** (not October).*
- to disagree or to contrast, e.g.
  *'Jack will win the race.' 'Jack **won't** win the race.'*
  *'I love chips.' 'Well, I **hate** chips!'*

5 🔊 *73* **Which words should be stressed in order to emphasise the information given in brackets? Listen and check. Practise saying the sentences.**

   1 Miss Jones is going to give us a test on Dickens on Friday. (not Mr Summers)

   2 Miss Jones is going to give us a test on Dickens on Friday. (not today)

   3 Miss Jones is going to give us a test on Dickens on Friday. (not a talk)

   4 Miss Jones is going to give us a test on Dickens on Friday. (not about Shakespeare)

6 🔊 *74* **Underline the syllable or word which you think Speaker B will stress in his/her responses. Listen and check. Practise saying the mini conversations.**

   1 **A** The tickets cost fifty pounds, don't they?
     B No, they cost fifteen pounds!

   2 **A** Is Harry's party this Friday?
     B No, it's next Friday.

   3 **A** Shall we go to the beach before dinner?
     B I'd rather go after dinner.

   4 **A** We need to write a longer article for the website.
     B No, it needs to be shorter.

   5 **A** Did you say that you can't download information from the site?
     B I said I can't upload information.

7 🔊 *75* **Choose the question which the second speaker is responding to. Listen and check.**

   1 **A** *What do you do? / What kind of teacher are you?*
     B I'm a **Maths** teacher.

   2 **A** *Do you live with your grandparents? / Do you live near your cousins?*
     B No, I live near my **grandparents**.

   3 **A** *Shall I cook fish or beef? / What's your favourite meal?*
     B I like fish **and** beef.

   4 **A** *Have you seen the new survival film? / Do you like the new survival film?*
     B Yes, we went **yesterday**.

UNIT VOCABULARY PRACTICE > page 109

9C **VOCABULARY** | Environmental responsibility

1 ⭐ **Choose the correct words to complete the sentences.**

1 Please *keep / avoid* damage to a minimum by walking on the paths.

2 It's important to *disturb / respect* the guidelines while you are in the national park.

3 Don't throw away *reduced / single-use* plastic products. Take them with you and recycle them.

4 We try to *minimise / sort* human impact by asking you to stay in certain areas.

5 If you have produced rubbish, please *collect / dispose* of it in the bins in the car park.

6 We have stopped selling snacks in plastic packets in order to *disturb / benefit* the environment.

2 ⭐ **Complete the sentences with the words from the box.**

avoid collect damage ~~disturb~~ reduce sort

1 If you switch on radios or loud music, you'll *disturb* the local wildlife.

2 Please _____ your rubbish into plastic, paper and glass.

3 It's a good idea to _____ breaking or cutting plants.

4 Try to _____ pollution levels by parking your car and proceeding on foot.

5 We ask you not to _____ any fences by sitting on them or letting children play on them.

6 Please _____ any paper or plastic packets you use and dispose of them in the bins.

3 ⭐⭐ **Complete the sentences with the correct forms of the verbs in brackets.**

1 Taking a big picnic and then leaving your rubbish there isn't exactly *respectful*. (**RESPECT**)

2 Don't cook too much and then throw away the food; it's really _____. (**WASTE**)

3 That was a stupid accident – with a little preparation it was totally _____. (**AVOID**)

4 This is a really _____ website with lots of advice about environmentally-friendly choices. (**HELP**)

5 It's better to use _____ plates and cups. (**REUSE**)

6 I think _____ energy is definitely a key to the future. (**SUSTAIN**)

4 ⭐⭐ **Complete the sentences with one word in each gap.**

1 You can throw these cups away – they're d*isposable*.

2 After considering the problem, Andy offered me some very t_____ advice on the matter.

3 Don't throw plastic into the sea. It's incredibly h_____ to the animals which live there.

4 A lot of damage we've done was totally unnecessary and a_____.

5 Solar power is a cheap and easily-available source of s_____ energy.

6 I think it would be h_____ if we distributed information leaflets.

5 ⭐⭐⭐ **Complete the conversation with the words from the box. There are two extra words.**

avoid damage dispose ~~impact~~ reduces respectful
reusable sort sustainable thoughtful

Tobias Lisa, did you just throw that plastic bottle on the ground? Don't you know there are bins over there?

Lisa Oh come on, Tobias! One bottle doesn't make a difference. What ¹*impact* will one bottle have?

Tobias A huge one if you multiply it by a million! A million people like you who don't behave in a ²_____ way really ³_____ the environment.

Lisa Look – I usually ⁴_____ my rubbish and recycle it, OK? I really believe in ⁵_____ energy, too. My parents have got solar panels for example.

Tobias Have they? I bet that really ⁶_____ your electricity bills!

Lisa Yes, it does, but we also ⁷_____ damaging the environment by using solar power. Anyway – calm down! I'll pick up my plastic bottle and ⁸_____ of it over there in the plastic bin.

6 ⭐⭐⭐ **Complete the text with one word in each gap which means the same as the words in brackets.**

When two surfers on holiday in Bali realised that the sea was full of ¹ s*ingle-use* (non-reusable) items such as ² d_____ (throw-away) cups and bottles, they decided to do something about it. They saw that local fisherman had to force their way through the plastic, which was very ³ h_____ (damaging) to the local wildlife, too. The plastic rubbish was having a devastating ⁴ i_____ (effect) on animals and birds. They decided to ask the fishermen to fish for plastic instead of fish, but obviously this was not economically ⁵ s_____ (possible in the long term) for the fishermen. So to finance the project they are selling ⁶ r_____ (that can be recycled) plastic bracelets. Each bracelet represents one pound of plastic removed from the sea. It ⁷ b_____ (is good for) the sea, the wildlife and the local population. Of course the ultimate goal is to ⁸ r_____ (cut down) plastic waste to zero.

7 ON A HIGH NOTE **Write a short paragraph about what you do to protect the environment. Is there anything more you think you should do? Would you need help from other people or groups to do this?**

9D GRAMMAR

I wish / If only for regrets

1 ⭐ **Choose the answer, a or b, which means the same as the first sentence.**

1 I wish my parents would listen to me more.
   a My parents listen to me a lot.
   b My parents don't listen to me much.

2 If only we'd chosen a quieter hotel!
   a This hotel is noisy.
   b We've got a very quiet hotel.

3 I wish I hadn't decided to cycle in this weather.
   a I decided to cycle.
   b I would like to cycle.

4 I wish you'd stop shouting.
   a You shouted at me!
   b You're shouting at me!

5 If only we could go to the Maldives.
   a We would like to go the Maldives.
   b We don't want to go to the Maldives.

6 I wish I had my own room.
   a I wanted my own room as a child.
   b I want a room of my own now.

2 ⭐⭐ **Complete the regrets about the present with the correct forms of the verbs in brackets.**

1 If only we *could* (can) stay in a hotel and not a tent!
2 I wish we _____ (live) in a bigger house.
3 I wish I_____ (not have to) get up at 6.30 every morning.
4 If only my friends _____ (not like) that terrible music!
5 I wish people _____ (take) more care of the environment.
6 If only I_____ (have) a dog.
7 I wish my eyes _____ (be) a different colour.
8 I wish our Maths teacher _____ (not give) us such difficult tests.

3 ⭐⭐ **Complete the regrets about the past with the correct forms of the verbs from the box.**

buy ~~find~~ meet never meet not move save

1 If only we *had found* a better campsite – this one's terrible!
2 I wish my friend _____ away from this area – I really miss him.
3 If only I _____ more money – now I can't afford to go out with my friends!
4 I wish I _____ you – you're horrible to me!
5 If only my parents _____ me a new bicycle last year.
6 I wish we _____ before!

4 ⭐⭐⭐ **Use the prompts to complete the sentences. Use *would*.**

1 I wish / you / stop whistling – it's really irritating.
   I wish you would stop whistling – it's really irritating.
2 If only my parents / book / a holiday in a hot country!
   _____
3 I wish my mum / not come / into my room without knocking.
   _____
4 If only people / respect / animals more.
   _____
5 I wish my boyfriend / call / me a bit more often.
   _____
6 If only my neighbours / not make / so much noise at night.
   _____

5 ⭐⭐⭐ **Complete the conversation with the correct forms of the verbs in brackets.**

Alex I wish you ¹*would stop* (stop) singing, Becky. I'm trying to study!

Becky Well, why don't you go up to your room? I wish you ² _____ (not use) the living room as a study.

Alex But my room is so small. I wish we ³ _____ (have) in a bigger house.

Becky I know what you mean, but we don't. And I'm fed up with not being able to sing in my own room. If only our parents ⁴ _____ (not buy) this tiny house – just because it has a garden. I wish they ⁵ _____ (choose) that other house – it was much bigger.

Alex Yes, I know. And it didn't have a garden. Who needs a garden? I wish they ⁶ _____ (not make) me do the gardening. I hate it! If only we ⁷ _____ (live) in a flat.

Becky And I wish I ⁸ _____ (can/go) to singing lessons! You have a garden and you hate it and I can't sing and I love it!

6 ON A HIGH NOTE **Write two short paragraphs beginning with the words given.**

I wish I had/hadn't ...
I wish I were/weren't ...

1 🔊 76 **Listen and repeat the phrases. How do you say them in your language?**

SPEAKING | Expressing and responding to regrets

EXPRESSING REGRETS

I wish/If only I had brought an umbrella.
I should(n't) have invited him.
It's a pity/shame that I didn't check the tyres.
How stupid of me!
I can't believe I forgot about this/didn't remember this.
It was so careless of me.

RESPONDING TO REGRETS

Forget it.
(It's) no problem.
It doesn't matter.
There's no point worrying about it.
It's not a big deal.
Calm down!/Chill out!
It's not the end of the world.
It's no use crying over spilt milk.
There's nothing you/we can do about it.

---

2 **Complete the second sentence in each pair beginning with the words given so that it means the same as the first sentence.**

1 I didn't bring a warm coat. How stupid of me!
I should *have brought a warm coat*.

2 I regret not taking out more money.
I wish _____.

3 I didn't know you liked cheese sandwiches, so I didn't make more.
It's a pity that _____.

4 It's a shame you didn't invite Charlie to the party.
If only _____.

5 I'm sorry I got angry with you. That was wrong.
I should _____.

6 I can't believe I ate all those potatoes. I feel ill now!
I wish _____.

3 **Choose the correct words to complete the short exchanges.**

1 **A** I forgot to buy milk.
B It's not a big *shame / deal*.

2 **A** How could you have left your bag on the bus?
B I know! It was so *avoidable / careless* of me!

3 **A** I accidentally deleted my essay.
B Well – it's no use crying over *spilt / dropped* milk. You'll just have to write it again.

4 **A** It's a *deal / pity* that we missed that film about earthquakes.
B Yes, but it's on again next week.

5 **A** I forgot to pass on your message to Katy.
B It doesn't *matter / worry*. I saw her myself and told her.

6 **A** I'm so sorry!
B *Forget / Calm* it. It's OK – really.

4 🔊 77 **Complete the conversations with the words from the box. Listen and check.**

~~believe~~ chill have how nothing point should
wish world would

A

Girl 1 Ah, what a beautiful view from up here!

Girl 2 Yeah – great! But – oh my goodness! My feet are killing me! I can't **¹*believe*** I wore these shoes!

Girl 1 Well, there's **²**_____ you can do about it now. Just rest for a while.

Girl 2 And I'm hungry. I **³**_____ have brought those energy bars like you suggested. I'm hopeless!

Girl 1 Hey! **⁴**_____ out! It's not the end of the **⁵**_____!

B

Boy 1 Oh, this is crazy. We're wasting this lovely day. I **⁶**_____ I'd checked these bike tyres before we left! My brother **⁷**_____ have changed this one for me.

Boy 2 There's no **⁸**_____ worrying about it. Take your time. You're doing fine. I've just been giving the horses over there some apples.

Boy 1 Oh no! You shouldn't **⁹**_____ done that. Look – they're coming over. They're looking for more.

Boy 2 Oops! **¹⁰**_____ stupid of me! They always say not to feed the horses. Come on! Let's go!

Boy 1 I can't! I'm still changing my bicycle tyre!

5 ON A HIGH NOTE **Think of something you regret doing/ not doing at the following times. Write about what you regret and why.**

1 yesterday evening at home

2 when you were out somewhere last weekend

3 this morning or today at school

1 Read the article quickly and tick (✓) the animals which are NOT mentioned in the text.

1 ☐ whale

2 ☐ cat

3 ☐ goldfish

4 ☐ crocodile

5 ☐ sea turtle

6 ☐ sea bird

7 ☐ snake

8 ☐ dog

2 Read the article again and match the topics a–f with the paragraphs 1–6. There is one extra topic.

a ☐ an unexpected source of inspiration

b ☐ an amazing memory

c ☐ a difficult decision

d ☐ a long term plan

e ☐ a long awaited holiday

f ☐ a chance to recover

3 Read the article again and choose the correct answers.

1 The writer didn't go to college immediately after school because she

a wasn't sure which course to take.

b had something else planned.

c wanted a break from studying.

d needed to earn some money.

2 What was the writer's reaction when she learned about Jenna's holiday?

a She was envious that Jenna was in Mexico.

b She was surprised by the number of activities Jenna could do.

c She was impressed by Jenna's photos on the beach.

d She was interested in something Jenna posted online.

3 Which of the following is mentioned in the text as a fact, not an opinion?

a Costa Rica is the main nesting place for sea turtles.

b Sea turtles are a threatened species.

c Eating turtle meat is illegal.

d Poachers earn a lot of money.

4 What is true about the writer's life in the UK?

a She lives with her parents.

b She enjoys the local night life.

c She volunteers in her local area.

d She would prefer to live in a town.

5 What is the writer's main purpose in writing the article?

a to encourage other people to take time out from studying

b to describe an important experience in her life

c to suggest ways of helping conservation projects

d to thank a friend for some important career advice

Vocabulary extension

4 Match the highlighted phrases from the article 1–6 with their meanings a–f.

1 ☐ taken their toll

2 ☐ won me over

3 ☐ before I knew it

4 ☐ something else

5 ☐ faded away

6 ☐ all too soon

a ☐ very soon

b ☐ slowly disappeared

c ☐ succeeded in persuading me

d ☐ more quickly than expected/wanted

e ☐ fantastic

f ☐ damaged/harmed her (physically or psychologically)

5 Complete the sentences with the phrases from Exercise 4.

1 I hope that on my beach holiday all the stresses of work and home will just _fade away_.

2 The early mornings last week have really _____ and now I'm absolutely exhausted.

3 I booked a flight to Madrid and _____ I was getting off the plane in the warm September sunshine.

4 I wasn't sure about staying at the city hotel my friend recommended, but the pictures on their website _____.

5 I knew the trip was going to be fun, but the reality was _____! It was the best holiday I've ever had!

6 My birthday celebration was wonderful, but _____ it was midnight and we had to go home.

ACTIVE VOCABULARY | Negative prefixes *il-* and *ir-*

Adjectives beginning with the letters *l-* or *r-* often take a negative prefix beginning with *il-* or *ir-*, e.g.

- legal → illegal
- reversible → irreversible

---

6 Complete the sentences with the negative forms of the adjectives from the box.

literate logical ~~regular~~ relevant responsible

1 I learned a list of _irregular_ verbs for my English test.

2 You can't buy something if you don't know what it costs – it's _____.

3 Can we focus on the main subject please? What you're saying is _____.

4 A hundred years ago there were many people who were _____ – they couldn't read or write.

5 Some _____ people dump rubbish in the countryside.

7 ON A HIGH NOTE Write an email to a friend telling him/her about the article. Start with these words:

Hi! Just read a really interesting article about a girl who ...

MY MONTHS IN
COSTA RICA

1 Animals have always been important in my life, starting with a birthday gift of five goldfish in a small tank when I was five years old. Throughout my childhood and teenage years I shared my life with a series of family cats and dogs. It therefore seemed inevitable that I would train to be a veterinary surgeon. I was accepted onto a course at one of the best veterinary colleges in Europe. However, all the studying and exam pressure had taken their toll and I just wasn't ready to start the course straight away after finishing school. So I decided to take a year off. But I had no idea how to spend that year. I couldn't sit back and do nothing. Should I travel with a friend, get a part-time job, learn something new? People suggested different ideas, but none of them appealed to me. All I knew was that I didn't want to waste the year and then think, 'Oh, I wish I'd done that ... or gone there ...'.

2 The solution came in a social media post. One of my best friends, Jenna, went on holiday with her family to Mexico for two weeks. She posted the normal pictures of herself in cafés, herself on the beautiful white beach sunbathing – you know the kind! I loved the one of a crocodile swimming up to her lakeside table at a restaurant! But then I saw the photo that helped me make my decision, and I guess changed my life in many ways. The photo was of her open hand with a tiny, baby sea turtle on it. Her post explained that one of the hotel activities had been helping to carry baby turtles from their nests on the beach to the sea. The reason was that every year many of them were taken by sea birds while they made that perilous short journey to the water.

3 The idea of going to a popular tourist resort didn't attract me, but the conservation idea did. So I went online to find out more. Statistics showed that sea turtles are becoming rarer and rarer. I started checking out volunteer programmes and then I found an amazing opportunity in Costa Rica! The local people work hard to protect the large female sea turtles, their eggs and the babies from poachers who catch them to sell illegally. Their dedication won me over. Before I knew it I was walking along white sandy beaches, looking at breathtaking scenery. In the UK I don't live in a busy, noisy area with vibrant night life. My parents' house is in quite an isolated village. However, the peace and quiet of the remote Costa Rican coast was something else! There's an atmosphere on the island that completely relaxes you and I felt the pressures of all the studying and exams just faded away.

4 I also became fascinated by the turtles. Every night we patrolled the beaches to scare off poachers and to find the nests. We moved eggs to a protected area so that they couldn't be stolen. Then when the eggs hatched we helped the babies get to the sea. I shall never, ever forget standing on a beach in full moonlight, the clear sky dotted with stars, watching a huge female turtle walk slowly out of the sea, up the beach and lay her eggs. They are really magnificent animals and it would be terrible if the damage to their numbers was irreversible.

5 All too soon my volunteering months were over and now I'm getting ready for college. I'm feeling so much better about getting back to studies again than I did a year ago. I also now have a clear idea of what I want to do with my life after college. My plan is to work with an international wildlife vets organisation. It trains local vets in different countries to help with conservation projects. So, I'm really grateful to Jenna for posting that particular photo. If I hadn't seen it I would never have had such a wonderful, life-changing experience. Thanks Jenna!

Begin with an eye-catching title.

Start with an engaging sentence.

Address readers directly to involve them.

Ask questions to make readers want to read on.

Give examples.

Ask personal questions to involve the reader.

Use imperatives.

Leave the reader with something interesting to think about.

ARE WE GETTING THE MESSAGE?

We are slowly destroying our planet. You know that, don't you? And you're probably doing what you can to help. But what about all those people who aren't aware how bad the situation is or those who don't know how to help, or those who perhaps don't even care? The message needs to reach everyone so that change can happen.

We need to be constantly reminded of the topic and in a way that makes us sit up and take notice. Sometimes when we're told something too often, we stop listening. But this issue is too important to be ignored. Articles must be shocking and memorable because they need to make us think. For example, I remember an online article about plastic waste and right in the middle of the article was a number that kept changing. It gave the number of plastic bottles that had been produced since I'd started reading the article! It made it personal.

Are you one of those people who respond to images? Then you'll understand the importance of documentaries or films which show vivid scenes of how the environment has been damaged by human habits. However, once again, we don't want people to become immune. New technology and creative approaches to documentary making will help here. In addition to this, people need to know the scale of the problem. For instance, a voice over an image of the Great Garbage Patch in the Pacific comparing it to an area three times the size of France is shocking, but it's something we'll remember.

So, addressing the problem is something we all need to be part of. Have you seen an impressive statistic, read a memorable article online recently? Share it on social media. We need to be aware and we need to act. Now!

---

1 Read the article. Which question do you think the writer is answering?

 a We are looking for articles about how to address environmental problems.
 b We are looking for articles about how to make people more aware of environmental problems.

2 Which of the words or phrases *cannot* replace the underlined part in the sentence? More than one answer may be possible.

 1 The documentary was very successful <u>because</u> it approached the problem from a different angle.
 as / so / since

 2 The cameras took us underwater down to the sea bed <u>so that they could</u> show us the damage.
 because / in order to / as

 3 Extreme measures must be taken <u>in order to</u> repair the destruction human activities have caused.
 so that we can / because we can / since we can

 4 <u>Since</u> it's a difficult topic, many people don't want to hear about it.
 in order / because / as

 5 Scientists can't make exact predictions <u>as</u> they don't have enough data yet.
 since / because / so

3 WRITING TASK **Read the advertisement on a webpage and write your article.**

> **ARTICLES WANTED!**
> • What has your town done to improve pollution or deal with waste?
> • Has your school or college made any changes to help the environment?
> • Have your family changed their habits in order to use less energy or water?
> Write your article today! We will publish the most interesting articles on our website.

ACTIVE WRITING | An article

1 Plan your article.
 • Make a note of your ideas to answer each question in the task.
 • Divide the notes into paragraphs.

2 Write your article.
 • Think of an eye-catching title and opening sentence.
 • Give examples to illustrate your points.
 • Address your reader directly and ask questions.

3 Check your article. Check that:
 • you have used linkers to connect your sentences.
 • there are no spelling, grammar and punctuation mistakes.

UNIT VOCABULARY PRACTICE

1 9A GRAMMAR AND VOCABULARY **Complete the sentences with one word in each gap.**

1 Many people have d<u>rowned</u> because they swam too far out and couldn't get back to land.

2 The fishing village was devastated when a ts_____ hit it – the huge wave destroyed everything.

3 Local people didn't know that deep u_____ an earthquake had struck.

4 We love walking along the sh_____ every morning and listening to the waves on the sand.

5 Be careful of the strong c_____ in this area – they can pull you out to sea before you know it.

6 Sometimes the s_____ of water looks perfectly calm, but underneath it can be very dangerous.

7 When the w_____ are very big, we advise you not to go into the sea unless you are an expert swimmer.

2 9B LISTENING AND VOCABULARY **Match the beginnings 1–8 with the endings a–h.**

1 ☐ No one had any water

2 ☐ That terrible forest fire

3 ☐ A lot of lava came out in

4 ☐ My cousin's house was blown down

5 ☐ Skiers had to stay off the mountain because

6 ☐ The tornado looked like

7 ☐ There was a severe earthquake, but

8 ☐ Because of the continual heavy rain

a the volcanic eruption.

b most buildings were anti-seismic.

c because of the drought.

d in that terrible hurricane.

e a column of twisting, black air.

f destroyed thousands of trees.

g we had a bad flood.

h of the danger of an avalanche.

3 **Choose the correct words to complete the sentences.**

1 The forest fire caused terrible *destruction* / *earthquakes* over a large area.

2 The fire services had to *warn* / *evacuate* an entire village as the forest fire approached.

3 We think it's a good idea to have regular fire *warnings* / *drills* to train people.

4 When they inspected the *flames* / *ruins* after the fire, they could see the damage.

5 The *survivors* / *victims* had managed to escape the forest fire by running into the sea.

6 The *drowned* / *trapped* people were rescued by firefighters.

7 When the earthquake struck, the whole building *panicked* / *shook* – it was terrifying.

8 Sadly, there were hundreds of *victims* / *survivors* when the tsunami struck the island.

4 9C VOCABULARY **Complete the sentences with the words from the box. There are two extra words.**

avoid dispose harmful impact minimum respect sustainable ~~wasteful~~

1 Throwing out all this plastic and glass instead of recycling it is really *wasteful*.

2 Why don't you _____ of your rubbish in a more responsible way?

3 We try to cut our non-recyclable waste to a _____.

4 Please _____ the rules while hiking in the national park.

5 I really think we should _____ these single-use plastic bags and take reusable ones.

6 Pollution is incredibly _____ to plants, animals and humans!

5 9F READING AND VOCABULARY **Complete the text with one word in each gap.**

When I lived in a city I was a teenager, and I really loved the hustle and [1] b<u>ustle</u> and the trendy [2] b_____ where I bought clothes, shoes and books. I was also a big fan of the city's vibrant [3] n_____ and I went out dancing with my friends every Saturday. We lived in a tower [4] b_____ where I knew most of my neighbours. However, as an adult I got tired of all the people. Suddenly it was too [5] c_____ and noisy for me. So I got a job an hour outside the city in a village. I found a lovely [6] p_____ little house – it's so pretty! I've met new neighbours, so I still have that sense of [7] c_____ which I had in the city. And when I look out of my window, I see fields, woods and the distant mountains – breathtaking [8] s_____ instead of traffic and buildings!

6 9G WRITING AND VOCABULARY **Match the phrases 1–7 with their definitions a–g.**

1 ☐ recycled building materials

2 ☐ sensor lights

3 ☐ geothermal heating

4 ☐ solar panels

5 ☐ a modest size

6 ☐ energy efficiency

7 ☐ rainwater collection

a It isn't very big.

b They make electricity from the sun.

c They switch themselves on and off automatically.

d You save water from the rain.

e These come from old wood, stone and bricks.

f It uses natural heat from the earth to warm your home.

g This means that you don't waste electricity.

7 ON A HIGH NOTE **Write a short text about what you think your school could do to make its energy use more efficient and to switch to sustainable energy sources.**

1 **For each learning objective, write 1–5 to assess your ability.**

1 = I don't feel confident. 5 = I feel very confident.

	Learning objective	Course material	How confident I am (1–5)
9A	I can use the third conditional to talk about unreal situations in the past.	Student's Book pp. 124–125	
9B	I can identify specific details in an interview and talk about natural disasters.	Student's Book p. 126	
9C	I can talk about environmental responsibility.	Student's Book p. 127	
9D	I can use *I wish* and *If only* to express regrets.	Student's Book p. 128	
9E	I can express and respond to regrets.	Student's Book p. 129	
9F	I can summarise a text and talk about places to live.	Student's Book pp. 130–131	
9G	I can write an article.	Student's Book pp. 132–133	

2 **Which of the skills above would you like to improve in? How?**

Skill I want to improve in	How I can improve

3 **What can you remember from this unit?**

New words I learned and most want to remember	Expressions and phrases I liked	English I heard or read outside class

GRAMMAR AND VOCABULARY

1 Choose the correct answers.

1 A lot of people suffered from lack of water in that terrible _____.
   a forest fire
   b hurricane
   c drought

2 You should learn to _____ of your waste in a more responsible way.
   a avoid
   b dispose
   c reuse

3 The petrol _____ from the traffic were terrible.
   a fumes
   b energies
   c harm

4 She lives in a very _____ community; everyone knows everyone else.
   a life-changing
   b tight-knit
   c single-use

5 You can use _____ if you want to benefit from the earth's natural heat.
   a geothermal energy
   b solar panels
   c recycled materials

/ 5

2 Complete the sentences with one word in each gap.

1 The strong sea c_____ often pull swimmers out to sea.

2 The firefighters carried out an amazing r_____ by pulling people to safety from the roof tops.

3 The use of plastic has had a terrible i_____ on our oceans.

4 I don't like where she lives – there are no neighbours for miles around! It's too i_____ for me.

5 I think we should all use s_____ energy and try to minimise our use of fossil fuels.

/ 5

3 Complete the sentences with the correct forms of the verbs from the box.

avoid install not know not move realise

1 If you hadn't told me, I _____ about the disaster.

2 If only people in the past _____ the damage they were doing to the environment.

3 The house would have been more energy efficient if you _____ solar panels.

4 She _____ getting trapped if she hadn't gone down into the cave alone.

5 I wish you _____ so far away – we hardly ever see each other anymore.

/ 5

4 Use the prompts to write sentences and complete the text.

If only ¹ we / have a house with a garden! If ² my parents / buy a little house with a garden, I ³ can / get a dog. I wish ⁴ my parents / let me have a dog, but they refuse. They say I can have a goldfish. ⁵ I / ask for a goldfish if I'd wanted one!

1 _____   4 _____
2 _____   5 _____
3 _____   / 5

USE OF ENGLISH

5 Choose the correct answers.

I think my local council are making a terrible mistake. They have built a new gym and they are installing traditional oil central heating, but I think they should use ¹_____ and benefit from the earth's heat. If they ²_____ to local architects, they ³_____ about it, and realised that it's perfectly possible. Also, they should have put solar panels on the roof. I wish they ⁴___ about it – it's still not too late. We are using too many harmful energy sources, and that has to stop. We need to use as much ⁵_____ as possible and stop harming the Earth!

1 a geothermal heating   4 a had thought
  b electric energy   b are thinking
  c single-use energy   c would think
2 a listened   5 a recycled material
  b were listening   b sustainable energy
  c had listened   c disposable plastic
3 a would learn
  b would have learned
  c might not learn

/ 5

6 Complete the text with the correct forms of the words in brackets.

The use of single-use containers is becoming very ¹_____ (HARM) as it increases the amount of plastic and paper waste in the environment. Too many people forget to take them to recycling ²_____ (COLLECT) points, and just drop them in the street. If you have to buy ³_____ (REUSE) plates and cups, at least put them in the plastic or paper bins! We get so many ⁴_____ (WARN) from environmental experts about the planet, but not enough of us actually listen. We can start by becoming a little bit more ⁵_____ (THINK) in our behaviour and putting the environment first instead of ourselves.

/ 5
/ 30

111

10 Justice for all

10A GRAMMAR AND VOCABULARY

Modal verbs for speculating about the present

1 ⭐ Read the sentences and write (C) for Certain, (P) for Possible or (I) for Impossible.

1 Ⓒ She must be the judge.
2 ☐ He might be guilty.
3 ☐ They must be very tired now.
4 ☐ The trial could be finishing.
5 ☐ The lawyer may be in the courtroom.
6 ☐ He can't be studying the case.

2 ⭐ Choose the answer, a, b or c, which means the same as the first sentence.

1 I think they could be in the judge's office.
   a I'm certain.
   b I think it's possible.
   c I think it's impossible.
2 He can't be Billy's lawyer – he doesn't even know him!
   a I'm sure he is.
   b I'm not sure.
   c It's not possible.
3 The judge might be listening to the witness now.
   a It's certain.
   b It's possible.
   c It's impossible.
4 She must be a police officer.
   a I'm sure she is.
   b I think it's possible.
   c I'm sure she isn't.
5 This case may be difficult to solve.
   a It's certain.
   b It's a possibility.
   c That's not possible.

3 ⭐ Complete the sentences with *must* or *can't*.

1 That was a long, difficult trial – you *must* be really tired now.
2 She only started reading the notes a minute ago – she _____ be finished already!
3 They were in a different town at the time of the crime – they _____ be guilty.
4 The lawyer looks very satisfied – he _____ have new evidence.
5 He hasn't eaten since the start of the day in court – he _____ be really hungry.
6 She's only nineteen – she _____ be a qualified lawyer.

4 ⭐ Choose the correct verb forms to complete the sentences.

1 Marion can't *know / be knowing* the facts – she wasn't there.
2 The escaped prisoner could *hide / be hiding* near his home town – police are searching there now.
3 The witness might *tell / be telling* the truth, but it's hard to say.
4 She's not answering the phone; she must *work / be working*.
5 I'm not sure where the lawyer is. I suppose she could *have / be having* lunch.
6 The jury have been gone for a long time – they must *discuss / be discussing* the evidence again.
7 The lawyer for the defence may *not have / not be having* time to interview all the witnesses today.
8 The jury must *be / being* exhausted.

5 ⭐⭐ Complete the second sentence in each pair so that it means the same as the first sentence.

1 It's possible that they are lying.
   They might *be lying* (lie).
2 Perhaps he's trying to understand the witness.
   He may _____ (try) to understand the witness.
3 There's a possibility that they are cancelling today's trial.
   They could _____ (cancel) today's trial.
4 I'm not sure if she's studying or not.
   She might _____ (study).
5 Maybe the lawyers are preparing the case.
   The lawyers may _____ the case.

6 ⭐⭐ **Complete the sentences with the correct negative forms of the verbs from the box.**

be have hide know ~~make~~ work

1 They seem a bit depressed about the case – they might *not be making* any progress with it.
2 You can try asking Belinda, but I'm afraid she may _____ the answer.
3 I think Kerry has got appointments all day, so she might _____ time to see you until tomorrow.
4 She may _____ information; perhaps she just doesn't know anything.
5 I haven't seen Yuri yet today – he might _____ here.
6 Rachel left the office – she may _____ this afternoon.

7 ⭐⭐ **Complete the sentences with the correct forms of the verbs in brackets.**

1 The witness *can't be lying* (can/not/lie). He made a promise that he would tell the truth.
2 It's possible that John _____ (might/read) through the documents at home.
3 The case _____ (must/be) fascinating – the courtroom is full of journalists.
4 That witness _____ (might/not/tell) the truth, but it's difficult to say.
5 I know you told the police what you saw, but they _____ (may/not/believe) you.
6 Rebecca is in the canteen – she _____ (could/have) lunch with a colleague.

8 ⭐⭐⭐ **Use the prompts to complete the sentences.**

1 She looks depressed.
could / think / about something sad
She could be thinking about something sad.

2 She hasn't eaten for twenty-four hours.
must / hungry
_____

3 Peter has got a law book in front of him.
must / study
_____

4 She has earphones on.
can / not / listen / to the judge
_____

5 He doesn't look relaxed.
might / be / worry / about his trial
_____

6 They keep looking around them.
may / wait / for someone
_____

7 Jessica isn't answering her phone.
may / discuss / the case / right now
_____

9 ⭐⭐⭐ **Choose the correct verbs forms to complete the newspaper article.**

NEWS FROM THE COURTROOM

The latest news from the courtroom is that the judge is listening to a new witness who [1]*must / might / can't* have new information, but that has not yet been confirmed. However, it [2]*must / could / can't* be important as the judge asked everyone to leave the room. The witness is a young woman, who [3]*must / could / can't* be a suspect as she is free and not under arrest. She [4]*must / may / can't* know the accused as he seemed to recognise her, but we can't be sure about that. If there is dramatic new evidence, the accused must [5]*feel / be feeling / feels* very worried right now.

10 ⭐⭐⭐ **Complete the second conversation so that it has the same meaning as the first. Use between one and three words in each gap.**

Lawyer Please tell us why you are sure the accused is the man you saw.

Witness It's impossible that he's another person. I'm certain!

Lawyer Is it possible that he is a *similar* person? It was dark. Maybe you made a mistake.

Witness The man I saw had dark hair, and this man has dark hair, so they are the same person for sure.

Lawyer Dark hair? Unless you can give me better proof than that, the court will think that you are possibly lying.

Witness But he looks so suspicious. It's impossible that he's telling the truth.

Lawyer Can we call the next witness, please?

• • •

Lawyer Please tell us why according to you the accused [1]*must* be the man you saw.

Witness He [2]_____ be another person. I'm certain!

Lawyer [3]_____ be a *similar* person? It was dark. Maybe you made a mistake.

Witness The man I saw had dark hair, and this man has dark hair, so they [4]_____ same person.

Lawyer Dark hair? Unless you can give me better proof than that, the court will think that you might [5]_____ .

Witness But he looks so suspicious. He [6]_____ the truth.

Lawyer Can we call the next witness, please?

11 ON A HIGH NOTE **Do you think that being a judge is a challenging job? Why/Why not? Write a short paragraph.**

10B VOCABULARY | Law and punishment

1 ⭐ Complete the sentences with the words from the box.

arrest bail caught charged custody ~~security~~ statement warning

1 He didn't escape because he was caught by the police on a _security_ camera.
2 There was a lot of evidence, so he was _____ with the burglary.
3 We decided to go the police station and make a _____ about what we had seen.
4 His crime was not serious, so he was released on _____ until his trial.
5 Detectives managed to _____ the burglar after several months of investigation.
6 The woman was arrested and held in _____ at the police station.
7 The newspaper reported that the police have _____ the thief with the stolen goods.
8 The boy was lucky. The police didn't arrest him – they just gave him a _____.

2 ⭐ Choose the correct prepositions to complete the sentences.

1 She was shocked to discover that she was *under / into* arrest for the crime.
2 The suspect was questioned *by / from* detectives all night.
3 The young woman was released *in / on* bail and she's living at home until her trial.
4 The man was charged *to / with* robbery and vandalism.
5 The drug dealers were held *at / in* custody overnight at the police station.
6 The police know that Mark stole the money because he was caught *from / on* a security camera.

3 ⭐ Match the beginnings 1–7 with the endings a–g.

1 ☐ Because his crime wasn't serious, he was given an electronic
2 ☐ The vandals were told to do community
3 ☐ The murder was brutal, so the killer was given a life
4 ☐ Since it was their first crime, they received a suspended
5 ☐ She parked her car in the wrong place and had to pay
6 ☐ The criminal was sentenced to three years of
7 ☐ Helping the victims of crime is

a imprisonment for his part in the robbery.
b sentence, but didn't go to prison.
c tag to wear and told to keep a curfew.
d part of the prisoners' rehabilitation.
e sentence as the maximum possible punishment.
f a fine of £100.
g service and clean up the area.

4 ⭐⭐ Complete the text with one word in each gap.

When a young person commits a crime, the judge is usually more interested in [1]*rehabilitation* than punishment. They want to help him or her to become a good citizen, so often they don't give an active prison [2]s_____; the judge might prefer to impose a [3]s_____ sentence. If the crime is not very serious, the authorities prefer to avoid prison completely and they might give a number of hours of community [4]s_____ and perhaps a [5]c_____, which would mean that the person can go out during the day, but must be at home in the evening and at night. The police might even decide not to [6]a_____ a teenager at all for a very minor offence, but to give him or her a [7]w_____ instead. For a teenager, having a criminal [8]r_____ has very serious consequences.

5 ⭐⭐ Choose the correct words to complete the text.

When police detectives first suspected the man of committing the bank robbery, they [1]*assaulted / questioned* him carefully, but they didn't arrest him. After five hours, he started to contradict himself, so at that point they [2]*fined / charged* him with the robbery and decided to hold him in [3]*custody / bail*. A short time later, the bank sent a film which clearly caught him on their [4]*security camera / electronic tag*. The judge decided that because the man was guilty, but this was his first offence, that he should be given the chance of [5]*rehabilitation / imprisonment*. He was given a [6]*community / suspended* sentence and he was also told to keep a [7]*curfew / statement service*. The judge decided that some hours of [8]*warning / community service* were also a good idea and for six weeks he will have to work in the local hospital. The man was warned: if he committed another crime, [9]*imprisonment / detectives* would follow.

6 ON A HIGH NOTE Write a short paragraph in answer to these questions.

For which crimes do you think people should
• go to prison?
• do community service?
• have a curfew?
• have an electronic tag?
• be given a warning?

10C GRAMMAR

Modal verbs for speculating about the past

1 ⭐ **Choose the answer, a or b, which means the same as the first sentence.**

1 She might have called the police.
  a I know she called the police.
  b It's possible that she called the police.

2 The burglars must have got in through the bathroom window.
  a I'm certain that they did.
  b It's possible that they did.

3 They can't have stolen very much.
  a I'm sure that's what happened.
  b I don't know if that's what happened.

4 They may have been local people.
  a It's definite that they were.
  b It's possible that they were.

5 They could have known about the flat's contents.
  a I think that might be true.
  b I know that's true.

6 She can't have locked the door properly.
  a From what I can see, that's what happened.
  b I don't really understand what happened.

2 ⭐ **Choose the correct verb forms to complete the sentences.**

1 The window is locked; the burglar *can't have climbed / must have climbed* out of it to get away.

2 The burglars *must know / must have known* that the home-owner had a lot of jewellery.

3 Be careful – the intruders *might not have left / must not have left*. They could still be here!

4 You *can't be / must have been* really shocked when you discovered the burglary.

5 The door *could have been / can't have been* left open, as there's no sign of a violent entry.

6 They haven't taken a lot of things – they *must have had / may not have had* time before the alarm went off.

3 ⭐⭐ **Complete the sentences with the modal verbs in brackets and the negative forms of the verbs from the box.**

get in go leave plan realise ~~see~~

1 He didn't say hello to me.
He *might not have seen* (might) me.

2 We saw the escape two minutes ago.
They _____ (can) very far in two minutes.

3 It was a very unprofessional robbery.
They _____ (may) it very carefully.

4 John heard noises upstairs when he got home.
The burglars _____ (might) the house before he got home.

5 The burglars took a lot of cheap plastic jewellery.
They _____ (can) it was worthless.

6 No one saw them.
They _____ (may) through the front door.

4 ⭐⭐⭐ **Use the prompts to write sentences about the past.**

1 they / can / not / have / break / any windows
They can't have broken any windows.

2 she / might / know / the thief
_____

3 the burglars / must / realise / the house was empty
_____

4 the burglary / may / not / happen / at that time
_____

5 they / might / not / use / a car to get away
_____

5 ⭐⭐⭐ **Complete the newspaper article with the modal verbs in brackets and the correct forms of the verbs from the box. More than one answer might be possible.**

~~be~~ feel go know look lose realise

THE WORST BURGLARS!

Two robbers were so unsuccessful that the police arrested them just one hour after they burgled a house. They made so many mistakes that police believe the robbery **1** *could have been* (could) their first job. First of all, they **2** _____ (can't) there was CCTV on the street. Why? Because they parked outside the house and their number plate was caught on the security camera!

And what did they take from the house? They stole some jewellery which they thought was valuable, but what they **3** _____ (can't) was that the rings were made of plastic! The jewellery **4** _____ (must) like it was real. Also they didn't take a collection of expensive watches which were worth thousands of pounds! The home-owner **5** _____ (could) a lot of money if the thieves had known that the watches were valuable.

As soon as the home-owner got back he phoned the police. 'Hurry,' he told them. 'The thieves **6** _____ (can't) far!' The police searched the area for the thieves' car and found it – outside a café. The thieves **7** _____ (must) hungry after their efforts because they had stopped for a snack!

6 ON A HIGH NOTE **Can you think of a famous unsolved mystery or crime? What do you think happened? Write a short paragraph.**

10D READING AND VOCABULARY

1 You are going to read an article about a crime. Look at the picture and decide which crime the article might be about. Read the article to check.

a a prison escape   **c** a kidnapping
b a burglary

2 Read the article again and for questions 1–8 choose from paragraphs A–D. Each paragraph may be chosen more than once.

Which paragraph

1 ☐ informs us that the men who carried out the robbery were experienced criminals?
2 ☐ implies that nobody knows exactly how much was stolen?
3 ☐ discusses in detail the attraction of this type of crime?
4 ☐ describes the mistake which lead to their arrest?
5 ☐ gives an example of another famous crime which also inspired film producers?
6 ☐ explains why the men were given a particular punishment?
7 ☐ suggests that the men could have prepared better for the robbery?
8 ☐ explains what was unusual about the robbers?

3 Read the article again and answer the questions.

1 What was it about the men that made this story unusual?

_____

2 What did the men steal from the boxes?

_____

3 What did they need to get during the burglary?

_____

4 What item did the police find which helped them to catch the men?

_____

5 What crime were they charged with?

_____

6 What hiding place did the criminals choose for some of the stolen valuables?

_____

Vocabulary extension

4 Complete the sentences with the highlighted words in the text.

1 Police used a _listening device_ to record the criminal's conversations.
2 The robbers were _____ through the wall of the bank when the alarm went off.
3 Boxes with valuable jewels and documents are kept in the underground _____ at the bank.
4 When the police checked the security cameras, they were able to see and identify the thieves' car _____.
5 The police couldn't find any _____ such as finger prints or other clues at the scene of the crime.
6 Perhaps the robbers' age was their _____ because they weren't up to date with the latest technological advances in police procedure.

5 Match the verbs 1–8 from the article with the meanings a–h.

1 ☐ plant
2 ☐ convict (somebody of)
3 ☐ immortalise
4 ☐ set off
5 ☐ crawl
6 ☐ plead guilty
7 ☐ trace
8 ☐ deactivate

a to cause something to start
b to make somebody famous, so that they are always remembered
c to find something by following clues/information/etc.
d to stop an electric/electronic device from working
e to officially find somebody guilty of a crime
f to put something in a person's car/house/etc. without their knowledge
g to admit to the court that you committed a crime
h to move forward on your hands and knees

ACTIVE VOCABULARY | Suffixes *-ion* and *-tion*

We can add the suffix *-ion* or *-tion* to a verb to create the noun form, e.g.

• attract → attraction

Sometimes we remove the *-e* at the end of the verb and add *-ion*, e.g.

• fascinate → fascination

Some verbs make other changes and these do not always follow a pattern, e.g.

• receive → reception
• produce → production

6 Complete the sentences with the correct noun forms of the verbs in brackets.

1 The examiner gives the students marks for their _interaction_ (interact) in the speaking task.
2 The _____ (describe) of the criminal given on the news said that he was tall and fair-haired.
3 I have a lot of _____ (admire) for the hard work that the police do.
4 It wasn't my _____ (intend) to cause any problems.
5 I need to get a _____ (prescribe) from the doctor and then I'll be home.
6 The police use advanced facial _____ (recognise) techniques to identify people in crowd photographs.

7 ON A HIGH NOTE Write a post for a forum giving your opinion about whether or not films should immortalise criminals by making them appear to be heroes.

From court
TO SCREEN

A Crime dramas on TV and in films have always been very popular, but they seem to attract an even bigger audience when they are based on true life crimes. This was certainly true when the film *The King of Thieves* was released in 2018. In addition to starring some of the UK's most popular actors, the film also tells a remarkable story. In 2015, four men planned and carried out a burglary at the Hatton Garden Safe Deposit Company, stealing what could have been between £14 and £200 million worth of valuable items from seventy-three boxes. Robberies and burglaries involving large amounts of money are not, in themselves, always great stories for the big screen. This burglary, however, became very famous for a different reason. Three of the four men were pensioners – in their 60s and 70s!

B These men were 'career criminals' and they had committed many burglaries over the course of their lifetimes. The Hatton Garden robbery was supposed to be their final job. They spent three years planning the attack on the vault of the Safe Deposit Company, which held boxes containing cash, gold and jewels. They chose a long holiday weekend in April 2015 when there would be no staff at the building. They had several days to break in. One reason for choosing this time might have been that they didn't want to use force, threats or injure innocent people. Another reason could be that they weren't as physically strong as they used to be and needed as much time as they could get! This was a very old-fashioned crime. It involved drilling through an underground concrete wall fifty centimetres thick to create a hole big enough to crawl through. But the plan didn't go smoothly! The thieves had to take a break at one point in order to get better equipment for the drilling. Another problem they had was that they set off the alarm before one of the team was able to deactivate it. Security guards came to check out the alarm, but luckily for the thieves, they couldn't see anything wrong and went away again.

C However, in the end it was modern technology that was their downfall. They had learned a lot about forensic evidence and they didn't leave anything behind to help the police. However, they weren't aware of the latest advances in CCTV security cameras and number plate recognition. The police noticed their car parked in the area, traced it and planted a listening device inside it. The criminals were heard discussing the crime and how the money was going to be divided. They were arrested a month later, charged and all four of the main team pleaded guilty. In 2016, they were convicted of burglary and sentenced to prison. Several people who helped them were also convicted, although two thirds of the money stolen has never been found. The sentences they received were much shorter than they would have been because the men used no weapons during the crime. This meant that they were charged with burglary and not robbery – a crime which carries a much longer prison sentence.

D Of course, the story made headlines and the film companies were soon planning their versions of the crime. It had all the ingredients of a sensational drama. The public love stories about criminals who take risks, steal lots of money but do not hurt anyone. These criminals had the extra appeal of being old as well as brave. And details such as hiding the valuables in a relative's grave only made the story more interesting. The idea of immortalising daring criminals in film is not new. The Hatton Garden job is believed to be the biggest theft in English legal history. However, another crime, known as 'The Great Train Robbery' which happened in 1963 led to more than forty books and a large number of movies and TV dramas. The public fascination with true life crime of this type is unlikely to fade.

10E SPEAKING

1 🔊 *78* Listen and repeat the phrases. How do you say them in your language?

SPEAKING | Comparing and contrasting photographs

DESCRIBE SIMILARITIES AND DIFFERENCES

Both pictures show crime scenes.

There are police officers **in both pictures**.

This one is in the street, **whereas the other one is** outside.

They are also alike in that they were both taken at the police station.

They are also different in that one was taken at the police station and the other one outside the police station.

In one respect they are similar because both show victims of an accident.

In one respect they are different because one shows a victim of an accident, and the other one a police officer.

The main/The most striking/Another obvious similarity is that both pictures show houses that have been burgled.

The main /The most striking/Another obvious difference is that one picture shows a house and the other one a shop.

SPECULATE

Perhaps/Maybe the burglars didn't have time to take everything.

It could be/might be/must be the girl's car.

This one looks/doesn't look as if it was taken from outside.

There might/might not have been another person there.

Someone must have taken this photo because they were shocked by the scene.

---

2 Complete the sentences with one word in each gap.

1 Both pictures *show* people protesting in different situations.

2 The two pictures are _____ in that they were both taken in city centres.

3 The most _____ similarity is that the pictures are both of juries in courtrooms.

4 There are policemen in _____ pictures.

5 In one _____ they are different because the policemen are clearly from different countries.

6 The first picture is of a policeman arresting a woman _____ the other one is of a policeman talking to two men.

3 Choose the correct words to complete the sentences.

1 The man *could / must* be about to steal something from the shop, but I don't know.

2 Someone *must take / must have taken* this photo because they thought the man was acting suspiciously.

3 There might not have *had / been* any security cameras inside the shop.

4 This picture doesn't look *as / like* if it was taken by a professional photographer.

5 *Maybe / Might* the person in this photo is a police detective, I'm not sure.

4 🔊 *79* Complete the conversation with a word or phrase in each gap. Listen and check.

Josh ¹*Both* pictures show crime scenes.

Kelly Yes, you're right. Because ²_____ broken glass in both pictures.

Josh They're ³_____ somebody – a thief or a burglar – has broken in and stolen things – from both places.

Kelly Yes, but ⁴_____ one is the inside of a house – somebody's home – and the ⁵_____ one is a shop.

Josh ⁶_____ it's a jeweller's – I can see some watches and necklaces in the window.

Kelly The thieves ⁷_____ have been disturbed though because otherwise they would have taken those things too.

Josh Yes, but the house looks ⁸_____ there's nothing left! The burglars have taken everything!

Kelly In that ⁹_____ the two situations are different. I think it must ¹⁰_____ much worse to have thieves in your home – you know – your personal space.

Josh Yes, I agree.

5 Look at the two photos and follow the instructions.

A

B

1 Write one sentence mentioning the similarities between the two photos.

_____

_____

2 Write two sentences mentioning the differences between the two photos.

_____

_____

3 Write two sentences speculating about the photos.

_____

_____

10F LISTENING AND VOCABULARY

1 Complete the sentences with the words from the box.

argue   certainly   ~~findings~~   might   show   survey

1 ☐ *Findings* confirm that young people today are very politically aware.
2 ☐ I would _____ that young people should be able to vote on what affects them directly.
3 ☐ There will almost _____ be a high turnout for the next general election.
4 ☐ The government _____ hold another referendum on the issue early next year.
5 ☐ According to a recent _____, more people are becoming bored with politics.
6 ☐ Statistics _____ that people would welcome more information before an election.

2 Read the sentences in Exercise 1 again. Write (F) for Fact, (O) for Opinion or (S) for Speculation.

3 🔊 80 Listen to an interview with Lara, a member of the National Youth Parliament, and choose the correct answer.

What is Lara doing in her interview?
a Encouraging people to vote for her in an election.
b Describing the policies the organisation have developed.
c Explaining the operation of the organisation.
d Advertising a campaign she is involved in.

4 🔊 80 Listen to the interview again and complete each gap with one or two words.

1 The members are aged between eleven and *eighteen*.
2 The NYP has _____ members.
3 Each MYP represents the young people from one _____.
4 The NYP has a four-day meeting every _____.
5 At this long meeting they create a _____ .
6 The NYP have a big debate once a year in the _____ Parliament.
7 Lara thinks she has become a more _____ person as a result of being an MYP.
8 One of this year's campaigns is to get cheaper _____.

Vocabulary extension

5 Choose the correct verbs, which you heard in the recording, to complete the sentences.

1 Our class is *managing / holding* a debate.
2 One of my former teachers is *putting / standing* for election to parliament next month.
3 Some politicians *make / do* a lot of good for their local communities.
4 She is taking part in a campaign to *raise / lift* awareness of the importance of sport for disabled people.
5 What *concerns / confirms* me is that more and more people are suffering from mental health problems.
6 Our debating club discusses issues *involving / ranging* from animal rights to youth crime.
7 The local community is *campaigning / defending* to have cars banned from the centre of the village.

Pronunciation

6 🔊 81 Look at these words from the listening containing the letter *s*. How is *s* pronounced in each word? Listen and repeat.

1 /s/ politic**s**
2 /ʒ/ deci**s**ion
3 /z/ politician**s**
4 /ʃ/ i**ss**ues

ACTIVE PRONUNCIATION | The letter *s*

The letter *s* can be pronounced in many different ways e.g. /s/ *looks*, /ʒ/ *television*, /z/ *his*, /ʃ/ *sugar*

When we use *s* at the end of a plural noun or as a third person singular ending, it can have three possible sounds:
• /s/ after an unvoiced consonant (e.g. *waits*)
• /z/ after a voiced consonant (e.g. *doors*)
• /ɪz/ after /ʃ/, /tʃ/ or /s/ (e.g. *washes, watches, misses*)

Double *ss* can be pronounced /s/ (e.g. *missing*) or /ʃ/ (e.g. *passion*).

---

7 🔊 82 Write the third person singular form of the verbs. Then circle the final sound of the verb forms. Listen, check and repeat.

1 hit ____   /s/ /z/ /ɪz/
2 choose ____   /s/ /z/ /ɪz/
3 feed ____   /s/ /z/ /ɪz/
4 rush ____   /s/ /z/ /ɪz/
5 seem ____   /s/ /z/ /ɪz/
6 stop ____   /s/ /z/ /ɪz/
7 kiss ____   /s/ /z/ /ɪz/
8 touch ____   /s/ /z/ /ɪz/
9 make ____   /s/ /z/ /ɪz/
10 kick ____   /s/ /z/ /ɪz/

8 🔊 83 Find one word in each group of words which has a different sound for the letter *s* from the others. Listen, check and repeat.

1 concerns   raise   this   lose
2 mission   reassure   measure   tissue
3 system   projects   loss   insure
4 thanks   represent   woods   organise

9 🔊 84 Practise saying these sentences from the listening. Listen and check.

1 We develop policies regarding these topics and include them in a manifesto – a statement of our views if you like.
2 We organise projects and campaigns to raise people's awareness of important issues.
3 It takes place over four days and we have speakers from the world of politics as well as important decision-makers.
4 I think it's that I've learned to see things from other people's point of view – not just my own.

UNIT VOCABULARY PRACTICE > page 121

10G **WRITING** | A formal letter

Use an appropriate greeting.	Dear Mr Barker,
Explain why you are writing.	I am writing on behalf of our group 'Students against Crime' which is made up of student representatives from all Year 11 classes. We would like to organise a 'Crime Education Day' at our school.
Use full forms and not contractions.	First of all, I should point out that our group is different from the 'Crime Awareness group' that contacted you last year. We appreciate all the hard work that this group did, but their focus was on measures like getting better security for bikes, etc. Our aim is to educate people more about the problems that lead to crime and the help that is available.
Indicate the main points.	We do not support the opinion that crime in certain areas is inevitable. For example, it is often thought that if a person lives in a community where there is a gang culture, that person will end up in a gang. We firmly believe that people can profit from learning about the consequences of crime and being encouraged to participate in certain projects.
State your opinion and give examples to support your view.	Secondly, I would like to explain what this Crime Education Day would involve. We would invite a range of speakers to talk to students, including an ex-prisoner, a volunteer community worker and the leaders of two social integration projects. These projects are shown to have helped the teenagers considerably and the rate of re-offending has decreased. We propose that this Education Day takes place at a weekend, probably on a Saturday in February.
Use impersonal structures and more complex vocabulary.	
Include suggestions.	To sum up, we would like to have your support for this Education Day and request funding to cover the cost of accommodating our visiting speakers. We really believe that the day would be a success.
Use an appropriate closing phrase.	Yours sincerely, Blake Harwood

1 Read Blake's letter. What is his aim in writing to the head teacher?

2 Complete the phrases with the words from the box.

all completely considered ~~express~~ favour fully
highlight option response sum

Explain why you are writing
I am writing to **1** _express_ my disappointment …
I am writing in **2** _____ to …

Divide the letter into clear sections
First of **3** _____ I would like to …
Secondly, I should point out that …
To **4** _____ up I would say that …
All things **5** _____, the best option …

State your opinion
I **6** _____ disagree with …
I am totally in **7** _____ of …
We **8** _____ support your idea to …
I do not support the opinion that …

Include suggestions
I propose that …
I would like to **9** _____ some ways to …
Perhaps … would be an interesting **10** _____ …

3 WRITING TASK Blake's letter was an answer to the task below. Read the task and write your own formal letter.

You are part of a group that wants to arrange a school event to help increase awareness of crime issues. Write a letter to your Head Teacher in which you:

- say how you differ from a previous group who tried to do something similar.
- outline your ideas and explain what help you need from the school.

ACTIVE WRITING | A formal letter

1 Plan your formal letter.
- Make a note of your ideas for both points in the task.
- Divide the notes into paragraphs.

2 Write your formal letter.
- Use full forms (not contractions or abbreviations).
- Use appropriate greeting and closing phrases.

3 Check your letter. Check that:
- there are no spelling, grammar or punctuation mistakes.
- you have used complex vocabulary and impersonal structures.

1 10A GRAMMAR AND VOCABULARY **Match the phrases 1–8 with their definitions a–h.**

1 ☐ the accused
2 ☐ the courtroom
3 ☐ the judge
4 ☐ the jury
5 ☐ the lawyer for the defence
6 ☐ the lawyer for the prosecution
7 ☐ a police detective
8 ☐ a witness

a twelve members of the public who give the final verdict
b the legal professional who argues that the suspect is innocent
c the person suspected of having committed a crime
d a person who has seen the crime
e the place where trials take place
f the person who is in charge of the trial and decides the sentence
g the legal professional who argues that the suspect is guilty
h a senior police officer who investigates crime

2 **Choose the correct words to complete the sentences.**

1 I hope you realise that you are *accused / innocent* of a very serious crime.
2 She needs to find a good lawyer to *defend / sentence* her husband at the trial.
3 There is *verdict / evidence* which proves that he was at the scene of the crime.
4 It's obvious that she is *evidence / innocent* – she wasn't even in the country at the time of the crime!
5 There's a lot of interest in this *jury / trial* because the accused is a famous footballer.
6 The jury is discussing their *witness / verdict* now, but I'm sure they will find Carl innocent.
7 The woman was found *guilty / accused* because her fingerprints were found at the scene of the crime.
8 The judge must consider many different aspects of the case before he or she *sentences / charges* a guilty person.

3 10B VOCABULARY **Complete the sentences with one word in each gap.**

1 The girls were given a *warning* about their noisy behaviour.
2 The suspect was thoroughly _____ by detectives for several hours.
3 The witness made a _____ to the police with details of what she had seen.
4 Since the crime wasn't serious he was released on _____ to wait for the trial.
5 Two people are _____ arrest for an attack yesterday in the town centre.
6 Police are holding someone in _____ at the police station in connection with the burglary.

4 **Complete the sentences with the words and phrases from the box.**

community service   curfew   electronic tag   fine
life sentence   rehabilitation   suspended sentence

1 I had to pay a(n) *fine* because I parked on a double yellow lines.
2 It was very hard for him to accept his _____ and the idea that he would never be free again.
3 She had to wear a(n) _____ on her ankle.
4 The boys were ordered to carry out _____ and from next week they will be cleaning up the local park.
5 They were very lucky to get a _____ and not be sent to prison.
6 The aim of the educational programme is the _____ of the prisoners.
7 Part of Simon's punishment is a(n) _____; he's not allowed to leave his house after six o'clock in the evening or before eight in the morning.

5 10D READING AND VOCABULARY **Complete the sentences with one preposition in each gap.**

1 The witness came *forward* with some important new information.
2 The burglars made _____ with a lot of jewellery.
3 We asked the police to look _____ the problem of vandalism in our street.
4 They are a very violent gang and have already beaten _____ several people.
5 The murderer turned _____ his accomplice.
6 We saw the burglar coming out of the window of our neighbour's house and chased _____ him.
7 They hoped to get _____ with the robbery, but they were caught and arrested.

6 10F LISTENING AND VOCABULARY **Complete the sentences with the words from the box.**

general election   opinion polls   parliament
referendum   turnout   voting age

1 Many young people would like to see the *voting age* reduced from eighteen to seventeen.
2 The latest _____ show that the opposition party is ahead of the government party by three percent.
3 Who will you vote for in the next _____?
4 In 2016, the British people voted in a _____ as to whether or not they wished their country to remain a member of the European Union.
5 How many representatives are there in your country's _____?
6 Unfortunately, there was a very low _____ in yesterday's election, with only forty eight percent of people coming out to vote.

7 ON A HIGH NOTE **Do you think that eighteen is the right age to start doing some things legally (e.g. drive, vote)? Should young people be able to do some things earlier? Write a short paragraph explaining your views.**

1 For each learning objective, write 1–5 to assess your ability.

1 = I don't feel confident. 5 = I feel very confident.

	Learning objective	Course material	How confident I am (1–5)
10A	I can use modal verbs to speculate about the present.	Student's Book pp. 138–139	
10B	I can talk about law and punishment.	Student's Book p. 140	
10C	I can use modal verbs to speculate about the past.	Student's Book p. 141	
10D	I can identify specific details in a text and talk about breaking the law.	Student's Book pp. 142–143	
10E	I can compare, contrast and speculate about the contents of photos.	Student's Book p. 144	
10F	I can tell the difference between a fact, an opinion and a speculation in a radio discussion and talk about voting.	Student's Book p. 145	
10G	I can write a formal letter.	Student's Book pp. 146–147	

2 Which of the skills above would you like to improve in? How?

Skill I want to improve in	How I can improve

3 What can you remember from this unit?

New words I learned and most want to remember	Expressions and phrases I liked	English I heard or read outside class

GRAMMAR AND VOCABULARY

1 Complete the sentences with one word in each gap.

1 The young man was held in c_____ for three hours before his lawyer arrived at the police station.

2 They weren't arrested – luckily they just got a w_____.

3 He committed a very violent crime and received a l_____ sentence.

4 Look at that! That girl took a bike and m_____ off with it! No one stopped her!

5 The t_____ in presidential elections was really high.

/ 5

2 Choose the correct answers.

1 During the _____ the judge listened carefully to all the lawyers and witnesses.
  a courtroom
  b trial
  c verdict

2 The detectives _____ the suspect for hours before he finally confessed.
  a accused
  b defended
  c questioned

3 The vandals received fifty hours of community _____ from the judge.
  a service
  b sentence
  c statement

4 They didn't manage to get _____ with the robbery – the police caught them.
  a off
  b forward
  c away

5 Women's suffrage is the right of women to _____ in elections.
  a charge
  b concern
  c vote

/ 5

3 Use the prompts to write sentences.

1 He seems to know them. he / might / be / involved with the gang.

_____

2 The police didn't question her. she / can / not / have / any useful information.

_____

3 It's one o'clock. they / must / have / lunch / now

_____

4 No car was seen. the burglars / could / get / away on a motorbike

_____

5 They didn't cover their faces. they / might / not / know / about the security camera

_____

/ 5

4 Complete the sentences with the modal verbs in brackets and the correct forms of the verbs from the box.

be (x2) feel have interview

> The accused **1**_____ (must) unwell because she fainted in court yesterday. I suppose I can understand that - the trial **2**_____ (must) very stressful for her. She continues to say she's innocent and that her lawyer **3**_____ (can't) the right witnesses. But it **4**_____ (might not) their turn now. Perhaps her lawyer is going to present them soon. He seems confident. He **5**_____ (could) some good news.

/ 5

USE OF ENGLISH

5 Complete the second sentence so that it has a similar meaning to the first one. Use between two and five words, including the word in bold.

1 It's possible that she's studying for her History exam. **MIGHT**
She _____ for her History exam.

2 It's impossible that you saw Jim – he's in Paris! **CAN'T**
You _____ Jim – he's in Paris!

3 I'm sure you were terrified! **MUST**
You _____ terrified!

4 He went to prison for the rest of his life as a punishment for his crime. **LIFE**
He received _____ as a punishment for his crime.

5 The police told her not to do it again. **WARNING**
The police _____ not to do it again.

/ 5

6 Complete the conversation with one word in each gap.

Terry Everyone thinks the suspect is guilty, but it can't **1**_____ been him who burgled the house!

Ed Why? The police found him there with a bag of jewels! It **2**_____ have been him. It's obvious.

Terry Yes, but did you read that the jewels were not the ones stolen from the house? He's going to trial and risks a prison **3**_____ for something that isn't definite.

Ed Well, I'm sure his **4**_____ lawyer will mention that in court. The people on the **5**_____ have to listen to the lawyers and witnesses before deciding the verdict.

/ 5

/ 30

PHRASAL VERBS

ask out: Do you think I should ask him out on a date?

be off to: I'm off to make some dinner.

beat up: How should society punish a child who beats somebody up?

boss around: He bosses me around and makes fun of me.

break into: The thief broke into their school during lunch break.

break up with: I've been feeling down since Tricia broke up with me.

build up: Lift weights and build up your muscles in our centre.

burn down: A shop in your street is burning down.

calm down: I was annoyed and my sister told me to calm down.

carry on: Thankfully, it wasn't serious so she decided to carry on.

carry out: So far, we've carried out three experiments.

catch up on: I have a lot of reading to catch up on.

cheer on: The crowd cheered the athletes on to win.

chill out: Stop being so stressed and just chill out!

come forward with: She hoped that someone would come forward with information about the stolen bike.

come round: What time are you going to come round to my house?

come up: I'm off to the library now. Got an exam coming up soon.

come up with: Have you come up with any good ideas?

cover for: If they ask you a question, I'll cover for you.

cut down: Cycling helps cut down pollution.

deal with: I find it easy to deal with many tasks.

dispose of: Sort your rubbish, then dispose of It In the recycling bins.

do with(out):   I could do with losing a kilo or two!

drop in: Why don't you drop in for a coffee later?

drop out: Sadly, a lot of teenagers drop out of college.

fall behind: You're going to fall behind if you miss any more classes.

fall down: Snow, ice and rocks fall down a mountainside.

fall for: They'll fall for it. But if you talk, they'll know you're lying.

fall out with: He often falls out with his sister because they've got very different personalities.

feel down: I've been feeling down since Tricia broke up with me.

figure out: Fifty-two percent of Americans believe doing their taxes is easier than figuring out how to follow a healthy diet.

find out: I'd like to find out more about the college by going to their open day.

get around: After the accident, he had to get around on crutches.

get away with: He got away with the crime and was never arrested.

get by: I don't consider myself rich, but I get by.

get down to: We'd better stop chatting and get down to work.

get dressed up: The girls are getting dressed up for the evening.

get into: She's started to get into healthy eating.

get on: How did you get on in your English exam?

get out: From nowhere, a lifeguard ran past her at full speed, shouting at people to get out of the way.

get together: We usually get together with friends at the weekend.

get up: I have to get up early on weekdays.

give away: The club is giving away one month's free membership to anyone who joins this week.

give up: What do you think of giving up our phones for a week?

give way (to):   Cyclists should always give way to pedestrians.

go away: My parents are going away for the weekend.

go on about (sth):   You know we can't afford a holiday in Florida so stop going on about it!

go on: These days you've got to be switched on all the time or you don't know what's going on.

go out: My boyfriend says we're in a serious relationship, but we've only just started going out!

go out with: I'd be heartbroken if she refused to go out with me.

go over: I need to go over my notes from today's lesson.

hand in: Please hand in your essay to the teacher at the end of the lesson.

head off: Grab the opportunity and, head off with your family on holiday.

hear from: I am really looking forward to hearing from you soon.

hold onto: If Maria hadn't held onto a tree, she might have drowned.

join in: Why don't you join in our game?

keep up with: The work isn't difficult and I'm able to keep up with the other students quite easily.

knock down: The girl was knocked down by a speeding car.

knock out: I love music and I could knock out some tunes in the evening.

knock over: Someone knocked me over on the ski slope.

leave behind: Leave your umbrella behind – it isn't raining.

let down: She makes lots of promises, but she always lets me down.

look after: You should look after your health by eating a balanced diet and getting plenty of exercise.

look back: A major publisher took it on and I haven't looked back since.

look down on: We tend to look down on people who dress badly.

look for: We looked for the missing earrings, but couldn't find them.

look into: Would the police in your country look into a minor crime such as bike theft?

look up to: I always looked up to my History teacher – he was such an inspiration.

make off with: The car thieves made off with six vehicles in one night.

make sth up: I'll make something up. I know! I'll say you've lost your voice.

make up with: After I fall out with someone, I'm usually the first one to try to make up again.

pay off: His dedication paid off when he managed to do a back flip.

pick up: I tend to pick up languages easily.

point out: I would like to point out that we have already wasted a lot of time and money.

put off: Don't put off your exam revision any longer – you've only got two days left!

put together: Two of my classmates put together a great presentation on the Amazon rainforest.

put up: I saw that more posters were being put up in the corridors.

put up with: I can't put up with his behaviour anymore.

read on: Read on to learn the rest of the story.

read up: She likes to read up on the country she's going to visit.

run out of: I've run out of money.

run over: A drunk driver runs over a man and seriously injures him.

send out: The lyrics of their rap send out their message loud and clear.

set off: What time do you set off?

set up: She set up a fashion blog called Engineering In Style.

settle into: After settling into my B&B, I walked around the island.

sit up: Everyone on the beach sat up and watched.

sort out: There was a problem with our website, but we've sorted it out.

speed up: Experts have proposed that we speed up research on safety.

split up: What's the best way to tell a boyfriend that you want to split up?

start out: Aaron started out as an amateur athlete.

stay in: Let's stay in. It's raining.

stay out of: Stay out of the cafeteria. It's extremely noisy.

stop off: Are you stopping off somewhere on the way?

sum up: Let's sum up everything we've talked about in the meeting.

switch on/off: I remembered to switch off my computer.

take off: The project really took off after it was shared on social media.

take out: Have you ever taken money out of an ATM?

take over: Are super-intelligent machines going to take over the world?

think ahead: It's important to think ahead before you take your final decision.

throw away: Please throw away all these old papers.

throw out: They were going to throw me out of college.

tick off: Consult our tips and tick off the items on your packing list.

turn around: It's only been ten minutes, so we can still turn the plane around.

turn back: We turned back and eventually found the castle.

turn in: She decided not to turn him in to the police.

turn into: The company turns unused land into farms and gardens.

turn out: What had seemed like a terrible idea, turned out to be a memorable experience.

turn over: She turned over to get some sun on her back.

wake up: If they want a lie-in, be careful not to wake them up too early.

warm up: Jackie pulled a muscle in her leg because she didn't warm up.

write back: Write back soon, please, because I really need to confirm our holiday plans.

PREPOSITIONS

PREPOSITIONS IN PHRASES

AS

as a result: It was clear that the children liked working with me, and as a result I felt more confident.

as for: As for food, could you confirm there are vegetarian options available during the expedition?

as long as: As long as I trust someone, I'm comfortable asking for personal advice.

as soon as: As soon as I see my best friend, I know how he or she is feeling.

AT

at a (bit of a) loss: I'm at a bit of a loss as to what they want. They're not clear about their intentions.

at first sight: I've fallen in love with a girl. It was love at first sight.

at risk from: Which jobs do you think are most at risk from automation?

at the same time: Too much screen time is bad, but at the same time these days you've got to be switched on all the time.

at the moment: Which clothes are the most fashionable for young people at the moment?

FOR

for ages: I hadn't watched the TV news for ages.

for sure: You've made the right decision for sure.

IN

in case of: I've got a little first aid kit in case of minor injuries.

in cash: Do your parents usually pay in cash?

in danger (of): The bald eagle is not in danger of extinction.

in favour of: Why is Maya in favour of advertising in schools?

in the end: In the end, we decided to cancel the holiday because Dad wasn't well.

in the red: He's got huge debts and his company is in the red.

in touch with: I'm still in touch with some of the teenagers I met on our family holiday.

in trouble: You'll be in trouble if you lose Mum's tablet.

in two minds (about sth): I'm in two minds about this – I really don't know what to do.

ON

on foot: Let's not get a taxi. It's quicker to go on foot.

on trial: She's on trial for kidnapping.

OUT

out of breath: I get out of breath when I run for the bus!

out of fashion: Those jeans are going out of fashion now.

out of shape: At first, I was totally out of shape, but I'm fitter now.

UNDER

under arrest: He's under arrest for attacking a woman.

PREPOSITIONS AFTER NOUNS

(dis)agreement about: There are disagreements about when artificial intelligence might become a reality.

access to: Have you ever spent a weekend without access to the Internet?

advice on: Can you give me some advice on saving money?

comment on: The film was meant to be a comment on corruption in Italy in the 1980s.

cost of: The cost of living has risen sharply in the last two years.

crime against: It's a crime against the environment to use a car.

demand for: There will probably be less demand for secretaries.

difference between: Will we be able to tell the difference between a human and a machine?

evidence of: It provides evidence of relevant skills and achievements.

example of: It is easier to recognise classic examples of fine art than of modern art.

impact on: We all need to consider living a greener lifestyle so that we minimise our impact on the environment.

lack of: Lack of sleep means you feel stressed and depressed and find it harder to concentrate.

mixture of: Smog is a mixture of smoke and fog.

north/south/east/west of: Oregon is the ninth largest state in the USA. It is north of California.

relationship between: What's the relationship between Sian and Louis?

source of: When I finish studying, I'd rather have two part-time jobs to have two sources of income.

support for: She wanted to express her organisation's support for a change in European election laws.

thanks to: Thanks to your contribution, the project will now be able to go ahead.

PREPOSITIONS AFTER ADJECTIVES

acceptable to: Should you always tell the truth or is it sometimes acceptable to lie?

afraid of: Do we have to fly so high? My wife's afraid of heights.

annoyed about: I was annoyed about something and my sister told me to calm down.

bad/good at: Millennials may have more distractions, but we're also way better at multi-tasking.

careful with: Please be careful with that book as it's an antique.

concerned about: He's concerned about his daughter's behaviour.

crazy about sb: It was love at first sight. I'm crazy about her.

determined to: He was determined to succeed, so he tried again.

eager to: Harold is eager to learn more about astronomy.

excited about: I'm really excited about starting college next year.

exposed to: Astronauts in space are exposed to radiation from the sun.

free from: Why can't schools be kept free from adverts?

full of: Junk food is full of salt, sugar and fat.

high/low in: Try eating foods which are high in fibre.

honest with: She can't always tell if people are being honest with her.

impressed by: Teenage visitors were impressed by many of the sophisticated and occasionally shocking works of art.

impressed with: She's impressed with what they do.

keen on: We're not keen on the idea of advertising in schools.

likely to: People who enjoy doing crosswords are more likely to maintain a healthy brain.

nervous about: When I'm nervous about something, I start sweating.

proud of: Let's build a more sustainable world together so that future generations can be proud of us.

satisfied with: I'm not satisfied with this laptop.

suitable for: I am not sure which expedition would be most suitable for me.

suspicious of: You should be suspicious of anyone who seems over-friendly.

willing to: I would be willing to travel in a drone taxi if it is possible in the future.

PREPOSITIONS AFTER VERBS

agree/disagree on sth: My parents and I disagree strongly on several important issues.

agree/disagree with sb: I'm not sure I agree with you.

allow (sb) to: Should sixteen-year-olds be allowed to take their driving test?

apply to: I don't know how to proceed with applying to university.

attempt to: We will attempt to beat the world record.

be against: Why is he against advertising in schools?

belong to: This house belongs to my mother.

call for: Could he have rescued his sons if they hadn't called for help?

care about: They say that girls care more about clothes than boys.

chase after: What are the dangers of chasing after someone who has just picked your pocket?

compete in: He said that about fifty dogs were competing in this year's championships.

complain about: If people don't vote in a general election, they shouldn't complain about the government.

connect with: Are these artists revealing their inner-thoughts and connecting with others?

contribute to: Thanks to all the volunteers who contributed to today's event.

PREPOSITIONS

cope with: If I lived alone, I don't think I'd be able to cope with the loneliness.

date from: The first online sale dates from 1994.

decide to: I decided to wear trainers and a T-shirt with my suit.

depend on: It depends on the individual artist.

donate to: She often donates money to charity.

dream of sth: I often dream of leaving my busy life and going to live in the countryside.

dress up as: Nobody is dressed up as a super hero at tonight's party.

drop to: By the 1960s, the population of the island had dropped to only four people.

emerge from: As they emerged from the ruins, the people cheered.

encourage (sb) to: They encouraged me to eat a healthy diet.

end in: I would never buy a lottery ticket because it is almost certain to end in disappointment.

enquire about: I am writing to enquire about the climbing expedition.

exchange for: I wonder if you could exchange these shoes for another pair?

fill with: It was filled with empty bottles and party decorations.

focus on: The movie focuses on the refugees in Italy.

gaze into: Trent gazed into her eyes.

glance at: He glanced quickly at the newspaper headlines.

go up/down: The price will go up before Christmas.

head for: We're heading for the top of that mountain over there.

head towards: Are we heading towards a cash-free society where all payments are made electronically?

insist on: Would you let them have a party? What conditions would you insist on?

interact with: Recent developments in AI have altered the way we interact with our electronic devices.

invite sb to sth: When my parents invited me to join them on holiday, I wasn't sure whether or not to go.

laugh at sth/sb: If I complain, he just laughs at me and insults me.

lead to: Remember that having a crush on someone doesn't always lead to a serious relationship.

lie about sth to sb: If you lied about where you got the money, would your friends and family believe you?

live without: Lots of young people today just can't live without their phones.

manage to: As long as the first and last letters of words are in the right place, most people still manage to read them.

move into: Trent and Freya moved into an apartment.

pay for: The money from ads is needed to pay for facilities like computers for the library.

play for: I play for a successful football team.

plug in: Take an adapter with you in case you can't plug in to charge your devices.

pour out: Hot gases pour out of the top of a mountain and lava covers the earth.

prefer to: I prefer to dress casually.

prepare for: What do children in Japan do to prepare for earthquakes?

proceed with: We will now proceed with the experiment.

qualify for: Katie Ormerod is a world-class snowboarder who qualified for the British Winter Olympic team.

queue up for: It's silly to spend hours queuing up for limited edition clothes or shoes.

save for: I'm saving for a holiday.

share sth with sb: There are many other important questions about a world shared with artificially intelligent beings.

spend on: The average US family spends nearly $1,000 per child on clothing.

stare at: Stop staring at that screen!

suffer from: I think she's starting to suffer from memory loss.

swap sth for sth: Swap junk food high in calories for natural food full of vitamins.

talk about: We're going to talk about the importance of accepting one's body shape.

tend to: These reports tend to be human interest stories.

think about: I've been thinking about our Physics project.

think of: What do you think of Hilary's prom dress?

upload to: Upload some videos to your own YouTube channel.

volunteer to: You could volunteer to do some shopping for a neighbour.

vote on: The students will vote on important issues during their elections.

wait for: Everyone is waiting for their exam results.

work for: My neighbour says she works for the police, but she doesn't wear a uniform.

work on: He would really like to work on a nature project.

worry about: Don't worry about your exams – I'm sure you'll pass.

WORD BUILDING

PREFIXES

Prefix	Examples
co- (= with, together)	coordination, co-pilot
inter- (= between)	international, Internet
multi- (= many)	multi-tasking
re- (= again)	rehabilitation, reuse
self- (= me)	self-employed, self-motivated

Prefixes that give an opposite meaning

Prefix	Examples
dis-	disabled, disagree
im-	impatient, impossible
ir-	irrelevant, irresponsible
non-	non-profit, non-existent
un-	unconscious, unfinished

SUFFIXES

Noun suffixes

Suffix	Examples
-ment	development, equipment
-tion/-sion	preparation, discussion
-ation/-ition	communication, definition
-ence/-ance	appearance, influence
-ty/-ity	activity, reality
-ness	fitness, goodness
-ing	meaning, revising
-al	proposal
-age	average, message
-sis	analysis, crisis
-ure	pressure, procedure
-hood	neighbourhood
-dom	freedom
-er/-or	author, voyager
-ist	artist, dentist
-ant/-ent	assistant, president
-cian/-ian	musician, pedestrian

Adjective suffixes

Suffix	Examples
-al	informal, artificial
-ic	artistic, scientific
-ive	active, attractive
-ful	helpful, successful
-less	harmless, useless
-ous	generous, serious
-y	chatty, temporary
-ly	curly, likely
-able/-ible	avoidable, possible
-ed	exhausted, relaxed
-ing	interesting, matching

Adverb suffixes

Suffix	Examples
-ly	effectively, probably

Verb suffixes

Suffix	Examples
-ate	calculate, create
-ise/-ize	organise, realise
-ify	clarify, identify

PRONUNCIATION TABLE

Consonants

p	pair, complete, appear
b	box, abbreviation, job
t	temporary, waiting, getting
d	dancing, wedding, sound
k	kind, school, think, section
g	girlfriend, again, baggy
tʃ	check, match, future
dʒ	judge, page, soldier
f	feel, difficult, laugh, physical
v	verb, nervous, move
θ	think, author, bath
d	this, father, with
s	same, sentence, sister
z	zero, amazing, choose, prize
ʃ	fashion, sure, occupation, ocean
ʒ	pleasure, occasion
h	habit, who, chocoholic
m	meaning, grammar, sum
n	name, know, skinny, sun
ŋ	reading, strong, thanks, young
l	like, really, article
r	respect, worry, arrival
j	year, use, beautiful
w	with, one, where

Vowels

ɪ	information, invite
e	sentence, belt
a	add, match, can
ɒ	not, documentary, wash
ʌ	love, but, luck
ʊ	footwear, look, put
iː	reading, three, magazine
eɪ	race, may, grey
aɪ	advice, night, cry
ɔɪ	boy, join
uː	two, blue, school
əʊ	coat, show, know
aʊ	about, how
ɪə	appear, here
eə	pair, various, square
ɑː	dark, father
ɔː	bought, draw, author
ʊə	floor
ɜː	hurt, third
i	happy, pronunciation, serious
ə	accessory, actor
u	situation, visual, influence

SELF-CHECK ANSWER KEY

Unit 1
Exercise 1
1 elegant 2 unshaven 3 underdressed
4 broad-shouldered 5 faded
Exercise 2
1 up 2 in 3 for 4 on 5 up
Exercise 3
1 are clothes sizes getting 2 have 3 don't come
4 are having 5 do I look
Exercise 4
1 The 2 a 3 0 4 a 5 the 6 an 7 a 8 the 9 the
10 the
Exercise 5
1c 2d 3b 4b 5a
Exercise 6
1 to sort this out 2 we are doing a / our group
is doing a 3 hardly ever go 4 am thinking of
taking 5 first time I have

Unit 2
Exercise 1
1 lack of sleep 2 achievement 3 changed
4 delivery 5 constellations
Exercise 2
1 development 2 recognition 3 broaden
4 ahead 5 law
Exercise 3
1 have been working 2 haven't finished
3 have we been doing 4 haven't been wasting
5 Have we made
Exercise 4
1 to launch 2 to increase 3 meeting 4 doing
5 to allow
Exercise 5
1 disagreement 2 procedure 3 identification
4 requirements 5 proposal(s)
Exercise 6
1 have been travelling 2 have been reading
3 refused to use 4 don't remember reading
5 stopped working

Unit 3
Exercise 1
1g 2d 3j 4i 5h 6a 7c 8e 9f 10b
Exercise 2
1 injury 2 bruise 3 organic 4 fizzy 5 junk
Exercise 3
1 were watching 2 hadn't tried 3 was the
player lying 4 Had you heard 5 wasn't
performing
Exercise 4
1 used to 2 didn't know 3 would always refuse
4 didn't use 5 did I use to
Exercise 5
1c 2c 3a 4b 5c
Exercise 6
1 fire 2 had 3 set 4 down 5 pitch

Unit 4
Exercise 1
1b 2a 3c 4c 5b
Exercise 2
1 luggage 2 got lost 3 travel adapter 4 easy
reach 5 toxic
Exercise 3
1b 2c 3d 4c 5a
Exercise 4
1 which 2 whose 3 where 4 which 5 who

Exercise 5
1 congestion 2 demonstration 3 beaten
4 sustainable 5 pollution
Exercise 6
1a 2c 3c 4a 5b

Unit 5
Exercise 1
1 hard-working 2 keep up with
3 self-employed 4 permanent 5 salary
Exercise 2
1 eager 2 off 3 catch 4 part-time
5 Unemployment
Exercise 3
1a 2a 3c 4b 5c
Exercise 4
1 will/'ll have finished 2 will/'ll be waiting
3 Will you have started 4 won't have done
5 will you be doing
Exercise 5
1 repetitive 2 determined 3 competitive
4 overconfident 5 sensible
Exercise 6
1 together a presentation 2 seeing/meeting
3 will be taking/doing/writing/sitting
4 is about 5 will have arrived

Unit 6
Exercise 1
1 up 2 through 3 glanced 4 eyes 5 loneliness
Exercise 2
1b 2c 3a 4b 5c
Exercise 3
1 will/'ll tell 2 wouldn't trust 3 would you do
4 won't get 5 would go
Exercise 4
1 Unless 2 provided 3 get 4 finish 5 As soon as
Exercise 5
1b 2a 3c 4d 5a
Exercise 6
1 through 2 won't 3 make 4 would 5 teeth

Unit 7
Exercise 1
1d 2f 3e 4g 5b 6a 7j 8c 9i 10h
Exercise 2
1 on-demand content 2 viral 3 sophisticated
4 set design 5 looked back
Exercise 3
1 hadn't wanted 2 had chosen 3 not to switch
on 4 if/whether I had auditioned 5 where
I had learned/learnt
Exercise 4
1 if/whether she was going to be 2 she had
heard that 3 thought she/Kerry was 4 to buy
a ticket 5 not to worry
Exercise 5
1 subscription 2 spoilers 3 atmospheric
4 lighting 5 shocking
Exercise 6
1b 2a 3b 4c 5c

Unit 8
Exercise 1
1 jingle 2 fortune 3 value 4 crowdfunding
5 rate
Exercise 2
1c 2d 3a 4e 5b

Exercise 3
1 made 2 were taken 3 been bought 4 being
5 sold out
Exercise 4
1 have their purchases delivered 2 get items
paid for 3 get renewed 4 get their tickets
booked 5 have their lessons taught
Exercise 5
1 was being advertised 2 been banned by
3 is/'s having/getting her 4 didn't get/have
5 is a rip
Exercise 6
1 exchange 2 currency 3 bank/prepaid 4 is
5 be

Unit 9
Exercise 1
1c 2b 3a 4b 5a
Exercise 2
1 currents 2 rescue 3 impact 4 isolated
5 sustainable/solar
Exercise 3
1 wouldn't have known 2 had realised 3 had
installed 4 would have avoided 5 hadn't
moved
Exercise 4
1 we had 2 my parents bought 3 could get
4 would let 5 I would have asked
Exercise 5
1a 2c 3b 4c 5b
Exercise 6
1 harmful 2 collection 3 reusable 4 warnings
5 thoughtful

Unit 10
Exercise 1
1 custody 2 warning 3 life 4 made 5 turnout
Exercise 2
1b 2c 3a 4c 5c
Exercise 3
1 He might be involved with the gang.
2 She can't/cannot have (had) any useful
information. 3 They must be having lunch
now. 4 The burglars could have got away on
a motorbike. 5 They might not have known
about the security camera.
Exercise 4
1 must have felt 2 must be
3 can't have interviewed 4 might not be
5 could have had/could have
Exercise 5
1 might be studying 2 can't have seen
3 must have been 4 life imprisonment/life in
prison/a life sentence 5 gave her a warning
Exercise 6
1 have 2 must 3 sentence 4 defence 5 jury